The English Cardinals

NICHOLAS SCHOFIELD & GERARD SKINNER

FAMILY PUBLICATIONS
OXFORD

ISBN 978 1 871217 65 0

Front Cover: Thomas Wolsey receiving
the red hat in Westminster Abbey
by George Henry Harlow.
Courtesy of the Accademia San Luca, Rome.

Published by
Family Publications
6a King Street, Oxford OX2 6DF, UK
www.familypublications.co.uk

Printed in England

ACKNOWLEDGMENTS

Many people have been most generous in their support of the writing of this book. Firstly the authors thank His Eminence the Cardinal Archbishop of Westminster for most kindly writing the Foreword. We are also most grateful for the generous support of Patrick Coll and Bill Loschert, without whose sponsorship some important illustrations would have been omitted from this volume. With sincere apologies to anyone who has inadvertently not been included in the following list, we would like to thank all those who have supported this project: His Grace the Duke of Norfolk, the Lord Acton of Aldenham, the Lord Clifford of Chudleigh, Abbot Aidan Bellenger, Mgr David Norris, Mgr Nicholas Hudson, Mgr Dr Philip Whitmore, Mgr Mark Langham, Mgr Mark O'Toole, Canon Charles Acton, Revd Dr Mathias Trennert-Helwig, Revd Dr Bruce Burbridge, Fr Mark Brentnall, Fr Christopher Cunningham, Fr Ian Dickie, Fr Stewart Foster, Fr Andrew Headon, Fr Marcus Holden, Fr Paul Keane, Fr Alban McCoy, Fr Peter Vellacott, Fr Mark Vickers, Fr Richard Whinder, Fr Alan White, The Fathers of the Birmingham Oratory, Sr Mary Joseph, Cressida Annesley, Matthew Austin, Mark Bateson, Dr Nicholas Bennett, Suzanne Evard, Paul Gillham, Jan Graffius, Dr James Hagerty, John Hardacre, Bryan McDonald, Alistair MacGregor, Simon McCormac, Vincent Murphy, Angela Prior, Margaret Richards, Dr John Martin Robinson, Martina Salieri, Dr Barbara Stark, Tamara Thornhill, George Wain, Robert Yorke.

A special word of thanks must go to all at Family Publications, especially Colin Mason, Denis Riches and Edward Reeves, for their encouragement and support in the publication of this book.

Contents

FOREWORD

When Pope John Paul II created me cardinal along with forty-three others, on 21 February 2001, he referred to the College of Cardinals as 'the first collaborators in the Roman Pontiff's ministry of unity', and steering the barque of the Church across the 'vast ocean that lies before her'.

This book takes us on a journey across the 'vast ocean' of history. It shows the important contribution of our cardinals in steering the barque of the Church, both in this country and in Rome. Different periods have thrown up different challenges and circumstances but the close collaboration between the cardinals of England and the Holy Father has remained, for the most part, very strong.

I am confident that reading about the English cardinals will give us a greater appreciation of the Christian heritage of these lands and of the universal Church.

Cormac Cardinal Murphy-O'Connor
Tenth Archbishop of Westminster

A cardinal's galero lies upon the high altar of Westminster Cathedral.

INTRODUCTION

'It was never merry in England while we had cardinals amongst us.'

This was the opinion of Henry VIII in Robert Bolt's play, *A Man for All Seasons*, in response to the Duke of Suffolk's supposed exclamation during the discussions about the King's divorce, held at Blackfriars, London in 1529. To be certain that in future the merriment could continue unabated, Henry cut off the head of the newly-elevated English cardinal, St John Fisher, before the red hat could be put on. The early Christian writer Tertullian noted that the blood of the martyrs was the seed of the Church. Fisher's death was an inspiration to thousands to hold fast to the faith which they had received from their parents and grandparents before them.

Times have indeed changed. Cardinal Hume concluded his life peacefully, having been honoured by Queen and country with the Order of Merit. The martyrdom to which many recent cardinals have been called has been a living one; their blood shed (as symbolized by the scarlet robes) in a more protracted and less obvious manner – the martyrdom granted to those who give prophetic witness.

Cardinals are chosen by the Pope, who alone has the power to appoint them. They should be priests of outstanding learning, piety, judgment and ability, ready to assist the Pope in the governance of the Church. They are ranked as Princes of Royal Blood, accorded the title of 'Eminence', and take precedence over bishops and all other prelates. It is hoped that the honours and precedence given are a natural consequence of the individual's outstanding attributes, as it is because of these qualities that members of the Sacred College are charged with the governance of the Church after the death of the Pope, and with the election of his successor.

Scholars disagree about the exact origin of the title 'cardinal', but seem broadly to agree that it comes from the Latin word *cardinalis* (*cardo* meaning 'pivot' or 'hinge'). Thus we speak of 'cardinal virtues', 'cardinal points' and 'cardinal winds'. However, although we could metaphorically describe the cardinals as the 'hinges' of the Holy Roman Church, there is another meaning. As Aidan Bellenger and Stella Fletcher explain in their recent study of the English cardinals: 'Clerics in the early Church were ordained to a particular post or "title" for life and, if transferred to another place, were "incardinated" into it: here the idea is not that of a hinge, but rather of a tenon wedging a piece of wood into a cavity.'

The term was used in Rome for the seven deacons of the city, the senior parish priests and the bishops of the sees surrounding the city. Thus three divisions or orders of cardinals came to be. The Cardinal Bishops were the bishops of the dioceses surrounding Rome, but currently are the most senior curial cardinals with one of these dioceses as a title. Today, these suburbicarian sees are Ostia, Albano, Frascati, Palestrina, Porto-Santa Rufina, Sabina-Poggio Mirteto and Velletri-Segni (see Appendix IV). Secondly, there are the Cardinal Priests, who were formerly the parish priests of Rome. Today these cardinals live all over the world, but are the titular priests of the Roman parish churches (see Appendix V). Finally there are the Cardinal Deacons, who were formerly in charge of the seven regions of Rome on behalf of the Pope, but are now cardinals with posts in the Roman Curia. Like the Cardinal Priests, they are each assigned one of the churches in Rome as their *diaconia* (see Appendix V).

If the origins of the word 'cardinal' can be found in the first Christian Millennium, the role of cardinal only became formalised in the reforms of the eleventh century, going far beyond its original pastoral meaning. They were now senators and princes of the Church and electors of the Pope. As Leo IX wrote: 'Like an immovable hinge which sends the door back and forth, Peter and his successors have sovereign judgment over the entire Church. . . . Therefore his clerics are named cardinals, for they belong more closely to the hinge by which everything else is moved.' In 1245, Innocent IV prescribed the *galerus ruber* (the red hat with fifteen tassels on each side) for his cardinals – and red has remained the cardinalatial colour ever since, although rather confusingly this is often referred to as the 'sacred purple'. Perhaps the characteristic garb of cardinals is most familiar to us from Renaissance paintings of St Jerome († 420), who was 'promoted' to the rank of cardinal not in his lifetime but by zealous devotees in the Middle Ages and Renaissance.

Cardinal Priests and Deacons 'take possession' of their titular or diaconal church, normally shortly after the consistory. Their coat of arms (see Appendix VI) hangs at the main entrance of the church, together with that of the reigning Pontiff, and their portrait can sometimes be found within the church. Until quite recently, the fact that the cardinals originated as the parish clergy of Rome was also reflected in the traditional form of address used by the Pope – whereas the bishop of even the smallest diocese was called a 'venerable brother', cardinals were addressed as 'beloved sons'.

In 1965 Paul VI added to the colourful array Oriental Rite Patriarchs, who rank as Cardinal Bishops, although they retain their patriarchal see.

The number of cardinals within the Sacred College has also steadily increased. Sixtus V fixed the total number of cardinals at seventy in 1586, and this remained the case until the 1960s. However, the number of voters in a conclave has now been limited to one hundred and twenty, excluding cardinals over the age of eighty.

Since the restoration of the Catholic Hierarchy in England and Wales in 1850, the Archbishop of Westminster has always been created a cardinal. Cardinal Murphy-O'Connor was promoted to the Sacred College within a year of his translation from the diocese of Arundel and Brighton; some of his predecessors, however, had to wait longer – Manning, for example, was appointed to Westminster in 1865 but only received the red hat in 1875. It should be noted that the red hat does not fall on the head of Westminster's Archbishop *ex officio*, although it has been thought fitting since Westminster is the seat of political power and the Archbishop is usually President of the Bishops' Conference of England and Wales. There is also the possibility of an individual being singled out: perhaps most famously John Henry Newman, created a cardinal in old age for his pioneering theological work, rather like his modern counterparts Henri de Lubac, Yves Congar, Hans Urs von Balthasar, Avery Dulles and Albert Vanhoye.

The most difficult thing about compiling a book about the English cardinals is the question of who is, or who is not, to be included. Almost every previous book on the subject has had its own peculiarities, and this book claims be to be no exception. Most of the entries are of Englishmen who became cardinals, even though many spent most of their lives out of the country. Thus, Hertfordshire born Nicholas Breakspear worked energetically in Scandinavia and then reigned as Pope Adrian IV; James II's grandson, Cardinal Stuart, never set foot in England and yet claimed to be Henry IX, King *de jure* if not *de facto*; and Cardinal Merry del Val, a priest of the Archdiocese of Westminster, is chiefly remembered as Pope St Pius X's Secretary of State who died in Rome in the odour of sanctity.

Some of our cardinals, however, had no claim to be English except that they were appointed to an English diocese. Henry VII and Henry VIII followed a policy of appointing useful foreigners to vacant sees – thus both Giulio de' Medici (later Clement VII) and Girolamo Ghinucci were Bishops of Worcester *in commendam*, whilst Lorenzo Campeggio was granted the See of Salisbury for his Legatine mission to England. However, we have not chosen to include cardinals who were granted non-episcopal benefices as a means of providing revenue, for this would unduly lengthen the book without any real benefit. During the 1370s and 1380s, for example, three Archdeacons of Suffolk were Princes of the Church: William Noellet (Cardinal Deacon of San Angelo), Eliziarius de Sabrano (Cardinal Priest of Santa Balbina) and Philip de Alençon (Cardinal Bishop of Sabina). Likewise, Gauscelin Jean d'Euse, the nephew of Pope John XXII, was Rector of Hackney (1328-34) as well as Vice Chancellor of the Holy Roman Church.

Some cardinals have been excluded from this book since their elevation to the Sacred College, or their claims as Englishmen, seem highly dubious. Boso Breakspear, for example, was Adrian IV's chamberlain and biographer and is traditionally assumed to have been a monk of St Albans. In actual fact, there is no evidence of his English roots and he was probably an Italian who used his great patron's surname. Another dubious English cardinal, Theobald Stampendis, is only mentioned as a cardinal in one source while Herbert of Bosham, though mentioned in several lists as a cardinal, remains equally mysterious. Like Boso, he remains in the shadow of a more famous ecclesiastic – St Thomas of Canterbury, whose biography he wrote. Perhaps the story of his red hat arose from either patriotic desire for a greater number of cardinals, or through some confusion with regard to his name.

Other cardinals cause the historian problems due to the complexities of papal history. Cardinals Langley and Hallam were both given the red hat by the anti-pope, John XXIII, at a time when there were three claimants to the Throne of the Fisherman. However these 'anti-cardinals' are given the ecclesiological benefit of the doubt and are included in their proper chronological place.

Appendix II deals with two nineteenth century 'might-have-beens' – Bishop Baines, who was seemingly cheated out of the red hat by the death of Leo XII, and the historian, John Lingard, who was convinced he had been made a cardinal secretly. The creation of cardinals *in petto* or *pectore* (in the Pope's 'heart') has been a regular feature of consistories down the centuries. The secrecy in such instances is normally due to political reasons. 'Secret' cardinals acquire no rights until the public announcement of their status, and if the Pope dies before such a declaration is made they do not become members of the Sacred College. John Paul II created four cardinals *in petto*. Three were subsequently announced (Cardinals Kung of Shanghai, Jaworski of Lvov and Pujats of Riga) but one was never publicly revealed.

The appendices also include two miscellaneous cases: the apostate Cardinal Odet de Coligny, who is buried in Canterbury Cathedral (Appendix I), and the prolific Servite theologian, Cardinal Lépicier, who was ordained in

London and worked for some years in England (Appendix III).

Ever since Christ chose fishermen and tax collectors to form his close circle of disciples, the Church has prided herself in offering opportunities to those of humble backgrounds – a meritocracy which in some ages and places was considerably counter-cultural. The English cardinals include those of blue blood or aristocratic pedigree, such as Beaufort, Pole, Stuart, Acton and the two Howards. Yet only in the Church would it be possible for Thomas Wolsey, the son of an Ipswich butcher, to rise to become England's wealthiest and most powerful prelate and statesman under Henry VIII. Nor was he alone; early modern colleges and universities were full of talented commoners who had attracted ecclesiastical patronage and could look forward to a glittering career at court or in the Church.

Cardinals have often had a negative press in English history. For a Protestant nation they were a potent symbol of the troubled relationship between England and Rome and were viewed with suspicion as representatives of an alien potentate and members of a foreign court. Such xenophobia was heightened by their strange appearance – blood red robes and large, slightly ridiculous hats. The likes of Castellesi, Bainbridge, and in particular Wolsey, with their sometimes sordid stories of poisonings, intrigue and illegitimate children, were seen to sum up the dark days of pre-Reformation England.

Yet a history of England's cardinals presents an interesting sidelight on the history both of England and of the Catholic Church. Generally speaking, they can be divided into three groups. Firstly, we have the powerful medieval and Renaissance prelates, embodied by Langton, Beaufort and Wolsey, involved as much with the throne as with the altar, but often drawn into controversy by conflicting loyalties between King and Pope. It was this tension that caused the comment that England had never been merry when there were cardinals – for the Crown they could pose a tremendous nuisance.

With the advent of the Reformation we come to the handful of cardinals created during 'penal times', such as Allen and Howard, trying to do as much as possible for their fellow countrymen from exile overseas. Indeed, it was the pan-European Catholic diaspora that was the beating heart of the Church during this period, centred in the English seminaries, colleges and religious houses which could be found in the Low Countries, France, Spain, Italy and Germany. It was an indication of their courage and of the Papacy's desire to welcome England back into the fold that Englishmen occasionally found themselves in the Sacred College.

Finally, with emancipation (1829) and the restoration of the Hierarchy (1850), there are the cardinals of a newly confident and increasingly mainstream Catholic Community, a far cry from the days of Fisher and Pole. Even Nicholas Wiseman, whose appointment to Westminster had caused such controversy, died as a greatly loved and respected prelate, whose funeral was compared to that of Wellington's, the procession watched by as many as a million Londoners.

The legacy of our cardinals continues to this day: scholars who are still widely respected, like Fisher, Lingard and Newman; politicians like Langton, the mastermind behind the Magna Carta; patrons of the arts, like Wolsey, who laid the foundations of the palaces of Hampton Court and Whitehall and employed musicians of the calibre of John Taverner; even engineers, such as Morton, a pioneer of drainage in the Fens. Moreover, whenever we open our Bible we have Langton to thank, for it was he who supposedly divided the great book into chapters. It is hoped that this brief introduction to the lives of the cardinals of England, aimed at the general reader, will prove that most of the English cardinals have served with great distinction both their country and the universal Church. Perhaps none have done so more than Cardinal John Fisher. Addressing the Sacred College of Cardinals for the first time on 18 October 1978, the newly elected Pope John Paul II held up the witness of this most renowned of the English cardinals as a model for all who are called to serve as cardinals of the Holy Roman Church:

> I remember, at this moment, the figure of the great Bishop, St John Fisher, created cardinal . . . when he was imprisoned for his faithfulness to the Pope. On the morning of the 22nd June 1535, while he was preparing to offer his head to the executioner's axe, he exclaimed facing the crowd: "Christian people, I am about to die for faith in the Holy Catholic Church of Christ." . . . May this unshakeable faithfulness to the Bride of Jesus be always the badge of honour and the pre-eminent boast of the College of Cardinals.

ROBERT PULLEN

† C. 1146

CARDINAL PRIEST OF SAN MARTINO AI MONTI (C. 1144)

There are many interesting stories about the origin of Oxford University. Some medieval historians claimed that the town emerged as an academic centre under Arviragus, a first century British King, or even under the ancient Trojans. Others dated its foundation to the reign of Alfred the Great and named St Neot and St Grimbald as professors. Whatever the truth behind these legends, we know that Oxford was a well-known centre of scholarship by the twelfth century. One of the University's early Masters may have been Robert Pullen, who is normally listed as England's first cardinal. This is almost certainly true, although some sources mention an English ecclesiastic named Ulric (or Wilfrid) who is said to have been created cardinal around the year 1100.

Pullen probably originated from the West Country and was educated at either Laon or Paris. He became a famous teacher, perhaps at the Cathedral School of Exeter before 1133 and then, according to an early source: 'He began to lecture at Oxford on the Holy Scriptures, which had been neglected in England.' He taught there from 1133 to 1138 and was praised for teaching without charging fees and supporting many poor students at his own expense.

We can be surer about his subsequent ecclesiastical career. He was made Archdeacon of Rochester in 1137 (or possibly before) and may also have been offered a bishopric by Henry I, but he spent a considerable time out of the country seeking academic pursuits in Paris, where he lectured in logic and theology, supported by his revenues from Rochester. It seems that this was a point of contention with his Ordinary, Bishop Ascelin. Even the great St Bernard wrote to the Bishop apologising for Pullen's absence, which was 'on account of the sound doctrine which is recognised in him'. His students at Paris included a future Pope (Blessed Eugenius III) and a future Bishop of Chartres and writer (John of Salisbury). John described Pullen as a man 'of joyful memory'.

Pullen was highly respected not only by St Bernard but also by successive Popes. He settled in Rome in the mid 1140s and was created Cardinal Priest of San Martino ai Monti around 1144. Despite lacking an administrative background he was made Chancellor of the Holy Roman Church. Indeed, John of Salisbury noted with surprise that the Pope (Lucius II) 'made a chancellor out of a scholastic doctor'.

When Pullen's former student, Bernardo Pignatelli, mounted the throne of St Peter as Eugenius III in 1145, St Bernard wrote to Pullen encouraging him to be the new Pope's 'consoler and counsellor':

> Watch over the Pope carefully, according to the wisdom God has given you, so that in the press of business he is not circumvented by the craft of evil-minded persons, and led into decision unworthy of his apostolate. Act in a manner that becomes your position and the high dignity that you have obtained. Labour prudently and manfully with the zeal God has given you, for his honour and glory, for your own salvation, and for the benefit of the Church; then you will be able to say with truth: "The grace he has shown me has not been without fruit." Heaven and earth are witness that hitherto you have faithfully and carefully devoted yourself to the instruction of many; but the time has come to work for God and to do all that you can to prevent godless men from defying his law. Take particular care, dear friend, to be found a faithful and prudent servant of the Lord, displaying dove-like simplicity in your own affairs, and in the affairs of the Church, the bride of Christ which has been entrusted to your care and loyalty; and the wisdom of the serpent against the cunning of that old serpent, so that in both God may be glorified. There are many things I want to say, but there is no need for a long letter when the living voice is at hand. In view of both your many occupations and mine, I have put my words into the brother who brings this letter. Hear them as you would myself.

Part of Pullen's appeal to these great men was undoubtedly his doctrinal orthodoxy. Together with the likes of St Bernard and Hugh of St Victor, he was involved in debates with Bishop Gilbert de la Porrée, whose 'realist' teaching on the Trinity was thought to tend towards tritheism. Pullen was also an opponent of Abelard, against whom he wrote his *Sentences*, covering a large range of subjects from angels to tithes – an impressive work of eight books that was to be overshadowed by Peter Lombard's own *Sentences*. Cardinal Pullen had little time to become the Holy Father's 'consoler and counsellor' for he died around 1147, and is thought to have been buried at Viterbo.

Pullen advanced the careers of his relatives. A nephew, known as Paris (Parisius), succeeded him as Archdeacon of Rochester and a cousin, Joseph, became Prior of Sherborne Abbey. John of Salisbury describes Pullen as a man 'whom his life and learning alike commended'. England's first cardinal set an impressive example of scholarship and loyalty to the Holy See that was followed by many of his successors.

SAN MARTINO AI MONTI (VIALE MONTE OPPIO)

Dedicated to St Sylvester and St Martin of Tours and cared for by the Carmelites, this fourth century church was also the *titulus* of Cardinal Allen. More recently, Achille Ratti (the future Pius XI), Blessed Ildefonso Schuster (Archbishop of Milan) and Giovanni Battista Montini (the future Paul VI) were the titular cardinals here.

Little remains to be seen of the ancient gathering place for Christian worship, the *Titulus Equitii*, over which Pope St Sylvester I built a church. Pope Symmachus built the body of the existing church in the early years of the sixth century. Outside the church, at the back, can still be seen the ruins of an ancient building into which the present church has been built. Inside the church the high altar is raised above a large crypt area which contains the relics of many martyrs whose names, an ancient inscription declares, 'are known only to God'. The ceiling was the gift of St Charles Borromeo and the church contains some rare sixteenth century frescoes of Old St Peter's and St John Lateran. Other frescoes in the church were painted by Gaspard Dughet (1615-75), the brother-in-law of the great French artist Nicolas Poussin.

NICHOLAS BREAKSPEAR
C. 1100 – 1159
CARDINAL BISHOP OF ALBANO (1146)
POPE ADRIAN IV (1154)

According to the prophecies of St Malachy, the twelfth century Archbishop of Armagh who listed the qualities of one hundred and eleven anticipated Popes, Adrian IV was to be *de rure albo* (i.e. from a white country, of the Alban country). This was certainly apt – for not only was he from the shores of Albion, but famed as the 'Apostle of the North' (Scandinavia) and Cardinal Bishop of Albano.

The first, and so far only, English Pope spent a fraction of his life in his homeland. His birthplace is normally given as Breakspear Farm in Bedmond near Abbots Langley, Hertfordshire. A 'holy well' on the property was believed to have curative properties and was visited until the farmhouse was demolished in the 1960s to make way for residential housing. The village's famous son is memorialised in a plaque and local street names such as Adrian's Road, Pope's Road and Breakspeare Road. Others, however, have claimed Brill, Buckinghamshire, and Harefield, Middlesex (where there was a manor called 'Breakspears') as the place of birth.

The future Pontiff was the son of Richard (or Robert), possibly a married priest who later became a monk at nearby St Albans. Tradition has it that young Nicholas also tried to join the abbey but was turned away. In later life, as Pope, he is said to have pointedly refused the rich gifts of the Abbot of St Albans while accepting a home-made mitre and sandals from the Hertfordshire recluse, Christina of Markyate. However, he also granted several privileges to the abbey.

Breakspear may have studied at the newly-founded Augustinian priory of Merton, Surrey – whose alumni also included St Thomas Becket – and went on to France, where he eventually joined the Augustinian Canons of St Ruf. By 1147 he had become their abbot, although complaints were later sent to Rome about his strict reformist tendencies. The Pope removed him to keep the peace, but it was clear that his talents had been noted. In 1149 Pope Eugenius III created him Cardinal Bishop of Albano, one of the prestigious suburbicarian sees outside Rome.

If Breakspear had not become the first English Pope, it is likely that he would have been chiefly remembered for his energetic apostolate in Scandinavia, where he was legate in the early 1150s. He facilitated the payment of 'Peter's Pence' by Sweden and Norway and created the bishopric of Nidaros (today's Trondheim), a huge see embracing Norway, Iceland, Greenland, the Faroes, Shetland, the Orkneys and Sudreys (including the Isle of Man). He also reorganised the Swedish Church under the primacy of the Archbishop of Lund, thus ending its previous German dependence. The Cardinal is supposed to have written catechisms for the Swedes and Norwegians and a history of his Scandinavian mission, although none of these have survived.

One of his entourage was St Henry (or Henrik), an Englishman whom Cardinal Breakspear consecrated as Bishop of Uppsala in 1152. St Henry travelled to Finland with the King of Sweden, St Eric IX, and was eventually murdered by an excommunicate called Lalli (c. 1156). The story goes that, having killed the Bishop, Lalli tried on his mitre, but when he removed it his scalp came off with it. The saint was later enshrined in the Cathedral of Abo (now Turku) and was soon venerated as the Patron of Finland. His feast on 19 January (*Heikinpäivä*) is a day of national celebration – a modern memory of the widespread evangelisation carried out by the English Cardinal and his companions.

Returning from Scandinavia, Breakspear soon found himself in conclave and he was elected as successor to Anastasius IV on 4 December 1154. According to John of Salisbury, he discovered that, metaphorically speaking, the pallium was full of thorns and the mitre seared his head. He would have preferred to remain a simple canon of St Ruf. Little wonder, because the See of Rome was as challenging as his legateship in Scandinavia: the city was in the control of a hostile commune, who killed one cardinal as he was on his way to visit the new Pope, and the Papal States were under attack from William I of Sicily. Adrian IV took immediate action, placing Rome under interdict and expelling and executing Arnold of Brescia, one of the commune leaders.

The Pope renewed a treaty with Frederick Barbarossa, King of Germany, which meant that both parties recognised the other's sovereign rights. On 18 June 1155 Adrian crowned him Emperor at St Peter's. At their first meeting – before the Pope had agreed to crown the Emperor – things got off to a bad start when Frederick refused to perform the customary service of holding the Pope's stirrup as he dismounted. Adrian, in retaliation, refused to give him the kiss of peace. Points of division went beyond such matters of etiquette, however. Adrian wished to assert the papacy's monarchical claims while Frederick wanted to rule the Empire like a 'second Charlemagne'. Moreover, the commune of Rome continued to cause trouble – it had independently offered Frederick the imperial crown and, shortly before Adrian's death, was hoping to gain the Emperor's recognition. It was clear that Frederick could not be trusted.

In June 1156 the Pope made a dramatic volte-face and made peace with William of Sicily, recognising him as King over much of southern Italy, with special rights over the Church in his domains. Frederick was furious and relations between Pope and Emperor grew increasingly strained, especially when Frederick was seen to infringe papal prerogatives at the diet of Roncaglia (1158). Adrian fled to Anagni for safety, where he negotiated an anti-imperial alliance with disgruntled Milan, Brescia and Piacenza, and considered Frederick's excommunication. However, he died at Anagni on 1 September 1159 and was buried in an ancient red granite sarcophagus at St Peter's. When his tomb was opened in 1607 he was found to be 'an undersized man wearing slippers of Turkish make, and a ring with a large emerald'.

Adrian's most famous involvement in English affairs was his bull *Laudabiliter* (1155) whereby the English Pope supposedly granted Ireland to the English King and sent him an emerald ring as a symbol of this investiture. According to John of Salisbury, the Pope was able to make this gift because: 'According to the Donation of Constantine all islands are the property of the Roman Church.' Around 1175 Gerald of Wales transcribed *Laudabiliter* into his *Expugnatio Hibernica*:

> Adrian the Bishop, servant of the servants of God, to his most dearly beloved son in Christ, the illustrious King of the English, greeting and apostolic benediction.
>
> Laudibly and profitably does your magnificence contemplate extending your glorious arm on earth and laying up a reward of eternal happiness in heaven, inasmuch as you endeavour like a catholic prince to enlarge the boundaries

of the Church, to expound the truth of the Christian faith to ignorant and barbarous peoples, and to root out the seeds of vice from the Lord's field; and for the better execution of this, you seek the advice and favour of the apostolic see. In which work the more lofty the counsel and the greater the discretion with which you proceed, so much the more do we trust that by God's help your progress may be fortunate therein, in that those things which have their beginning in ardent faith and love of religion always tend to work out to a happy ending. . . .

We, therefore, supporting with due fervour your pious and praiseworthy desire, and granting our generous assent to your petition, are well pleased to agree that, for the extension of the boundaries of the Church, for the restraint of vice, for the correction of morals and for the implanting of virtues, and for the increase of the Christian religion, you may enter that island and perform therein the things that have regard to the honour of God and the salvation of that land. . . . If, therefore, you deem fit to carry through what you have in mind, strive to imbue that nation with good morals . . . that the Christian religion may be implanted and made to grow, and the things which pertain to the honour of God and the salvation of souls may be so ordered that you may deserve to obtain from God the crown of everlasting reward and on earth a name glorious throughout the ages.

Whether or not *Laudabiliter* was really produced by Pope Adrian, Ireland was not occupied by the English until the late 1160s.

The Hertfordshire Pope remained a vivid figure in the English imagination. Seven hundred years after his pontificate his successor, Blessed Pius IX, agreed to a scheme for the English to erect a monument to him in the Basilica of St Peter's, although insufficient funds prevented it from being completed.

Boso 'Breakspear' is sometimes listed as an English cardinal. He was created Cardinal Deacon of Santi Cosmo e Damiano in 1155 by Adrian IV and later promoted as Cardinal Priest of Santa Pudenziana (1166). However there is no evidence for his English origins and he was probably an Italian attached to the Breakspear household who enjoyed the patronage of the English Pontiff and wrote his biography.

Stephen Langton

c. 1150 – 1228

Cardinal Priest of San Crisogono (1206)

When John Paul II became the first reigning Pope to celebrate Mass on English soil in Westminster Cathedral on 28 May 1982, he quoted Cardinal Langton in his homily:

> We are on the eve of Pentecost, the feast of the Holy Spirit who descends on us at Baptism. One of the finest passages in the Pentecost liturgy was written by an Englishman, Stephen Langton, an Archbishop of Canterbury. In six short and vivid lines he calls upon the Holy Spirit to work in us:
>
> > Wash what is unclean.
> > Water what is parched.
> > Heal what is diseased.
> > Bend what is rigid.
> > Warm what is cold.
> > Straighten what is crooked.
>
> Most of the ills of our age or of any age can be brought under that prayer. It reflects a boundless confidence in the power of the Spirit whom it invokes.

Had Langton not risen to high office in the Church, it is likely that he would still be remembered as a scholar and the writer of the 'Golden Sequence' for Pentecost, the *Veni Sancte Spiritus*.

Born sometime in the 1150s, his father, Henry de Langton, was Lord of a small Lincolnshire manor and had enough means to send his son to the University of Paris, where he was joined by his brother, Simon (later Archdeacon of Canterbury). Stephen remained in Paris until 1206, teaching and producing many works, including commentaries on Scripture and collections of *Quaestiones*. Langton is credited with dividing each book of the Bible into chapters, while his contemporary, Hugh of St Cher, organised these chapters into verses. These changes made their way into codices and, later, all printed versions, and are still used today.

The Elevation of the Host and chalice at Mass are also said to be due partly to Langton. Some Masters at Paris, such as Peter Manducator and Peter Cantor, held that transubstantiation only occurred after the words of consecration for both the bread and wine. Langton was one of the leading opponents of this view and, as a sign of protest, his 'party' adored the Host immediately after the words *Hoc est enim corpus meum*. It is not difficult to see how this developed into the Elevation so that the people could adore the sacred species as well.

In 1206 the academic was sent to Rome where Innocent III, a friend from university, made him the Cardinal Priest of San Crisogono. Soon afterwards, the Pope appointed him Archbishop of Canterbury and consecrated him at Viterbo on 17 June 1207. However, King John had his own nominee for Canterbury – John de Gray, Bishop of Norwich – and, like Pope Innocent, was keen to stress his own authority and prerogatives. The Pope wrote to the King warning him that it was dangerous to 'fight against God and the Church in this cause for which St Thomas, that glorious martyr and Archbishop, recently shed his blood'. When he refused to accept Langton's appointment, the Pope placed England under Interdict on 28 March 1208. John responded by seizing Church property and was promptly excommunicated in November 1209. Meanwhile, Langton waited at Pontigny, a daughter house of Cîteaux. This famous abbey has been called 'the asylum of great men', for no less than three Archbishops of Canterbury received hospitality there during political crises: Becket, Langton and Rich (who is buried there).

Finally, John relented, England and Ireland were declared papal fiefs and Langton absolved the King from excommunication at Winchester on 20 July 1213, some six years after his original appointment and consecration. The King's reasons for this change in policy were not as straightforward as they first seemed – the French were planning an invasion and John needed the Pope's injunction against King Philip Augustus. John, now absolved from his excommunication, could rely upon full papal support since he was the Pontiff's faithful liegeman.

England was now in the grips of rebellion. Instead of trying to replace the King with a more attractive alternative – difficult since John was the only adult Plantagenet – the disgruntled aristocracy tried to push reforms in front of the King to diminish Angevin power. Langton was at the heart of these proposals, acting as mediator, even though he had been away from England for forty years. Shortly after his arrival in England, he was already looking back to the laws of St Edward and Henry I as possible models. This led the way to the Magna Carta, half-heartedly approved by the King after the rebels had captured London in 1215. However, the peace achieved by the 'Great Charter' of Runnymede lasted only a couple of months. A letter was received from the Pope excommunicating all 'disturbers of King and Kingdom', but Langton ignored the sentence due to the Pope's ignorance of the charter. However, Archbishop Langton was suspended and Innocent declared Magna Carta null and void, since it had been forced upon the King. The disgraced Langton went to Rome, where he kept a low profile during the Fourth Lateran Council, and his situation was only resolved when both Pope and King died the following year.

Langton returned to Canterbury in 1218. In 1220, he presided at two solemn ceremonies: the boy-King Henry III's second coronation (his first had been at Gloucester four years earlier) and the translation of Becket's bones to a magnificent new shrine in the cathedral's Trinity chapel. Organised for the fiftieth anniversary of the martyrdom, the translation was one of the most spectacular events of thirteenth century England and Langton provided barrels of free wine at each of the city's gates. He returned to Rome the same year to negotiate the recall of a papal legate, Pandulf, who was threatening Langton's influence, and having arranged this he carried on unchallenged during the last years of his life. Langton's reassuring presence, together with that of Hubert de Burgh, the Earl of Kent, was crucial in preserving the peace and stability of the Kingdom during the minority of Henry III.

Langton encouraged the newly founded Franciscans and Dominicans to set up houses in England and he passed Church reforms – indeed, a provincial synod held at Osney Abbey, outside the walls of Oxford, in 1222 is sometimes called 'the ecclesiastical Runnymede'. Langton had been inspired by his attendance at the twelfth Ecumenical Council (the Fourth Lateran Council), convened by Pope Innocent in 1215. Most of the canons of the Council are contained in the Decretals of Gregory IX. The opening words of Canon 27, *Cum sit ars artium regimen animarum*, give the flavour of the intentions of the Council as a whole – 'The government of souls is the art of arts.' The 'Langtonian' vision of the Church is deeply inspired by this lofty vision: the Church should be administered by zealous priests, properly trained at the universities and avoiding the temptations of court and politics. This ideal remained an inspiration for generations of English prelates, including Cardinals Fisher and Pole.

On the evidence of the many sermons of Langton that have survived, he was a clear and illuminating preacher and was nicknamed 'Thunder-Tongued' in some manuscripts. He once remarked: 'An illustrative anecdote is very often more effective than a polished subtle phrase.' Two examples of this are given in P G Maxwell-Stuart's study of *The Archbishops of Canterbury*:

> In a ship, the prow and the stern are narrow, and the keel is wide. The beginning of life is narrow, the end of it likewise. . . . The middle of life is wider. At this point a person is physically strong, and just as all the cargo is in the middle of the ship, so a person bears his or her own burden in the middle of life.

Likewise clear imagery is used to communicate effectively the blessing of living the Christian life:

> If someone wants to make his way safely through the Kingdom of France and carries the King's seal with him, he will be safe anywhere in the Kingdom. But suppose he were to throw away the seal and take some nobody's seal instead – he'd be regarded as a lunatic, wouldn't he? So how much more of a lunatic is someone who throws away the seal of the everlasting King and takes the seal of the Devil.

Langton died at his manor of Slindon, Sussex, on 9 July 1228 and was buried at Canterbury Cathedral.

SAN CRISOGONO (VIALE TRASTEVERE)

The church of Cardinals Langton and Castellesi is run by the Trinitarian Order and contains the shrine of the nineteenth century mystic and Trinitarian tertiary, Blessed Anna Maria Taigi. Another English cardinal, Robert of Somercotes, is buried here.

The façade of the present church was designed by Giovanni Battista Soria (1581-1651). As with so many Roman churches, the Romanesque campanile reaches up to the right of the church promising greater antiquity inside. This hope is not disappointed at San Crisogono. The main body of the church was built in 1123 by Giovanni da Crema, legate of Honorius II to England. However, even the most ancient decoration came after the lifetime of Cardinal Langton. The antique granite columns that support the nave were in place by Langton's day, but the stunning thirteenth century cosmatesque pavement of the nave and the exquisite mosaic from the school of Pietro Cavallini (c. 1250–1330) of the Madonna and Child with Ss Crisogono and James behind the high altar could certainly have been enjoyed by Cardinal Castellesi.

In the Middle Ages an English Hospice dedicated to St Edmund stood nearby. It was later merged with the Hospice of St Thomas on the other side of the Tiber (now the English College).

ROBERT DE CURZON
† 1219
CARDINAL PRIEST OF SANTO STEFANO IN MONTE CELIO (1216)

Robert Curzon (sometimes called Robert de Courçon) was the only English cardinal to die on a battlefield. He succumbed to sickness while ministering to the crusaders as they besieged Damietta, a port at the mouth of the Nile that was under the control of the Ayyubid Sultan of Egypt. The crusaders were heavily out-numbered and hostilities continued for fifteen months. Curzon did not live to see the Christian forces enter the city in November 1219.

Curzon was probably educated at Oxford and then certainly at Paris in the early 1190s under the tutelage of Peter, the precentor of Notre Dame. Here Curzon was joined in his studies by the future Pope Innocent III, who later created him a cardinal.

Having gained his doctorate in theology, Curzon continued to teach in Paris and produced several works, including a *Summa*. He became a canon of Noyon in 1204 and of Notre Dame in 1209. In 1211 he became Chancellor of the University of Paris and on 9 June 1212 was created Cardinal Priest of Santo Stefano in Monte Celio. The following year he was sent as papal legate to France to preach the crusade against the Cathars that was proclaimed by Innocent III in *Quia maior*. He also set about a reform of the French Church, which made him increasingly unpopular. He organized the syllabus of the University of Paris, prohibiting the works of Aristotle on metaphysics and natural philosophy, and tried to remedy the problem of usury, which he saw as one of the chief issues facing the Church. Curzon's campaign against usury was zealously pursued in his preaching which, according to one source, was exceptional, describing

Curzon as 'a star in the firmament of heaven'.

Following complaints from senior French clerics and accusations of an English bias, Curzon was recalled to Rome where he took part in the Fourth Lateran Council of 1215. One of the fruits of the Council was the promotion of an expedition to the Holy Land. Curzon joined the ill-fated Fifth Crusade in 1218, setting out on 28 July 1218 and died at Damietta on 6 February 1219. He did not live to meet St Francis of Assisi, who arrived in Damietta in the summer of 1219 on a dangerous mission to convert the Sultan.

SANTO STEFANO ROTONDO AL CELIO (VIA SANTO STEFANO)

Cardinal Curzon's *titulus* was established in the fifth century by Pope St Simplicius (468-83) and its circular shape echoes that of the Holy Sepulchre in Jerusalem.

Three concentric circles of ancient columns once formed the 'nave' of this church. The outermost circle of these columns was walled in during the restoration of Pope Nicholas V in 1450. This new wall is decorated by late sixteenth century frescoes executed by Pomerancio (Cristoforo Roncalli c. 1552-1626) and Antonio Tempesta (1555-1630), showing, in graphic detail, scenes of martyrdom through the ages. From 1589 the church was owned by the Hungarian College (later merged with the German College) and the frescoes provided reflection for students who faced martyrdom in their future missionary work.

Dedicated to St Stephen the Proto-martyr, the church became the Hungarian church in Rome and gained a secondary patron in St Stephen of Hungary. An Irish King, Donough O'Brien, who died in 1064 during a pilgrimage, is said to be buried in the church. Santo Stefano was the *titulus* of the Scottish prelate, Cardinal Beaton (1538-46), and the saintly Cardinal Jozsef Mindszenty (1892-1975), a twentieth century icon of the Church's resistance to communism.

Robert of Somercotes
† 1241
Cardinal Deacon of Sant' Eustachio (1239)

Hailing from the Lincolnshire village of Somercotes, the future cardinal was educated at Paris. He gained his first ecclesiastical preferment from Cardinal Langton, who gave him a rent in the church in Croydon, and seems to have acted as a confessor to Henry III in the mid 1230s. Subsequently Robert went to study at Bologna and entered the service of the Papal Curia as papal subdeacon in 1236.

In 1239 Pope Gregory IX created Robert a Cardinal Deacon with the *diaconia* of Sant' Eustachio. However, these were tense times in Rome. The Holy Roman Emperor, Frederick II, had commenced aggressive moves against the Lombard towns, a move which the Roman Curia understandably saw as a prelude to an attack on the Papal States. Firstly in 1227, and again in 1239, Gregory IX excommunicated him. When the Emperor advanced on Rome in 1240, the English cardinal was one of the few to remain with the Pope.

On 22 August 1241 the Pope died. With a crisis looming, Senator Matteo Rosso Orsini decided that the cardinals needed encouragement in order to secure a new Pope quickly. He therefore gathered the handful of cardinals who were present in Rome at the time, including Robert, and locked them in the squalid Septizonium Palace with an armed guard surrounding them. They did not reach the two-thirds majority required until, with the heat rising and the lavatories overflowing, they elected the elderly theologian Goffredo da Castiglione as Pope Celestine IV on 25 October.

Robert thus participated in the first conclave in which the cardinals were literally locked in, and it seems that he died during the conclave itself. Robert was said to have been a favourite for election and there were rumours of his being poisoned. As it happened, the new Pope lived for only seventeen days and it was to be two years before the cardinals reconvened in Anagni to elect his successor. Meanwhile, Robert of Somercotes was buried at the church of San Crisogano. A contemporary plaque in the church records:

> Here rests in the Lord, Robert of happy memory, Cardinal Deacon of S Eustachius, Englishman, who died on 26 September 1241.

Sant' Eustachio (Piazza Sant' Eustachio)

The origins of Sant' Eustachio, situated near to the Pantheon, possibly date back to the fourth century. In the eighth century a church was built over the site of the resting place of the bodies of St Eustachius and his wife and children, Ss Theopista, Agapius and Theopistus, who were roasted alive in a brazen bull during the reign of the Emperor Hadrian.

The campanile and portico were built in the twelfth century but the interior and the façade, surmounted by its distinctive stag's head (the artistic symbol of St Eustachius), date from the otherwise total rebuilding work of the eighteenth century.

JOHN OF TOLEDO O CIST

† 1275

CARDINAL PRIEST OF SAN LORENZO IN LUCINA (1244)
CARDINAL BISHOP OF PORTO AND SANTA RUFINA (1262)

Despite his misleading name, John of Toledo was originally from England. He was a cardinal *in curia* for over thirty years. According to Matthew Paris, John first won fame through his medical and alchemical skills having studied medicine at Toledo; other records suggest that John was actually a theologian, not a physician. It is possible that he has customarily been confused with an early medical scholar, Johannes Hispanus, who was also dubbed John of Toledo.

The English John, who was to be created a cardinal, entered the Cistercian Order and eventually became Abbot of L'Epau in Maine. After visiting the Eternal City on abbatial business, John was persuaded to remain in the Papal Curia.

On 28 May 1244 the Pope created him Cardinal Priest of San Lorenzo in Lucina. He was known as 'the White Cardinal', because of his white Cistercian habit, and on 24 December 1261 he was promoted to be Cardinal Bishop of Porto and Santa Rufina. As a cardinal, John promoted the interests of the Cistercians and encouraged the establishments of theology schools in each of the Order's provinces. He also founded Cistercian houses in Rome, Perugia and Viterbo.

Despite his links to the university town of Toledo, it is clear that he was considered an English cardinal and several fellow countrymen were found in his household, including Richard Gravesend (later Bishop of Lincoln), Henry of Evesham, William of Peterborough and Roger Luvel (a royal clerk). He also acted on behalf of English interests at the papal court.

Among his most notable deeds was the promotion of the canonisation of St Edmund of Abingdon, the Archbishop of Canterbury who died in 1240 and was canonised in 1246. In the political sphere, he supported Henry III against the aggressive ambitions of his barons. When the King's brother, Richard of Cornwell, became 'King of the Romans' in 1257, John of Toledo obtained a senatorial office in Rome for him.

The 'White Cardinal' died on 13 July 1275 at San Germano, having served the Church and, at a distance, his country faithfully for three decades.

SAN LORENZO IN LUCINA (PIAZZA SAN LORENZO IN LUCINA)

The original church on this site was built in the fourth century on the ruins of a house that reputedly belonged to a Christian lady called Lucina and it was here that Pope St Damasus was elected in 366. Restoration and rebuilding occurred a number of times before the church was completely rebuilt in the twelfth century. The portico and campanile constructed at this time can still be seen.

Like so many of the Roman churches the interior is completely Baroque, the work of Cosimo Fanzago (1591-1678). Below the altar is preserved the gridiron on which, according to tradition, St Lawrence was martyred; the church also claims other grisly relics of its patron – vessels containing his body fat, blood and burnt flesh, and a cloth purportedly used by an angel to clean his body. In the apse stands the throne of Pope Paschal II; the church also boasts Guido Reni's *Crucifixion* and the tomb of the great French painter, Nicolas Poussin (1594-1665).

San Lorenzo was also the *titulus* of Hugh of Evesham (who is buried in the basilica) and the burial place of yet another papal physician, Gabrielle Fonseca. Fonseca was physician to Pope Innocent X and is commemorated by some fine busts by Bernini.

Robert Kilwardby OP

c. 1215 – 1279

Cardinal Bishop of Porto and Santa Rufina (1278)

Cardinal Kilwardby ushered in a golden age for the English Dominicans. Between 1278 and 1305 there were no less than four English Dominican cardinals, reflecting the Order's success and its use by the King in providing royal confessors.

Kilwardby's early life is shrouded in mystery but he certainly studied at Paris, graduating in 1237. At Paris he taught grammar and logic and his students may have included St Bonaventure. Around 1245 Kilwardby joined the Dominicans, probably in England. The Dominicans had been founded earlier that century and quickly flourished, producing within a few decades leading intellectuals such as St Albert (the *Doctor Universalis*) and St Thomas Aquinas (the *Doctor Angelicus*). Although Aquinas' theological synthesis came to dominate Catholic thought for many centuries, it caused much opposition from his contemporaries, including members of his own Order. Indeed, Kilwardby became a prominent 'anti-Thomist' and, as Archbishop of Canterbury, visited Oxford to condemn certain Thomist propositions which were being taught there. With the gift of hindsight it is tempting to criticise such action, but at a time when Aquinas' thought was considered progressive, Kilwardby was doing his best to preserve the purity and orthodoxy of doctrine at England's oldest university.

Kilwardby was a gifted philosopher and theologian and his most important philosophical work was in the area of logic and philosophical grammar. His *De ortu et divisione philosophiæ* is one of the most important medieval treatises on the classification of the sciences.

At Oxford Kilwardby turned his mind to theology, lecturing on Peter Lombard's *Sentences* and producing the *Quaestiones in libros sententiarum*. Kilwardby's knowledge of the Church Fathers was detailed and among the many works in this field that he produced is a single concordance of Ambrose, Anselm, Augustine, Boethius, Isidore and Lombard, and alphabetical subject indexes for works by Augustine, Anselm and John Damascene.

In 1261 Kilwardby became the English Dominican Provincial, with responsibility over some six hundred friars. He implemented a chapter decree of 1261 that made Oxford a *studium generale* for the Order and dealt with disputes with the Franciscan Friars over such issues as recruiting and the nature of poverty. One Dominican, Solomon of Ingham, went so far as saying that all Franciscans were damned because, contrary to their vows, they held possessions. On the other hand, the followers of St Francis continued to claim a higher state of perfection.

On 11 October 1272 Kilwardby was appointed Archbishop of Canterbury by Pope Gregory X, the first English friar to hold such high office, and was consecrated by the saintly Bishop William Bytton (the Younger) of Bath and Wells (who after his death was popularly invoked against toothache). As metropolitan, Kilwardby undertook a thorough visitation of the whole province, and held provincial synods in 1273 and 1277. On 16 June 1276 he attended the translation of the body of St Richard of Chichester to a new shrine behind the high altar of Chichester Cathedral, in the presence of Edward I and his Queen. Kilwardby had a great devotion to St Richard, canonised at Viterbo in 1262, and had encouraged a fellow Dominican, Ralph Boecking, to write his *vita*. In 1275 he consecrated another future saint as bishop – his friend, St Thomas of Hereford.

Kilwardby remained a son of St Dominic and did his utmost to enable the further consolidation of the Order in England. In 1275 he helped them purchase a site at Barnard's Castle, London, where the Dominicans built a splendid priory and a church, two hundred and twenty feet in length, destroyed by the Great Fire of 1666.

The Archbishop was also plunged into the political world and famously excommunicated Prince Llewelyn of Wales for refusing to pay homage to Edward I. The Archbishop also had an important role on the international stage. He attended the Second Council of Lyons (1274), which briefly restored unity between East and West. At the Council he made his name as a vigorous supporter of papal authority.

On 12 March 1278 Kilwardby was created Cardinal Bishop of Porto and Santa Rufina, which involved residence at the papal court. He was one of two Dominican cardinals created that day by Nicholas III, the other being the Pope's nephew, Blessed Latino Orsini. A homily ascribed to Kilwardby about this time indicates that he saw the journey to Rome as a return to his spiritual father: 'I will arise and go to my father, and I will arise in confidence, for I know that my return and my concern for the clergy of England are joined together.'

Having resigned his See of Canterbury, Kilwardby left England for Viterbo on 25 July, but the journey was too much for an already elderly man. He fell ill and died on 11 September 1279 – though some suggest that his sudden death was due to poison. A saintly and largely unworldly man, who still wore his Dominican habit as cardinal, Kilwardby was laid to rest in the Dominican church of Santa Maria in Gradi at Viterbo. A French Dominican historian, Étienne de Salanhac, praised Kilwardby as *scientia perfectus, moribus ornatus* – 'perfect in knowledge, excellent in character'.

*All four early Dominican cardinals are represented on the walls
of the Chapter Room of San Nicolò in Treviso.*

HUGH OF EVESHAM

† 1287

CARDINAL PRIEST OF SAN LORENZO IN LUCINA (1281)

While John of Toledo may have been a physician, Hugh of Evesham was certainly a 'medical cardinal'. Hugh stayed in Rome at the request of the Pope (Martin IV) and, like John of Toledo, was created Cardinal Priest of San Lorenzo in Lucina on 23 March 1281.

Hugh originally came from the market town of Evesham in Worcestershire, where he may have been educated. He first achieved prominence by acting as a peacemaker during various disputes at the University of Oxford between 1267 and 1274. He held a number of appointments before his summons to Rome, including the archdeaconry of Worcester, a canonry of York and the parish of Bugthorpe. He was also a long-standing clerk of Edward I.

Hugh, having travelled to Rome, was commissioned by either Pope Nicholas III or Martin IV to find a cure for the perennial Roman problem of fever. Martin may have appointed him as his personal physician in 1280.

Whereas John of Toledo had been known as 'the White Cardinal', Hugh was called *il nero* or *atratus*, 'the black' – either because of his clothing or perhaps because of his advocacy of the Dominican Order in his Oxford days. He died on 27 July 1287, possibly due to poisoning, and was buried near the sacristy of his titular church.

Hugh is known to have written several works including a commentary on the Jewish physician Isaac ben Solomon Israeli's book of fevers. Faye Getz, in an article on Hugh of Evesham, notes a recipe to which the approval of both John of Toledo and Hugh of Evesham is ascribed. The recipe is for '*Aurum potabile* (a medical/alchemical concoction) . . . which is said to have been a secret ingredient used in the food of all the cardinals, to liven them up and improve their memories.'

For details of the Basilica of San Lorenzo in Lucina see p. 32.

William of Macclesfield OP
† 1303
Cardinal Priest of Santa Sabina (1303)

William of Macclesfield was the second of four English Dominicans raised to the sacred purple in the space of just twenty-five years. At least that was the intention of the Dominican Pope, Blessed Benedict XI, who named William a cardinal before news reached him of the Englishman's death.

William was a distinguished academic, having studied at the Universities both of Paris and Oxford, gaining his doctorate from the latter and becoming Regent Master of Blackfriars in 1300. Various works attributed to him survive, including several sermons, *quaestiones* on angels and the prologue to the *Sentences* and the *Contra corruptorem Thomae* (attacking the Franciscans). He was known in Rome from having been sent by his Order on various missions and he was sent as *definitor* of the English province to the Dominican General Chapter at Besançon in 1303, dying, probably during the summer, at Canterbury on his way home. Before word of his death reached the papal court, William was created Cardinal Priest of the Dominican church of Santa Sabina on 18 December 1303.

Santa Sabina (Piazza Pietro d'Illiria)

This great Dominican basilica on the Aventine Hill, the *titulus* of a further two English Dominican cardinals, Walter Winterbourne and Thomas Jorz, is one of the best remaining examples of the Roman basilica structure – it really does still look much like its builders intended it to look. The church as it appears today is a fifth century structure with ninth century additions and a little Baroque art more or less out of view as one's gaze stretches down the mighty nave.

Standing magnificently and proudly atop the Aventine Hill, Santa Sabina's severe exterior seems solid against the bright Roman sunlight. Yet this light streams through the ninth century windows into the vast open space of the nave and down upon the mosaic image that marks the tomb of Munoz de Zamora, a Master General of the Dominicans who died in 1300.

The basilica is the station church for Ash Wednesday, on which occasion the Pope normally celebrates Mass with the imposition of ashes, and also is famous for its carved fifth century wooden doors (with Biblical scenes) and Sassoferrato's (Giovanni Battista Salvi, 1609-85) *Our Lady of the Rosary*. An orange tree planted by St Dominic still flourishes in the cloister, and visitors can ask to see the rooms of St Dominic and St Pius V (whose titular church, before his election as Pope, was Santa Sabina) in the *convento*.

WALTER WINTERBOURNE OP
C. 1230 – 1305
CARDINAL PRIEST OF SANTA SABINA (1304)

A year after the posthumous elevation of William Macclesfield to the Roman purple, another English Dominican was created cardinal by the Dominican Pope, Benedict XI. The new Prince of the Church was Walter Winterbourne, who had been Provincial of the English Dominicans (1290–96) and confessor to Edward I since 1298. Winterbourne was accompanying the King on his Scottish campaign when he received news that he had been created Cardinal Priest of Santa Sabina, in succession to Cardinal Macclesfield, on 19 February 1304. The King sent word to the Pope thanking him for the preferment of his confessor but also stating that he could not dispense with Winterbourne's services so that he could move to the papal court.

Benedict XI died shortly afterwards and Edward allowed Cardinal Winterbourne to travel to the conclave at Perugia which, after eleven months, elected the Archbishop of Bordeaux, Bertrand de Got, as Clement V. The new Pope was crowned at Lyons on 15 November and it was during the journey there that the aged Cardinal Winterbourne died. He was buried first at the Dominican house in Genoa before being translated to Blackfriars, London. His epitaph praised him by noting that for all his duties as friar, scholar and cardinal, his hours of prayer were never shortened.

The only authenticated writings of Winterbourne to have survived are business letters to the royal Chancellor, John Langton. Other works ascribed to him have not been definitively identified, including a commentary on the *Sentences* of Peter Lombard, a theological *Summa*, a treatise on original sin and a collection of sermons preached in the presence of the King.

For details of the Basilica of Santa Sabina see p. 38.

THOMAS JORZ OP
C. 1260 – 1310
CARDINAL PRIEST OF SANTA SABINA (1305)

Cardinal Jorz was the last of the Dominican quartet. There would not be another English Dominican cardinal until Philip Howard in 1675. Born into a wealthy London family (or possibly hailing from Nottinghamshire), Jorz was one of six brothers who were to become Dominican friars, two of whom, Walter and Roland, were to succeed each other as Archbishop of Armagh. It is thought that Thomas (also known as *Thomas Anglicanus* to distinguish him from Thomas of Wales) studied at Oxford and subsequently at Paris, where he was a contemporary of St Albert the Great and St Thomas Aquinas. He became Master of Theology at Oxford, lecturing there as well as in London and then Paris. He was elected Prior of the Oxford Dominicans and English Provincial (1296) and acted as a confessor to Edward I.

As the Dominican English Provincial Jorz eagerly encouraged his friars in their mendicant way of life, preaching and hearing confessions whilst moving from parish to parish and diocese to diocese. Not surprisingly, some of the friars needed reminding of exactly how far their special commission ran and Jorz did this with courteous yet firm instructions.

In 1304 he went to Rome on Dominican business and on the 'secret business' of Edward I. The following year he was dispatched to Lyons on a royal mission to the new Pope, Clement V. At Lyons, the Pope created Jorz a Cardinal Priest on 15 December 1305 with the title of Santa Sabina. The Cardinal's remaining years were spent representing English interests at the papal court. These included the promotion of the canonisation process for Thomas of Hereford, which reached its desired conclusion ten years after Jorz's death. Less successful was the attempt to canonise

Robert Grosseteste, the scholarly Bishop of Lincoln.

Although Jorz was a renowned academic – he too wrote a commentary on the first book of Lombard's *Sentences*, and other works – the Pope chose to entrust him with juridical and administrative affairs. In 1310 he was sent as Papal Envoy to the future Emperor, Henry VII, but died suddenly at Grenoble on 13 December 1310. His body was brought home to Oxford for interment under the choir of the Dominican priory.

For details of the Basilica of Santa Sabina see p. 38.

Panoramic view of Rome as seen from Santa Sabina. In the foreground (bottom left) is seen Santa Cecilia in Trastevere; right of this is the 'pyramid' at the top of the San Crisogono bell-tower, and on the horizon the dome of St Peter's rises. All these basilicas have strong connections to the English cardinals.

SIMON LANGHAM OSB

C. 1315 – 1376

CARDINAL PRIEST OF SAN SISTO (1368)
CARDINAL BISHOP OF PALESTRINA (1373)

England has had four Benedictine cardinals – two in the fourteenth century and two in the twentieth – and the first of these was Simon Langham (or de Langham). Born at Langham in Rutland around 1315, he joined the famous Abbey of St Peter's, Westminster, which then held the manor of Langham with Barleythorpe. After studies at Oxford, he was appointed prior on 10 April 1349, but on 27 May of that year was elected abbot – a meteoric rise due to the ravages of the Black Death which was at its fiercest at this time. Ruling what had become a somewhat unruly community with great skill, he saw that the abbey's accounts were once more established on a sure footing, and continued to beautify this royal mausoleum, erecting its perpendicular cloister. He was an excellent administrator and has become known as the abbey's 'Second Founder'. In close contact with the monarchy, he caught the attention of Edward III and became Treasurer of England on 23 November 1360.

In 1362 he was named Bishop of Ely, turning down the See of London to which he was also elected (probably because Ely was a Benedictine see). He was consecrated a bishop at St Paul's Cathedral, London, on 20 March 1362. The following year Langham took up office as Lord Chancellor.

A somewhat stern administrator, his opening speech to the 1363 Parliament is remembered by posterity because it was the first to be given in English.

In 1366 he was translated to Canterbury and two years later created Cardinal Priest of San Sisto. There had not been an English cardinal for nearly sixty years, largely because the Pope resided in Avignon at a time when France was at war with England. The elevation of Langham, however, displeased the King since he had not been consulted. As far as Edward was concerned, Langham had now forfeited his see and so the King seized his substantial revenues. The Archbishop promptly resigned and left for the place where he felt cardinals truly belonged: at the side of the Holy Father, Blessed Urban V.

Langham later returned to the King's favour but he stayed at the papal court where he was known as the 'Cardinal of Canterbury', and continued to hold the archdeaconries of Wells, Taunton and the West Riding of Yorkshire. He was also involved in negotiations between England,

Effigy of Cardinal Langhan over his tomb in Westminster Abbey.

France and Flanders. In 1373 Gregory XI made him Cardinal Bishop of the prestigious suburbicarian See of Palestrina. He was re-elected as Archbishop of Canterbury in 1374, but Gregory refused to confirm the appointment. Langham finally decided to return to his homeland in 1376 as the Pope was making preparations to move back to Rome, but he died of a stroke on 22 July 1376 before he set out on the return journey. He was buried first at a Carthusian church near Avignon and moved three years later to the chapel of St Benedict at Westminster Abbey, the only cardinal, or indeed archbishop, to be interred in that great church. He left the abbey a legacy of £200,000, which financed the rebuilding of the nave, and, not forgetting his origins, he left vestments to his home parish of Langham.

SAN SISTO VECCHIO (PIAZZALE NUMA POMPILIO)

Cardinal Langham's church was established in the fourth century and rebuilt by Innocent III in the twelfth century. In the sixth century the relics of Pope St Sixtus II were moved from the Catacombs of San Calisto to this church.

In the early thirteenth century the church was given into the care of the Dominican sisters by Pope Honorius III and ever since it has had many Dominican Cardinal Priests. Of the twelfth century church only the campanile and apse is visible from the outside, as the rest of the exterior was remodelled during the reign of Pope Benedict XIII, as was the interior of the church. Inside the church, however, there is also a thirteenth century fresco cycle depicting scenes from the New Testament and the Apocrypha.

ADAM EASTON OSB
C. 1330 – 1397
CARDINAL PRIEST OF SANTA CECILIA (1381)

A scholar rather than a politician, Cardinal Easton's rise and dramatic fall from papal grace clearly illustrate the turmoil within the Church of the late fourteenth century.

He was probably born at Easton near Norwich, the son of humble parentage. Having entered the Benedictine priory in Norwich he was sent to study at Gloucester College, Oxford, where he gained a doctorate in theology and repute as a scholar of Greek and Hebrew. On 20 September 1366 Easton was appointed as prior of the students (dean of studies) of Gloucester College, an appointment which was often followed by further important preferments. Easton may have come to the attention of Simon Langham, the Benedictine Archbishop of Canterbury, who included him in his entourage as *socius* when he moved to the papal court at Avignon.

We know little of Easton's activities within the Papal Curia until 1375, but the best glimpse we have of his status is the fact that his name heads the members of the household in Langham's will, of which he was both a beneficiary and an executor.

For a scholar of Easton's finesse, Avignon must have been a most exciting place in which to work. There were many fine libraries and a Jewish ghetto noted for its learning. He started to study Hebrew and translated the Old Testament (excluding the Psalms) into Latin, since he held the translation of St Jerome to be inaccurate. His condemnation of the Lollard heresy, the *Defensorium ecclesiasticae potestatis*, was completed in 1381 and dedicated to Urban VI.

With the death of Langham in 1376, Easton had to reconsider his career. After administering Langham's will he travelled to Rome (where the Papacy had returned) and witnessed the election of Urban VI on 8 April 1378.

The cardinals in the conclave lived in fear of the Roman mob that was gathered outside protesting against any possibility of the cardinals electing a French Pope. An Italian, Archbishop Prignano of Bari, was elected. As a bishop he had been an excellent administrator and generally admired, but as Pope he turned out to be violent and paranoid. Within six months the cardinals had fled Rome, declared Urban's election invalid because of the great duress under which it was held, and elected the Cardinal Bishop of Geneva as Pope Clement VII. This became known as the Great Schism. Pope Urban retaliated by appointing twenty-nine cardinals from all over Europe. On 21 December 1381 Urban created Easton a Cardinal Priest with the title of Santa Cecilia. He was subsequently known as the *Cardinalis Angliae* ('the Cardinal of England') and gained the Deanery of York, the wealthiest English benefice without a mitre.

By 1384 Pope Urban was considered to be insane by many cardinals. The Pope had fled to Nocera where some members of the Sacred College came up with a scheme by which the Pope would be ruled by a committee. In January 1385 Urban discovered the plot thanks to the ever growing fear of one of the plotters themselves, Cardinal Orsini. On 11 January the cardinals arrived for what they thought was to be a routine consistory only to find that the Pope arrested six of them, including Easton, and submitted them to the torturers to extract confessions. Easton vowed that were he to survive he would advocate the canonisation of a recent holy woman, Bridget of Sweden, with all his might. Urban dragged the unfortunate cardinals around with him as he moved from place to place. By 16 December 1386, when Urban left Genoa, only four of them, including Easton, were still alive. His benefices had been confiscated and he was no longer a cardinal, but he was to escape with his life. Urban had never credited the politically naive Easton with anything more than keeping knowledge of the plot secret. After appeals for clemency from both the Benedictine Order and the English Government (which supported Urban), Easton was released and restored to the College of Cardinals by Boniface IX within a month of his election. He was granted other benefices, including Precentor of Lisbon Cathedral (1390) and Archdeacon of Shetland and Orkney (1391).

In his later years Easton worked for the promotion of the feast of the Visitation of the Blessed Virgin Mary – he may have even composed the Office of this feast – and for the canonisation of Bridget of Sweden, which was accomplished on 7 October 1391. He died on 15 September 1397 and lies buried in a splendid tomb at the back of the nave of his titular church,

Santa Cecilia in Trastevere. He did not forget his East Anglian roots and his library was given to the monks of Norwich.

SANTA CECILIA IN TRASTEVERE (PIAZZA DI SANTA CECILIA)

The church of Cardinals Easton, Wolsey and Howard (1676-79) is an ancient foundation, built to honour the third century Virgin Martyr, St Cecilia, who was executed in her bathroom (now beneath the basilica). On the site of the ancient church Pope St Paschal I (817–24) built a larger and grander church. The great mosaic in the apse dates from Pope St Paschal's reign. The fine baldacchino over the high altar was made by Arnolfo di Cambio around 1292, and Pietro Cavallini's fresco *The Last Judgment* in the choir gallery also dates from this time. All these treasures could have been seen by Cardinal Easton and, indeed, Cardinal Wolsey, if the latter had ever made it to Rome.

Yet another treasure, though, could only have been known to Cardinal Howard – Stefano Maderno's beautiful statue of St Cecilia. When St Cecilia's tomb was opened on the orders of Cardinal Sfondrati in 1599, the saint's body was found to be incorrupt. The Cardinal asked Maderno to make a sculpture of the body as it was found and this effigy now rests at the foot of the high altar.

Cardinal Easton's tomb – originally constructed as free standing but now moved up against a wall – can be found to the right of the main entrance.

PHILIP REPYNGDON OSA

C. 1345 – 1424

CARDINAL PRIEST OF SANTI NEREO E ACHILLEO (1408)

Believed to have been born in Wales, Philip Repyngdon (or Repington) became an Augustinian canon first at Repton, then at Leicester where he was ordained a priest on 26 May 1369. He was further educated at Broadgates Hall, Oxford. At Oxford he became a Doctor of Divinity in 1382 but was soon embroiled in a dispute that brought about his excommunication.

In Oxford Philip Repyngdon had a reputation for being humble, good natured and likeable. Yet in 1382 when he delivered a series of sermons and engaged in a disputation at Oxford defending John Wyclif's rejection of the belief in transubstantiation, opinions quickly changed. He first preached on this theme in Brackley in Northamptonshire, but it was his sermon of 5 June 1382 that particularly caught the attention of the ecclesiastical authorities.

Despite a Church council held at Blackfriars, London in May 1382, that condemned Wyclif's heresies, and the Archbishop of Canterbury's letter to the Chancellor of Oxford demanding that the erroneous teachings must not be disseminated through the University, Repyngdon was invited to preach the Corpus Christi sermon at the preaching cross in St Frideswide's churchyard in the city. According to a Carmelite compilation, the *Fasciculi zizaniorum*, Repyngdon not only defended Wyclif's Eucharistic theories but also stated that God would eventually cause the hearts and minds of Wyclif's opponents to be enlightened and find truth in his teachings. According to *Fasciculi zizaniorum*, Repyngdon said:

> Whosoever offers up to the Pope or bishops before temporal lords [in prayers of petition] goes against holy scripture, and that his master, Master John Wyclif, is a most catholic teacher, and that Wyclif has never determined or taught with regard to the Eucharist other than what the whole Church of God holds, and that his opinion on the Eucharist is most true.

Repyngdon was first suspended from preaching by the University's Chancellor and subsequently excommunicated by Archbishop Courtnay. However, Repyngdon's Lollard sympathies were short lived. On 23 October 1382 he recanted his erroneous beliefs before the Archbishop, doing the same before the Chancellor of Oxford the following month.

Henceforth, Repyngdon rose steadily, being elected Abbot of Leicester in 1393 (receiving royal assent on 12 January 1394) and Chancellor of Oxford (1400-3). He became Henry IV's confessor, and it was because of the King's prerogative to nominate the occupant of a see for election by the Dean and Chapter that Repyngdon was appointed Bishop of Lincoln in 1404, succeeding Henry Cardinal Beaufort. He was consecrated bishop at Canterbury Cathedral on 29 March 1405 and enthroned at Lincoln on 8 April.

On 18 September 1408 Pope Gregory XII raised Repyngdon to the dignity of cardinal under the title of the church of Santi Nereo e Achilleo. However, this was not recognised in England and Gregory XII's creations of cardinals were revoked after he was deposed in 1409. In any case, Repyngdon never used the title.

Repyngdon had a great concern for the poor and Margery Kempe, who met him in 1413, was impressed by his daily gift of a penny and a loaf to thirteen individuals. On 10 October 1419 Repyngdon made the unusual decision to resign as Bishop of Lincoln on the grounds of frailty. His resignation was accepted on 21 November but it was not until 1 February 1420 that he was finally and formally able to give up his see. He was given a pension by Pope Martin V.

Repyngdon continued to be influenced by the writings of Wyclif and maintained contacts with Lollard circles. This is perhaps most evident in his will, which states his desire to be buried naked in a sack with the minimum of ceremony. His money was to be given to the poor and even the funeral pall was to be used to make clothing. He gave orders that his Requiem Mass should be celebrated in the parish church of St Margaret near Lincoln Cathedral, if possible while he was dying. After his death in 1424 Repyngdon was buried simply in the southeast transept of Lincoln Cathedral.

SANTI NEREO E ACHILLEO (VIA DELLE TERME DI CARACALLA)

The fifth century church was the *diaconia* of Cardinal Pole (1536-40) and the *titulus* of Cardinals Repyngdon and Godfrey. The church is sometimes called the *Titulus de Fasciola* (Church of the Bandage) on account of the tradition that, as St Peter was fleeing Rome, a bandage on his foot (covering a wound caused by his prison chains) fell off at this spot.

Unfortunately this church is nearly always closed, but if persevering visitors are able to make their way to it on a late spring afternoon, during a wedding, they might be lucky to get a glimpse of the apse and triumphal arch decorated during the reign of Pope Leo III (795-816). From the Pomarancio frescoes of the nave to the sparkling mosaics of the apse this church is a blaze of colour and artistic activity.

One of the church's most famous cardinals was Cesare Baronius, the great Oratorian historian, who was responsible for much of its restoration at the end of the sixteenth century. Since then, the Congregation of the Oratory has looked after the church.

THOMAS LANGLEY
C. 1360 – 1437
CARDINAL PRIEST – NO TITULUS (1411)

The next two English cardinals, Thomas Langley and Robert Hallam, were both raised to the sacred purple on 6 June 1411 by the anti-pope, John XXIII (the only 'pope' to have studied at Oxford University). They lived in difficult and confusing times. In 1378 Gregory XI died, having brought the Papacy back to Rome from Avignon. Urban VI was elected as his successor, but many non-Italian cardinals declared his election invalid and elected Clement VII in his place, who set up court in Avignon. The schism lasted forty years and divided Christians – St Catherine of Siena, for example, was 'Urbanist' while St Vincent Ferrer was 'Clementine'. Many attempts were made to end this state of affairs, culminating in the Councils of Pisa (1409) and Constance (1414–18), in which our two English cardinals were heavily involved.

Thomas was the son of William and Alice Langley of Middleton, Lancashire and was educated at St Mary's Priory, Thetford (Norfolk), and Corpus Christi, Cambridge. Langley's career got off to a prodigious start thanks to the patronage of John of Gaunt, son of Edward III and brother of the famous 'Black Prince'. His first office was the rectory of Radcliffe, Lancashire (1385) and others soon followed: St Martin-le-Grand and St Alphege in London, St Asaph and Meifod in Wales, and Castleford in West Yorkshire.

On 17 March 1397 Langley was ordained priest at Coventry. Meanwhile, Langley worked in Gaunt's chancery and was heavily involved in the legitimization of the four Beauforts, Gaunt's children by Katherine Swynford. This was a crucial act and led not only to the rise of Henry Beaufort, a future cardinal, but also of John, thus allowing his great-grandson, Henry VII, to claim the throne in 1485. The legitimization also won Langley some influential friends for the future and gave him an early taste of diplomacy with the papal court.

Langley became secretary to Henry of Bolingbroke and, following Bolingbroke's coronation as Henry IV in 1399, he became Archdeacon of Norfolk, Dean of York and Keeper of the Privy Seal. In October 1404 he was elected Bishop of London upon the recommendation of the King, but this was overruled by Pope Innocent VII, who also rejected the King's recommendation the following year for Langley to succeed the executed Archbishop Richard Scrope at York. In 1405 Langley followed Beaufort as Lord Chancellor (until 1407) and was at last enthroned as a bishop – at Durham on 4 September 1406.

In 1409 Langley represented the northern province at the Council of Pisa, which deposed the two rival 'popes' and unanimously elected Alexander V. However, since the deposed pontiffs paid no attention to the Council, there were now in effect three 'popes'. Alexander V died in 1410 and was replaced by John XXIII. In need of as much support as he could muster the anti-pope made Langley a Cardinal Priest on 6 June 1411, though he received no titular church and Henry IV overruled the decision, having no desire for Langley to move to the papal court. Langley was never addressed as a Prince of the Church, nor did he wear the insignia of a cardinal; he is included here for the sake of completeness.

Langley was, above all, a servant of the Crown and he spent most of his time away from Durham at court or on diplomatic missions. Just as he worked intimately with Henry IV, he became in turn Henry V's most trusted minister and acted as Lord Chancellor once again between 1417 and 1424, one of the longest chancellorships of the Middle Ages. By the time of Henry VI's succession, he was highly respected as the elder Lancastrian statesman. Langley's biographer, Ian Sharman, has called Langley 'de facto England's first Foreign Secretary' and 'the first Spin-Doctor', since 'from the justification for the usurpation [of Richard II], through Agincourt and the Treaty of Troyes, and throughout the minority of Henry VI, a "spin" was put on events', in order to legitimise the House of Lancaster.

As a man of considerable wealth, Langley was able to embellish his cathedral at Durham. He founded a chantry, completed the roof, established a grammar and song school on Palace Green and rebuilt his manor at Stockton-on-Tees.

He died at Bishop Auckland on 20 November 1437, aged seventy-four, and was buried in the Galilee chapel of his cathedral, not far from the shrine of St Bede the Venerable.

Langley's birthplace of Middleton (near Rochdale) still remembers its distinguished son. The chantry school which he founded continued as the Middleton Grammar School and, more recently, the Queen Elizabeth School. The local Catholic High School is named after the fifteenth century Cardinal, as is the Langley housing estate, which won fame as the setting for Ken Loach's film *Raining Stones* (1993).

The tomb (bottom centre) of Thomas Langley in Durham Cathedral.

ROBERT HALLAM
† 1417
CARDINAL PRIEST – NO TITULUS (1411)

Like Thomas Langley, Robert Hallam (or Hallum) was created a cardinal by an anti-pope who was desperate for English support. This has led to much debate about whether he truly was a cardinal – indeed at the Council of Constance (1414-18) he was ranked only as a bishop. In these difficult times there were two, and, after 1409, three rival 'popes', each with their own curia, and 'obediences' depended largely on political and diplomatic alignments – the Papacy had become little more than a puppet at the hands of pan-European politics. Even religious orders were split in their loyalties, according to national groupings. At the time it was difficult to see who the right papal candidate might be, and people's choices were restricted by politics.

Robert Hallam was born sometime in the 1360s and received his education at Oxford. In 1400 he was named Archdeacon of Canterbury and three years later Chancellor of Oxford University. After a succession of appointments including prebends at Chichester, Salisbury and York and the archdeaconry of Canterbury (1400), Hallam was the papal nominee for the archbishopric of York following the execution of Archbishop Scrope (1405) and was consecrated by Innocent VII. However, the King, who had nominated Langley to the see, objected and Hallam had to wait until 1407 to gain the bishopric of Salisbury, with its new cathedral and soaring spire.

Hallam was a competent administrator at Salisbury and did much to promote the Use of Sarum as the standard liturgy for the Province of Canterbury and the campaign for the canonisation of St Osmund. He liked to call himself *ecclesiae Sarum servus humilis et minister* ('humble servant and minister of the church of Salisbury').

Much of the rest of Hallam's episcopate revolved around the councils held to resolve the Great Schism. At Pisa (1409), Hallam was one of the English ambassadors and preached at the sixth session on the theme of the unity, of the Church. In Council he was given the first seat among the bishops, to the left of the cardinals, on the grounds that England was, according to tradition, evangelised by St Joseph of Arimathea before any other nation. Two years later, on 6 June 1411, the Neapolitan anti-pope, John XXIII, created Hallam a Cardinal Priest (though without a titular church). However Henry IV quashed the nomination, pleading that he could not spare Hallam's useful service to the Crown.

The Council of Pisa only achieved further division in the Church, resulting in three 'popes' instead of two. Thus there was need for another Council, which was called by the King of Hungary, Sigismund. (He had been elected King of the Holy Roman Empire in 1410, but could not be called Emperor until he had been crowned in Rome by an authentic Pope.) Turning up to the Council of Constance in 1415 with a large retinue, Hallam made a name for himself. A citizen of Constance, Ulrich von Richental, described in his *Chronicle* the arrival of the English delegation:

> On Thursday at the hour of vespers on the eve of the festival of Our Lady there rode in two archbishops and seven bishops from the Kingdom of England, with vii wagons and twenty-two sumpter horses bearing the luggage and other gear: and there was forty-two learned clerks from the universities ... twelve of whom were doctors of Holy Writ and the others masters of civil and canon law: and with them came the noble Earl Richard of Warwick with three trumpeters and four pipers: and when this same Earl rode in the tourneys at Constance he rode the course on a horse with trappings of gold with a padded lining, and when he had ridden once in a tourney, he never used the same again: and the trumpeters blew their trumpets in a scale of three voices as is used in singing: and the Earl lodged in the painted house in the upper market.
>
> They had with them five hundred horses and a great company: and the foremost among them was Bishop Robert the Archbishop of Salisbury and he lodged in the house of the minster, by the steps, the house with a door into the cloisters. . . .
>
> This embassy came to Constance both by reason of the Council and also at the behest of the King of England, to tell of his good name and of his rights against the King of France, for they two were fighting mightily together and laying waste each others' lands and people.

There are inaccuracies in this account – most obviously, Hallam was not an archbishop – but it suggests that Hallam was indeed held in high regard. A keen supporter of the Council and of reform *in capite et in membris* (in head and members), Hallam forgot his personal ties to John XXIII in his desire for the election of one new Pope. The anti-pope even listed Hallam's hostility as one of the reasons for his departure from Constance for Schaffhausen in March 1415, two months before his deposition on charges of simony, perjury and gross misconduct.

The Council was also concerned with the rooting out of heresy, and Hallam found himself in an international committee that tried to urge the Bohemian reformer, Jan Hus, to recant before he went to the stake. Hus had travelled to Constance under the promise of safe conduct, hoping to influence the reforms, but found himself arrested and condemned to death as a heretic. Hallam, however, was more concerned with the reform of the whole Church rather than extremists in a far-flung kingdom in the East. Yet Hallam well understood the power of some of the wayward thinkers of his time. During the trial of one of the supporters of Hus, Jerome of Prague, someone cried out that Jerome should also be burned like Hus. Jerome responded saying: 'If you wish my death, so be it in God's name,' to which Hallam replied, 'Nay, Jerome, for it is written "The Lord desireth not the death of a sinner but rather that he should turn from his wickedness and live."' Jerome did not 'turn from his wickedness' and a year later he too was burnt.

The Council of Constance dragged on, despite the departure of Sigismund and his court in July 1415. In the same month Gregory XII was made to abdicate. Still the Council continued, but it was not all hard work, as Ulrich von Richental records:

On the eve of St Thomas after Christmas [1416] the English celebrated the feast of St Thomas of Canterbury: their four trumpeters went through the town and bade all to vespers: and from their trumpets were hung the Arms of England: and they proclaimed that the English were going to hold a great feast: and they began to celebrate the feast of St Thomas at the Minster right beauteously and well with great peals of bells, with great lighted candles and with sweet English singing, with the organ and with the trumpets, the tenor, the descant and the medium: this was at vespers. And in the morning on St Thomas' day they had High Mass in the Minster and the Archbishop of Salisbury sang the Mass and two other bishops from England were his servers at the altar: and there were at this Mass three Patriarchs and other lords . . . and after this Mass the trumpeters went through the city and bade many lords to a feast. But the cardinals ate with no man.

And on the 24th day of the month of January the Archbishop of Salisbury and the Bishop of London and five more bishops from England invited all the city council and many other worthy burghers to Burckhart Walter's house. . . . And they gave a great and rich feast: there were three courses one after the other, each course having eight dishes of which four were of gilt and four of

silver. During the meal between the courses they made a mime with scenes of
Our Lady and the birth of our Lord God, her Child, with most rich garments
and drapery: they stood Joseph beside her and the Holy Kings bringing their
gifts to Our Lady and her Child: and they made a star of pure gold which went
before them on a thin wire of iron: and they showed King Herod and how he
sent messengers after the three Holy Kings and how he slew the little children.
All this was done with most rich garments, with wide golden and silver girdles,
most beauteously and devoutly.

It is not surprising that von Richental records that 'the cardinals ate with
no man'. The Anglo-German axis was meeting increasing opposition
from the contingent of cardinals as a formidable block, second only to the
French, both opposed to reform first. The French said that 'MARS' ruled
the Council – the letters standing for the sees of the principal prelates
demanding reform (the Archbishop of Milan, the Patriarch of Antioch, the
Archbishop of Riga and the Bishop of Salisbury). The crisis was heightening;
the sharp point of dispute being that some, like the English and German
delegations, thought that reform of the Church should be pursued before
a new Pope was elected. Others, including the cardinals and the French,
Italian and Spanish delegations, desired that the Pope be elected first. The
fear of those who wished to discuss reform first was that as soon as a Pope
was elected the Council would disperse, its work left incomplete.

In July 1417 Benedict XIII was finally deposed and the papal throne was
at last completely vacant. Hallam continued to campaign for reform first,
the French Cardinal Fillastre bitterly recording in his diary of this time
that, to his mind, Hallam used 'haughty speech, as is his wont, mingled
with threats', and that he and those who supported him were 'notorious
enemies of the Roman Church, the Curia and the cardinals'. It would seem
that ire at his effective opponent inspired these words but he need not have
worried – death would suddenly put a stop to Hallam's great schemes. Von
Richental records:

On the fourth day of the first month of harvest [September] at the eighth
hour after noonday, there died in the Castle of Gottlieben the high and mighty
Lord Archbishop Robert of Salisbury from England. And on the next day, a
Sunday, at vesper time they rang a bishop's peal of bells for him right nobly
and they brought him in by ship and the bearers bore him from the ship with
the honours of a bishop: and he had a mitre on his head and he wore the
Mass vestments of a bishop: one could see his face uncovered and his hands
lay before him: and he had two maniples and a most costly ring was on his
middle finger and the double cross lay beside him: he was laid on a beauteous

cloth of gold and he was borne with many great candles and laid in the Choir of the Minster, where he now lies buried under a marble stone: they stood a waxen chalice and a paten on his breast: and as he came thither a priest all the time threw pennies into the street under the feet of the people: and they bore on high before him three pieces of cloth of gold which are in the Minster to this day: there went with the bier all cardinals, patriarchs, archbishops, bishops, all priests, prelates and clerks and the learned clerks from the schools and our Lord the King, all electors, dukes, counts, knights, and squires and besides a great mass of the people. And before him and behind went eighty great lighted candles: the candles and the bier were borne by poor unmarried men and each was given a new grey coat: and in the morning there was a rich Mass. . . .

Monday the thirteenth day of September was the day when they held the funeral Mass of the Bishop of Salisbury in the Minster of Constance: he was placed in the midst of the Minster on a bier covered with cloth of gold and there stood at the head a great lighted candle and likewise at the foot: and around the bier stood twenty-four worthy old men with new white garments and with white caps with long white liripipes and each had a lighted candle in his hand: and there stood on the pulpit thirty-six great candles all alight and each was of more than five pounds weight of wax: and there were at this service all cardinals, all patriarchs, all archbishops and bishops as before written, our Lord the King of the Romans, all electors, princes, dukes, counts, knights, and squires: and the service was very grand, but not as grand as that of the afore written Cardinal [of Bar].

And this was the Bishop who at mid Lent, when Pope John was still at Constance, dared to tell him to his face that he was not worthy to be Pope, because of the great wickedness which he had practised, such as simony and other sins which cannot be written, and he told these things to his face and feared him not. He, too, was the Bishop who dared to address the mighty Elector of Mainz openly before the whole Council and told him that he was worthy to be burned. And he put up in Constance at the house by the steps which has a door into the cloisters: and the white robes and the white caps they gave at his behest to the twenty-four old men and they wore them after his death for many a day.

The Bishop of Salisbury was buried before the high altar of Constance Cathedral where his grave is still marked by an impressive memorial brass of English workmanship. Buried with him were the hopes of the 'reform first' party. By the end of September news reached Constance that an English bishop, seemingly making a pilgrimage to the Holy Land, had arrived in Ulm. This Bishop, who was the uncle of Henry V, helped to persuade Sigismund against the 'reform first' policy of Hallam and his like. A conclave was called and a Pope, Martin V, duly elected. The new Pope was soon to show his gratitude to that English Bishop by naming him – Henry Beaufort, Bishop of Winchester – a cardinal.

HENRY BEAUFORT
C. 1375 – 1447
CARDINAL PRIEST OF SANT' EUSEBIO (1426)

Henry Beaufort was the first of England's royal cardinals, but as an illegitimate child his life might have turned out very differently. His father was John of Gaunt (i.e. Ghent), one of Edward III's younger sons, but his mother was John's long-term mistress, Catherine Swynford. At the time of the future cardinal's birth in Anjou, his father was married to Constance of Castile, his second wife, who had given Gaunt the royal title of 'King of Castile and Léon' and plunged him into the murky world of Iberian politics. Constance died in 1394 and Gaunt married Catherine in February 1396, after which Richard II and the Pope declared Henry and his siblings legitimate, though barred from the royal succession.

Beaufort was educated at both Cambridge (Peterhouse 1388-9) and Oxford (The Queen's College 1390-c.1393). Having commenced further studies in theology he was ordained deacon on 7 April 1397 being made Chancellor of the University of Oxford in the same month.

In 1398 Beaufort became Bishop of Lincoln, aged just twenty-four. He would serve as a bishop for almost half a century. About this time he made his one major indiscretion – after a brief affair with the widowed Lady Alice Fitzalan a daughter, called Jane or possibly Joan, was born in 1402. He remembered her in his will.

In 1403 he was made Chancellor to his half-brother, Henry IV, though he resigned when he was translated to Winchester the following year. He became a close friend and confidante to his nephew, the Prince of Wales and future Henry V, and a staunch opponent of the Archbishop of

Canterbury, Thomas Arundel. This led to conflict with the King, and when Prince Henry proposed that his father should abdicate in his favour, both the Prince and his bishop-friend were dismissed from the Royal Council.

Beaufort was back in power in 1413 when Henry V, Beaufort's nephew, succeeded to the throne, and he served as Chancellor again. He served the King faithfully, acting as Regent during the long military campaigns in France. On 18 December 1417, just over one month after his election as Pope, Martin V created Beaufort a cardinal and appointed him legate *a latere* for life in England, Wales, Ireland, and in all other lands overseas that were under the authority of Henry V. Pope Martin permitted Beaufort to retain the See of Winchester *in commendam* and to be exempt from the jurisdiction of the Archbishop of Canterbury. The King would have been happy to have had an English cardinal in the Roman Curia promoting the interests of the English in Rome but he was not pleased with the thought of a cardinal in England, with such authority as had been given Beaufort, serving first and foremost the needs of the Pope. According to Humphrey, Duke of Gloucester (no friend of Beaufort's), Henry exclaimed on hearing of his uncle's elevation that: 'He had as lief set his crown beside him as to see him [Beaufort] wear a cardinal's hat, he being a cardinal.'

The Pope's offer was largely in recognition of Beaufort's involvement at the conclusion of the Council of Constance (1414-18). At a crucial moment, Beaufort had united all the factions in agreeing that a commission should be set up to organise the papal election, that all the decrees now ready should be published and that once the Pope was elected, reform would be the main concern of the Papacy. Henry V had particularly wanted a Pope elected who would be sympathetic to England's cause in her continuing struggle with France. During the election Beaufort himself was considered as a candidate for the papacy, but ultimately Odo Colonna was elected as Martin V.

It is unclear as to what extent Beaufort might have promoted himself to receive the red hat – he was a cautious man who knew well the King's mind, and that he would lose his profitable see if sent to Rome as a curial cardinal. Martin V had not published the bulls that concerned Beaufort's promotion and when the aspiring cardinal met the King at Rouen on 3 March 1419 he was left in no doubt that the King did not desire him to become a cardinal. Beaufort returned to England under something of a political cloud but the King's need for Beaufort's great wealth was to be most important in reinstating the Bishop in public life.

Beaufort was finally allowed to accept the red hat on 24 May 1426 with the title of San Eusebio. The consistory that day included two future *beati* – Blessed Louis Allemand (Archbishop of Arles) and Blessed Niccolo Albergati (the Carthusian Bishop of Bologna). Beaufort travelled to France, where he was made legate to Germany, Hungary and Bohemia and led a doomed crusade against the reformist Hussites. In 1429 he raised another army to fight the Hussites but, with the end of his legateship imminent, used the troops to relieve the English in France.

Beaufort has received a bad press. He was reputed to be the richest prelate in Christendom and his contemporaries were impressed by the fact that even the kitchen utensils in his household were made of silver. He may have had a portrait painted by Van Eyck, now in the Kunsthistorisches Museum, Vienna, although it has traditionally been thought to be of Cardinal Albergati. On his deathbed, Beaufort is supposed to have cried, 'Why should I die, having so many riches?'

Beaufort's frequent loans to the Crown made him a crucial champion of the Lancastrian supremacy and gained him the name 'banker of the State'. Throughout his life Beaufort granted astonishing loans to the Crown to support the cost of the army – £14,000 in 1417, £17,666 in 1421, £9,333 in 1424, £8,333 in 1430 – usually lending more money before the previous debt had been paid. Moreover, posterity remembers Beaufort as one of the key actors in the trial of St Joan of Arc. Though he is said to have wept as he watched her burn, it is unlikely that he had much sympathy for the French visionary. Her relief of Orleans effectively denied the Lancastrians the crown of France that was so nearly theirs.

Shakespeare vividly portrayed Beaufort's opposition to Humphrey of Gloucester during the reign of Henry VI. Gloucester tried to deprive Beaufort of his bishopric in 1426 (on grounds of treason), 1429 (whilst away as legate) and 1431 (when Beaufort went to Paris to crown Henry as 'King of France'). Beaufort survived each attempt – though he had to resign his third term as Chancellor in 1426 – and continued with his conciliatory 'pro-peace' policy. Together with the future Cardinal Kemp, he went to the Congress of Arras (1435) and managed to secure the release of Charles of Orleans in 1439.

Gloucester died of a stroke in 1447 while awaiting trial for treason and instantly became a 'martyr' for the war in France. Many saw his death as suspicious – people speculated that he had been smothered, poisoned or even that, like Edward II, 'a hot spit was put to his fundament'. Beaufort died in Winchester the same year and Shakespeare, in *Henry VI, Part II*, has him hallucinating and writhing on his deathbed in remorse over Humphrey's murder. Warwick observes: 'See, how the pangs of death do make him grin,' and that 'So bad a death argues a monstrous life.' Indeed, this deathbed scene later became a favourite with artists such as Sir Joshua Reynolds. Two very different accounts have come down to us of Beaufort's last days, both claiming to have been eyewitnesses. One is melodramatic, the other describes Beaufort dying 'with the same business-like dignity in which for so long he had lived and ruled'.

Undoubtedly the account most extraordinary to modern ears, probably written by a monk of Croyland Abbey, claims convincingly that: 'He who wrote this was present, and both saw and heard these things, "and we know that his testimony is true"'.

> There occurs to my memory as I write this a notable action, and one worthy of imitation by others, of that glorious and catholic man, the said Cardinal of Winchester. When he was languishing at the point of death in his palace of Wolvesey beside his Cathedral Church of St Swithun in the said year 1447, on the Saturday before the Sunday of the passion of our Lord, on which day the Office *Sitientes* is sung, he caused all the ecclesiastics of the parts adjacent, both regular and secular, to be collected in the great chamber of the same palace. Here he had his solemn exequies with the Mass of Requiem chanted in his presence as he lay in bed. On the fifth day thereafter the prior of his cathedral church as executor of the whole office celebrated Mass in full pontificals. In the evening after the exequies had been performed the testament of his last will was read aloud before all; and early on the morrow of the Mass, when he had added certain corrections and codicils, all these testamentary matters were once more recited, and publicly and in a audible voice he confirmed them. And thus he bade farewell to all and died at the time above-mentioned.

The royal Cardinal was buried in a magnificent chantry chapel at his cathedral, and the shrine of St Swithun was moved to adjoin his tomb. He asked that the inscription 'I should tremble did I not know Thy mercies' be written on the tomb. After making provision for his relatives, Beaufort's will cancelled the debts of some noble borrowers and left generous sums to his household, tenants officials, executors, the monks of Winchester and of St Augustine's, Canterbury. The vast bulk of the rich Cardinal's wealth, however, was left to make provision for Masses to be said and charitable works done – Masses were to be said forever at Lincoln and Winchester Cathedrals, the monasteries at Canterbury and the mendicants' houses in London as well as in Hyde Abbey, Eton, King's College, Cambridge, the house of the Bonhommes (or Bluefriars) at Ashridge, Hertfordshire and wherever else his executors might decide. To his trusty executors he finally asked that the residue of his estate should be disposed of on pious uses 'as they should believe to be of the greatest possible advantage to the safety of my soul'.

SANT' EUSEBIO (PIAZZA VITTORIO EMANUELE)

If ever a Roman church needed a benefactor today like Beaufort it would be this church. Built by St Eusebius of Bologna in the fourth century and dedicated (probably) to St Eusebius of Vercelli, it was rebuilt in the twelfth and eighteenth centuries. Beyond the plaque that recalls the consecration of the church and the fleeting glimpse of a Romanesque campanile, extraordinarily little remains in this church that transmits a sense of its antiquity.

Arms attributed to English Cardinals:

by

Dom Anselm Baker:

a monk of the Cistertian Order:

Painted by him at the Abbey of

Saint Bernard in the Forest of

Charnwood Leicestershire· circa 1875:

Given to the College of Arms by William Henry Weldon Norroy King of Arms· 1906:

The title page from Dom Anselm Baker's The Armorial Bearings of English Cardinals from Earliest Times, *with the arms of (left to right) Pullen, Somercotes, John of Toledo and Hugh of Evesham below.*

Cardinal Nicholas Breakspear – Pope Adrian IV

TOP LEFT: *Cardinal Langton crowning King Henry III.*

TOP RIGHT: *Rather than move Cardinal Langton's tomb for the construction of St Michael's chapel at Canterbury Cathedral, the architects simply built around it, the stone coffin protruding under the chapel's altar inside the building, and leaving the other half outside.*

LEFT: *Cardinal Langton presiding over the translation of St Thomas, from a vestment at Stonyhurst.*

THIS PAGE AND FACING PAGE: *Representations of the four early Dominican cardinals from the Chapter Room of the Dominican Convent of San Nicolò, Treviso, painted by Tomaso da Modena from 1351-2. From left to right, Cardinals Kilwardby, Macclesfield, Winterbourne and Jorz.*

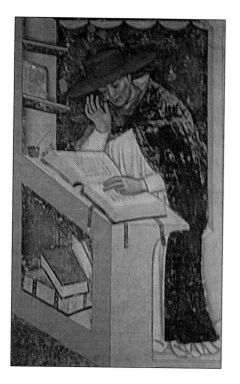

The tomb of Cardinal Langham in Westminster Abbey.

The tomb of Cardinal Easton in the Basilica of Santa Cecilia, Rome.

The seal of Cardinal Langley. His image is represented on both sides of the seal: enthroned (above), and as the warrior Prince-Bishop (below).

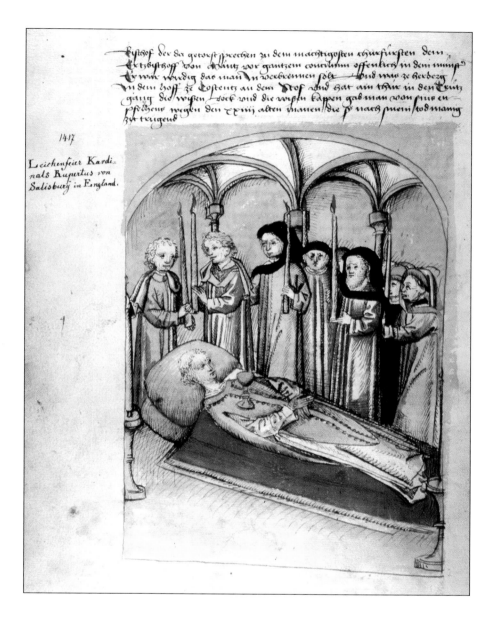

FACING PAGE: *At the Council of Constance, Cardinal Hallam is to be seen (third bishop from the right) before 'Pope' John XXIII.*

THIS PAGE: *Cardinal Hallam lying in state, from Ulrich von Richental's illustrated record of the events surrounding the Council of Constance.*

FACING PAGE: *Paul Dela-roche's representation of the interrogation of Joan of Arc by Cardinal Beaufort, painted in 1824.*

LEFT: *Effigy of Cardinal Beaufort from Bishop's Waltham Palace.*

BELOW: *The tomb of Cardinal Beaufort in Winchester Cathedral.*

A nineteenth-century engraving representing Cardinal Kemp.

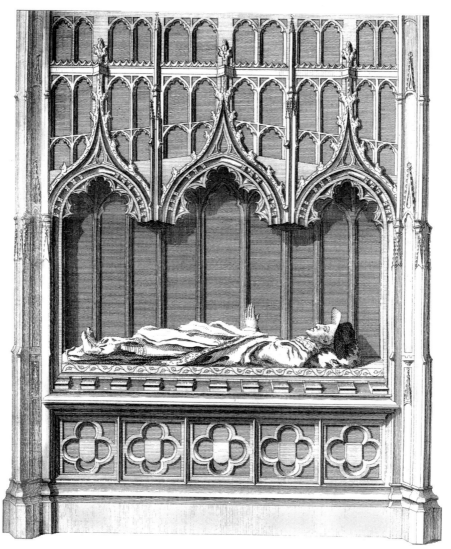

The tomb of Cardinal Louis of Luxembourg in Ely Cathedral, and (below) his arms in stained glass.

1438 — 1443
LOUIS OF LUXEMBURG

The coronation of King Edward IV by Cardinal Bourchier on 28 June 1461. Bourchier was not – as depicted – a cardinal at the time, receiving the red hat only in 1465.

The tomb of Cardinal Morton, in Canterbury Cathedral.

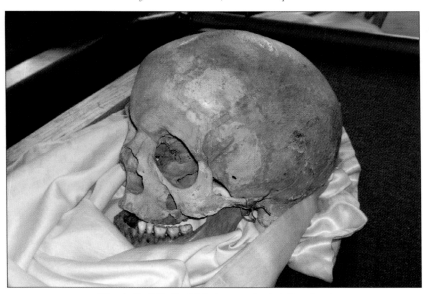

The skull of Cardinal Morton, now kept at Stonyhurst.

The bishops of England taking part in the Royal Procession to Parliament on 4 February 1512.
Adrian Castellesi is the third bishop from the left.

JOHN KEMP

C. 1380 – 1454

CARDINAL PRIEST OF SANTA BALBINA (1439)
CARDINAL BISHOP OF PORTO AND SANTA RUFINA (1453)

John Kemp held a peculiarly long list of bishoprics: Rochester (1419), Chichester (1421), London (1421), York (1425) and Canterbury (1452), but it has to be said that he was more a statesman than a pastoral leader. He was born at Olantigh, a mile north of Wye, Kent, where he later founded a collegiate church and school (which was to become Wye College in the University of London). He was ordained subdeacon on 14 April 1403 and a priest on 21 May 1407. After completing his studies at Merton College, Oxford, Kemp made his name as an ecclesiastical lawyer at the Court of Appeal of the Archbishop of Canterbury, becoming in 1415 Dean of the Court of Arches. Soon he was involved in diplomatic work with Aragon, Sicily and France and acted as Henry V's Keeper of the Privy Seal and Chancellor in Normandy.

Kemp was elevated to the poor See of Rochester, being ordained a bishop at Rouen on 3 December 1419. Henry V died suddenly of dysentery in the summer of 1420. He left a nine-month old heir, Henry VI, and Bishop Kemp became a prominent member of the council that ruled the Kingdom during the King's minority. He also served, in swift succession, as Bishop of Chichester (1421), Bishop of London (1421) where he was enthroned on 26 October, as Archbishop of York (from 1425) and Chancellor (1426–32). The period was characterised by its comparative peace and stability when compared to the later years of Henry's reign. However, as ever, squabbles between factions were a key factor in politics. Kemp joined Cardinal Beaufort's pro-peace 'party', opposed to the group behind Duke Humphrey of Gloucester, who, as last surviving brother of Henry V, desired to complete the late King's policy of conquest over the Channel. Kemp headed an embassy to the ill-fated Congress of Arras (1435). Despite France offering concessions, England remained intransigent and stuck to the earlier Treaty of Troyes (1420) whereby Henry V was made heir to the French throne. However, this resulted in an increasingly close relationship between France and England's former ally, Burgundy, and proved a decisive development in the 'Hundred Years War', to England's disadvantage.

On 18 December 1439 Kemp was created Cardinal Priest of Santa Balbina by Pope Eugenius IV (1431–47), much to the disgust of Archbishop Chichele of Canterbury. He was not the only English subject created cardinal on that day, as Louis of Luxembourg, the Archbishop of the English controlled Rouen, was also elevated to the sacred purple on the same day.

At home Cardinal Kemp had an important part to play in putting down Cade's Rebellion of 1450. Originating from Kent, the rebels managed to enter London and kill some of the King's courtiers. The last years of his life also saw him as Chancellor again and Archbishop of Canterbury (from 1452), the King's trusty servant and mainstay against the rising Yorkist party. He died suddenly on 22 March 1454 at Lambeth Palace – some say of poisoning – and was buried in his cathedral.

SANTA BALBINA (PIAZZA DI SANTA SABINA)

Dedicated to the second century virgin martyr who is buried here, the basilica was also the *titulus* of Cardinal Ghinucci (1535–37). Overlooking the baths of Caracalla the basilica is itself built upon the remains of an ancient Roman palace belonging to the consul Lucius Fabius Cilo. Originally built in the fourth or fifth century, its exterior, thanks to twentieth century restoration, appears much as it would have in the fifteenth century. Inside the usually locked church is the splendid tomb of Cardinal Surdi that was constructed in 1291 by Giovanni di Cosma and an altar that was taken from the old Basilica of St Peter in the Vatican.

LOUIS OF LUXEMBOURG
† 1443
CARDINAL PRIEST OF SANTI QUATTRO CORONATI (1439)

Although not an Englishman by birth, Louis of Luxembourg was a subject of the English Crown and administrator of the See of Ely (1438-43). He was appointed Bishop of Boulogne in 1415. He later became Archbishop of Rouen in 1436 and Chancellor of France. Both Boulogne and Rouen were in English hands. On 18 December 1439 Louis was created a Cardinal Priest of Santi Quattro Coronati by Eugenius IV in 1439.

The wars between England and France left little revenue for the Cardinal to maintain the customary household of a Prince of the Church. The situation was alleviated by Henry VI when he petitioned the Pope in 1438 to allow Louis to become perpetual administrator of the See of Ely, thus providing him with revenues. Louis was not guilty of absolute absenteeism and died at his Hertfordshire mansion in Bishop's Hatfield on 18 September 1443. His body was buried in Ely Cathedral and his heart sent to Rouen. Meanwhile the see passed into the hands of another future cardinal, Thomas Bourchier.

SANTI QUATTRO CORONATI (VIA SS QUATTRO CORONATI)

The *titulus* of Louis of Luxembourg is one of Rome's most charming medieval churches, yet seen from the road that winds up to it from the area of the Coliseum it appears like an impregnable fortress. The basilica is named after four martyrs (Ss Severus, Severianus, Carpophorus and Victorinus) who refused to worship the Roman god of healing, Aesculapius. It was built during the reign of Pope Leo IV (847-55) and reconstructed by Paschal II (1111-16).

This tranquil basilica is famous for its twelfth century Cosmatesque floor, a thirteenth century cloister and the frescos of the legend of Constantine that decorate the chapel of St Silvester. It is the home of enclosed Augustinian nuns and, from the end of the twentieth century, a second community of religious called the Little Sisters of the Lamb. The church was briefly the *titulus* of Cardinal Giacomo della Chiesa who was elected Pope Benedict XV in the very year he was created a cardinal (1914).

THOMAS BOURCHIER
C. 1411 – 1486
CARDINAL PRIEST OF SAN CIRIACO (1467)

Thomas Bourchier, the great-grandson of Edward III, was the highest born prelate of his age and so the red hat must have seemed almost inevitable. He was the third son of William Bourchier, the Count of Eu, and his wife, Anne of Woodstock (a granddaughter of Edward III). He was educated at Oxford, but does not seem to have dazzled anyone with particular academic gifts; being born of such a well-established family, this was not important. Clerical advancement moved swiftly for Thomas. By 1427 he was Dean of St Martin's-le-Grand in London as well as holding lesser benefices. In 1433 he was Beaufort's candidate to be the Bishop of Worcester, despite being under the canonical age. The Pope had already nominated Thomas Brouns, the Dean of Salisbury, to the See of Worcester, but subsequently changed his nomination appointing Brouns to Rochester and Bourchier to Worcester in 1434. Bourchier was consecrated bishop on 14 March 1435, Pope Eugenius IV declaring that he had 'hitherto promoted no one of the like age to a cathedral church'. Around the same time, Bourchier was elected Chancellor of Oxford University.

In 1435 the Cathedral Chapter of Ely petitioned the Pope for the translation of Bourchier to that see. This was agreed upon by the Pope but there was a problem: Ely was a means of revenue for Archbishop (Cardinal from 1439) Louis of Luxembourg due to his service as Chancellor of France for the English King. An arrangement was therefore made, with the Pope's approval, by which Bourchier did not immediately become the Bishop of Ely and by which Louis was regarded as the administrator of that see. With the death of Louis in 1443, Bishop Bourchier was translated to become Bishop of Ely.

When Archbishop Kemp of Canterbury died in 1454, Bourchier succeeded him as Primate of All England. He was enthroned on 24 January 1455. In the same year as his enthronement, he was appointed Lord Chancellor and the War of the Roses began. There ensued years of careful diplomacy and pragmatism as Bourchier attempted to further the cause of peace in England whilst not losing his own position as archbishop. Thus in 1465 the Yorkist King, Edward IV, petitioned Pope Paul II to create Bourchier a cardinal. On 18 September 1467 the King was granted his request, but due to further dynastic upheavals it was not until 31 May 1473 that Bourchier actually received the red hat – the Pope then being Sixtus IV (who had been named a cardinal the same day as Bourchier) – being given the titular church of San Ciriaco.

As Archbishop of Canterbury, Bourchier carried out a visitation of the diocese. He condemned the malpractices that he discovered but none so strongly as the heresy of Reginald Pecock, Bishop of Chichester. Having heard the report of a commission that had been set up to study the Bishop's writings he wrote to him:

> Seeing you are convicted of not only holding what is contrary to the saying of all [the Church] Doctors, but moreover, to be a contradicter of them; it behoves us, according to the doctrine of the said Doctor Jerome, to cut you off from the body of the universal Church, as rotten flesh, and to drive you from the fold as a scabbed sheep, that you may not have it in your power to corrupt or infect the whole flock. Choose, therefore, for yourself one of these things; whether you had rather recede from your errors, and make a public abjuration, and so, for the future, agree with the rest of Christ's faithful ones in your opinions; or whether you will incur the penalty of the canons, and not only suffer the reproach of degradation, but also, moreover, be delivered over to the power of the secular arm, that, because you have attempted by force to plunder the treasury of faith, you may become, according to the saying of the prophet, as well the fuel of the fire, as the food of the burning. Of these two choose for yourself, for this is the immediate division in the coercion of heretics.

Pecock was thus persuaded to confess his mistake and plead forgiveness – he was not burnt but he was imprisoned by the Archbishop because he would not resign his see.

Bourchier's position as Archbishop of Canterbury for thirty-two years kept him at the centre of all the dynastic struggles which befell England then. It was he who crowned the first Yorkist King, Edward IV, in 1461 and Edward's consort, Elizabeth Woodville in 1465. With Edward's death he found himself having to crown Gloucester as Richard III in 1483 and finally, two years later, crowning Henry VII whom in January 1486 he joined in matrimony to Elizabeth of York, thus uniting the two Houses of York and Lancaster. Two months after the wedding, on 6 April 1486, Bourchier died at his manor of Knole in Kent and was subsequently buried near the high altar of Canterbury Cathedral.

The tomb of Cardinal Bourchier in Canterbury Cathedral.

SAN CIRIACO ALLE TERME DIOCLEZIANE

Cardinal Bourchier's *titulus* was suppressed in 1587 and changed to Santi Quirico e Giulitta – Quirico being interchangeable for Ciriaco, a three year old martyr in the time of Diocletian, who suffered with his mother Giulitta.

John Morton

c. 1420 – 1500

Cardinal Priest of Sant' Anastasia (1493)

A quick glance at John Morton's life gives the impression of a smooth rise up the echelons of the politico-ecclesiastical world of late fifteenth century England. Born at Milborne St Andrew or Bere Regis in Dorset, he was educated at nearby Cerne Abbey and then Oxford as a lawyer and soon attracted the attention of Cardinal Bourchier. He subsequently served as Privy Counsellor, Chancellor of the Duchy of Cornwall, subdeacon of Lincoln (1450), Principal of Peckwater Inn, Oxford (1453), Prebendary of Salisbury and Lincoln (1458), Master of the Rolls (1472), Archdeacon of Winchester and Chester (1474) and Bishop of Ely (1479), Archbishop of Canterbury (1486) and Lord Chancellor (1487), and Chancellor of Oxford University (1494). In 1493, at Henry VII's request, Pope Alexander VI raised him to the sacred purple as Cardinal Priest of S Anastasia. It was the sort of career structure to be expected of a late medieval Primate of England.

However, the truth is more complex. Fifteenth century England was in the grips of a civil war between the Lancastrian and Yorkist factions, both fighting for the Crown. Morton was a staunch Lancastrian and was briefly imprisoned in the Tower of London after the battle of Towton (1461). Morton is, in fact, unique amongst the English cardinals in having escaped from this formidable fortress-prison. He spent several years in France with the Lancastrian government-in-exile. It was only with Henry VI's final defeat at Tewkesbury and subsequent murder in 1471 that he was able to give himself to Edward IV's Yorkist regime: hence his promotion to the See of Ely in 1479. One of the more unexpected results of his rule in the fenland see was the building of a twelve-mile dyke from Peterborough to Wisbech known as 'Morton's Leame'. This was a pioneering feat and, later in Canterbury, Morton turned his mind to the drainage of lands in Kent. He also rebuilt the mansion of the Bishops of Ely at Bishop's Hatfield, Hertfordshire, which, after the Reformation, passed to the Crown and then the Cecil family as Hatfield House.

With the accession of Richard III in 1483, Morton's fortunes changed for the worse. He was involved in 'Buckingham's Rebellion', a revolt involving disgruntled members of Edward IV's household following rumours that Richard had murdered the 'Princes in the Tower'. He was arrested but managed to escape across the Channel. In the comparative safety of the Low Countries he intrigued on behalf of Henry Tudor, by now the hope not only of the Lancastrian faction but also of many disillusioned Yorkists. Morton was a central figure in arranging Henry's marriage to Elizabeth of York, thus uniting the rival houses.

In 1485 Henry Tudor landed in England and defeated the King at Bosworth Field. Henry found it difficult to assert his authority, especially in the North, and understandably distrusted many of the nobles. His cause was not helped by the emergence of pretenders to the throne, such as Lambert Simnel (defeated at Stoke in 1487) and Perkin Warbeck (captured in 1497). Henry increasingly relied upon a small circle of advisers, including Morton. The Cardinal served his King well as Archbishop of Canterbury (after the death of Bourchier in 1486) and Chancellor. Morton was held responsible by many for the high taxation that marked the first decade of Henry VII's reign, and so it was easy for the early seventeenth century historian Francis Bacon falsely to ascribe to Morton a notorious principle for tax assessment that he called 'Morton's Fork'. This device involved 'persuading prodigals to part with their money because they did spend it most, and the covetous because they might spare it best'. The Italian chronicler Polydore Vergil († 1555) left posterity a quite different impression of Morton, commenting that after his death it was soon seen that the Cardinal had actually been a restraining, rather than a driving, force when it came to taxation.

Morton was named a cardinal on 20 September 1493 by the infamous Borgia Pope, Alexander VI. He shared the honour of being given the red hat that day with the Pope's son, Cesare Borgia, and Ippolito d'Este, who commissioned the famously fountained Villa d'Este near Rome. Alessandro Farnese, the future Paul III, was also elevated to the sacred purple that day. As Pope he was to convene the reforming Council of Trent.

Morton kept a magnificent court at Lambeth, where the young St Thomas More, from the age of twelve, served as a page and attended the small private school. It was thanks to Morton's nomination that the future martyr got a place at Canterbury College, Oxford. More was clearly influenced by Morton, as can be seen most clearly in his controversial *History of Richard III* – his old mentor would have undoubtedly approved of his account of the 'croke backed' tyrant and usurper. Although Francis Bacon said that Morton was 'in his nature harsh and haughty ... envied by the nobility and hated of the people', this comment does not at all agree with the more reliable witness of Thomas More, who held him as the model of an astute and prudent administrator. In a semi-autobiographical section of his celebrated book *Utopia*, More has one of his characters reminisce about his old master:

> During my stay I received a lot of kindness from the Most Reverend John Morton.... He was a person that one respected just as much for his wisdom and moral character as for his great eminence. He was of average height, without a trace of a stoop, although he was fairly old. He had the sort of face that inspires reverence rather than fear. He was quite easy to get on with, though always serious and dignified. Admittedly he was rather inclined to be rude to people who asked him for jobs, but he meant no harm by it. He only did it to test their intelligence and presence of mind, for he found these qualities very congenial, so long as they were used with discretion, and considered them most valuable in public life. He was a polished and effective speaker, with a thorough knowledge of the law. He also had a quite remarkable intellect, and a phenomenal memory – two natural gifts which he'd further developed by training and practice.
>
> Apparently the King had great confidence in his judgment, and at the time of my visit the whole country seemed to depend on him. This is hardly surprising, since he'd been rushed straight from the University to court, when he was not much more than a boy, and had spent the rest of his life in the public service, learning wisdom the hard way, by having to cope with a long series of crises. And what one learns like that isn't easily forgotten.

William Roper's biography of Sir Thomas More recalls that Morton also had a high estimation of the young Thomas More:

> In whose wit and towardness the cardinal much delighting, would often say of him unto the nobles that divers times dined with him: "This child here waiting at table, whosoever shall live to see it, will prove a marvellous man."

Morton died at the manor of Knole, near Sevenoaks, on 15 September 1500 during a plague epidemic, and was buried in the crypt of his cathedral, close to the shrine of Our Lady of the Undercroft. There his bones remained until the time of the English Civil War, when his grave was looted and skull removed. It subsequently passed into Jesuit hands and is kept at Stonyhurst College.

SANT' ANASTASIA (PIAZZA DI SANT' ANASTASIA)

Cardinals Morton and Campeggio (1519-28) were given this titular church built on the site of the house of the martyr, St Anastasia († 304), and rebuilt in the seventeenth century. The church houses the relics of Our Lady's veil and St Joseph's mantle, which were supposedly brought from the Holy Land by St Jerome. Sant' Anastasia was also the titular church (1894-1921) of Blessed Andrea Ferrari, the Cardinal Archbishop of Milan.

ADRIAN CASTELLESI
c. 1461 – c. 1521
CARDINAL PRIEST OF SAN CRISOGONO (1503-18)

The only Cardinal Bishop of Hereford, Adrian de Castellesi, was born in the village of Corneto (now Tarquinia) in Lazio. He came to the attention of Pope Innocent VIII who commissioned him as his nuncio to Scotland to make peace between James III and his nobles. However, James III died before Castellesi's arrival, but not before the latter had arrived in England and had been well received by Henry VII. Archbishop (later Cardinal) Morton advised Henry that Castellesi would be a good English agent in Rome and so he was thus employed. For his good services the King gave him the prebend of Ealdland of St Paul's Cathedral in 1492 to which Archbishop Morton added the rectory of St Dunstan-in-the-East. He also acted as collector of Peter's Pence, the annual tribute of local churches for the works of the Pope, a post which he retained *in absentia* for over twenty years.

Roderigo de Borgia succeeded Innocent VIII as Alexander VI in 1492, and Castellesi eventually rose to become his secretary and, consequently, a very rich man. Castellesi's immediate predecessor as secretary, Bartolomeo Flores, the Archbishop of Cosenza, had also been a wealthy man but had been made a scapegoat by Pope Alexander in response to the report of a commission that had suggested some radical reforms of papal government and life. Flores was arrested, condemned of serious malpractice and, according to Johann Burchard, Pope Alexander VI's Master of Ceremonies, 'taken from his room to eat the bread of affliction and drink the water of sorrow for the rest of his life in another more squalid dungeon' in Castel Sant'Angelo, were he was to die. Flores' wealth was confiscated further to enrich the Pope.

In 1498 Castellesi was able to offer twenty thousand ducats to buy a red hat, though his bid was unsuccessful. However, he continued representing English interests in Rome, despite an aggressive relationship with Silvestro Gigli, Bishop of Worcester – with whom he was admitted into the confraternity of the English Hospice of St Thomas (the main English base in Rome) in 1499.

In 1502 Castellesi was nominated Bishop of Hereford and on 31 May 1503 he was created Cardinal Priest of San Crisogono. By now he was living in his palace near St Peter's, what is now the Palazzo Torlonia on the Via della Conciliazione, and became a patron of the likes of Polydore Vergil, the renowned scholar who acted as his sub-collector in England and Archdeacon of Wells. Indeed, Castellesi was a scholar in his own right, producing works such as *De Vera Philosophia ex Quatuor Doctoribus Ecclesiae* (1507), which was dedicated to Henry VII, and *De Sermone Latino* (1513), on how to write Ciceronian Latin.

By the time he received the red hat he had eclipsed the Cardinal Protector of England, Francesco Todeschini Piccolomini (soon to be elected Pius III), in terms of wealth and magnificence and was able to maintain a lavish lifestyle. On 10 August 1503 he was able to entertain Alexander VI and his son, Cesare, to a sumptuous banquet in his villa just outside Rome. According to the often-told story, the Pope was envious of Castellesi's position and intended to murder him by means of a pot of poisoned jam. Castellesi heard of this and paid the hired assassin to offer the jam to the Pope and his son instead. They fell gravely ill and the Pope died eight days later. It is more likely, however, that he succumbed to the dreaded Roman fever. Castellesi was also taken ill and his skin was said to have sloughed off, although he recovered. The circumstances of the celebrated banquet still remain mysterious. The dead Pontiff, meanwhile, was buried in Santa Maria in Monserrato, a stone's throw away from the English Hospice.

During the brief reign of Pius III, who died ten days after his coronation in October 1503, Castellesi was named Cardinal Protector of England. However, under the succeeding Pope, Julius II, the Cardinal quickly lost favour in Rome. In an attempt to secure English support, he presented Henry VII with the Palazzo Torlonia as a residence for royal ambassadors. He hoped to regain the Cardinal Protectorship but this title went, instead, to Galeotto della Rovere, Julius II's nephew. By way of consolation, Castellesi was nominated Bishop of Bath and Wells, though (just as with Hereford) he never set foot in this wealthy see.

A disagreement with the Pope led Castellesi temporarily to flee to Venice in 1507. Ten years later, he was implicated in a plot, allegedly organised by Cardinals Petrucci and Sauli, to poison Leo X. Castellesi, who was almost certainly a victim of factional rivalry, panicked and once again fled to Venice in disguise. He was deprived of his cardinalate and the See of Bath and Wells, which was given to Wolsey. Little is known about Castellesi's final years: after Pope Leo's death he emerged from hiding in Venice, and he is believed to have been murdered by a servant as he made his way back to Rome.

For the entry on San Crisogono see p. 25.

CHRISTOPHER BAINBRIDGE
1462/3 – 1514
CARDINAL PRIEST OF SANTI MARCELLINO E PIETRO (1511)
CARDINAL PRIEST OF SANTA PRASSEDE (1511)

Christopher Bainbridge appears to be the quintessential Cardinal of Renaissance Rome – a worldly prelate who spent most of his last years on the battlefield and died at the hands of a poisoner, probably in the pay of his arch-rival, the Bishop of Worcester. However, the intrigues of papal Rome were far removed from Hilton, near the Westmorland county town of Appleby, where he was born in 1462/3. He was educated at Oxford, Ferrara and Bologna, where he obtained a doctorate in law. In 1496 he was appointed Provost of The Queen's College, Oxford.

Like many Renaissance prelates, Bainbridge owed his fast promotion to the patronage of a relative – his uncle, Thomas Langton, who was Bishop of St David's (1483), Salisbury (1485) and Winchester (1493). Bainbridge's first offices were prebends linked to Salisbury: South Grantham, Chardstock and Horton. He also became Prebendary of North Kelsey (Lincoln). In 1497 he was named Treasurer of St Paul's, followed by other important posts: Archdeacon of Surrey (1501), Prebendary of Strensall and Dean of York (1503), Dean of Windsor (1505) and Master of the Rolls (1506). On 12 December 1507 he was consecrated Bishop of Durham and shortly afterwards, on 20 September 1508, was named Archbishop of York.

However, he was not to remain in England for long. At the accession of Henry VIII, Bainbridge was sent to the Palazzo Torlonia in Rome as royal ambassador, and was plunged into the complexities of papal diplomacy. In March 1509 Julius II had joined the 'League of Cambrai' with France, Germany and Spain against Venice. However, realising that France posed a greater threat to the balance of power in Italy, Julius made peace with the Serene Republic and turned his attentions to driving out the French forces. Louis XII counter-attacked by calling the Council of Pisa in 1511 to depose the Pope. The Pope, in turn, called the Fifth Lateran Council (1512) and formed the Holy League of Venice (1511) against France. Henry VIII joined the League in 1511 and petitioned the Pope through Bainbridge for the title of 'Most Christian King', forfeited by Louis.

The same year, on 17 March, Julius created Bainbridge a Cardinal Priest, one of many Julian cardinals created to stabilise the papal authority in the aftermath of the Council of Pisa. A favourite of the warrior Pope, Bainbridge was entrusted with command of papal troops at the siege of Ferrara, and was made legate *a latere* to the Papal States after the city fell. Peace was declared in 1514 and Louis withdrew support from the schismatic Council of Pisa. He was restored with his title, 'Most Christian King', to Henry's frustration.

In 1513 Bainbridge became the first English cardinal to take part in a conclave since Simon Langham in 1370 and even received a handful of votes. He never returned to his See of York and stayed in Rome, where he acted as warden to the English Hospice, though he appointed William Burbanke to do much of the work. He would have liked to have returned to England with legatine powers but the rising and powerful Thomas Wolsey ensured this never happened. Wolsey also did his best to undermine Bainbridge's influence in the Curia.

Bainbridge was said to have been a quarrelsome and contentious man, who ruled his household with a regime of fear. He died on 14 July 1514, having drunk poisoned soup on the feast of Corpus Christi. The culprit seems to have been a member of his household, an Italian priest called Rinaldo de Modena who acted as the Cardinal's bursar or steward. Accounts differ as to the motivation of this crime: some say that Rinaldo was seeking revenge after the Cardinal had hit him during one of his violent rages, others that he was hired by Bishop Silvestro Gigli of Worcester – Bainbridge's rival and the English Ambassador in Rome. While Gigli took control of the Hospice and Thomas Wolsey reached out for control of his diocese, Bainbridge was buried in the church dedicated to St Thomas attached to the hospice, where his fine tomb has survived the ravages of the centuries and can still be seen today.

The historian William Wilkie, in his book *The Cardinal Protectors of England*, provides this analysis of the fall of Bainbridge:

It is not necessary to seek poison as an explanation of Bainbridge's death. His death perhaps aroused but little grief even among the members of the English Hospice in whose church he was buried, and perhaps his fall from favour under Leo X was in some measure due to his own attitudes and personality. But whatever his faults he did not deserve the treatment he received from those whom he served. It was Wolsey who destroyed him, not by poison but by policy, with the connivance of the King and the Pope, and using Gigli as the pliant instrument of his will. Because Bainbridge's influence in Rome was an obstacle to him, Wolsey undermined him. Because his return to England would have been intolerable to him, Wolsey prevented it. It was not only the smaller ambition of Gigli but the larger ambitions of Wolsey which brought final ruin to Bainbridge. The supple and wily insincerity which pervaded the Rome of the de' Medici Popes encouraged Wolsey as much as it eluded Bainbridge. A humbler man could have survived, but Bainbridge's spirit was broken. Like Wolsey's his nature required power and pomp. Henry VIII permitted Wolsey to destroy Bainbridge, as Wolsey would one day be destroyed by the King himself.

The tomb of Cardinal Bainbridge.

SANTI MARCELLINO E PIETRO (VIA MERULANA)

The title, briefly, of Cardinal Bainbridge (1511) was built by Pope Siricius in the fourth century and rebuilt most recently by Benedict XIV in 1751. Very little remains that would have been known in 1511 except an image of Saints Marcellinus and Peter near the back of the nave that dates from the thirteenth century.

SANTA PRASSEDE (VIA DE SANTA PRASSEDE)

The entrance to this church is unpromising, whichever way you go in. But then, upon entering the church itself, one is aware of great antiquity present on a large scale. This church was built by Pope St Paschal I (817-24) near the site where tradition relates that St Prassede sheltered twenty-three persecuted Christians who were martyred. This early foundation, near Santa Maria Maggiore, boasts some fine ninth century mosaics and, in the chapel of St Zeno, part of the Pillar of the Scourging. Named after St Praxedes, sister of St Pudentiana, this basilica was also the *titulus* of Cardinal Merry del Val, St Robert Bellarmine and St Charles Borromeo.

THOMAS WOLSEY
C. 1470 – 1530
CARDINAL PRIEST OF SANTA CECILIA IN TRASTEVERE (1515)

Variously called 'a butcher's cur' and 'vainglorious far above all measure' by his contemporaries, when we think of Wolsey today the mind often goes back to Orson Welles in the 1966 film *A Man for All Seasons*. This image is hardly flattering, as Peter Gwyn puts it: 'An overweight and overdressed spider occupying the centre of a web of intrigue and bearing a much closer resemblance to the emperor Nero than to anyone remotely religious.' But there was much more to Thomas Wolsey than his flamboyant scarlet robes and 'unbounded stomach'.

Thomas Wolsey was born in Ipswich, the son of a prosperous butcher, and was educated at Magdalen College, Oxford. He was elected a fellow there in 1497 and may have served as bursar. After his priestly ordination, he became rector of Limington, Somerset in 1500 and, according to his first biographer, George Cavendish, was put in the stocks after displeasing the local landowner, Sir Amyas Paulet – drunkenness or fornication are the reasons normally given. In 1501 he became chaplain to Archbishop Deane of Canterbury and then, after the Archbishop's death in 1503, entered the service of Sir Richard Nanfan, governor of Calais, during which time he made his first appearance at court.

Advancement was secured now that he had been 'noticed' – the King sent him on diplomatic missions to Scotland and Flanders and appointed him as Dean of both Lincoln and Hereford. Enjoying the support of the Lord Privy Seal, Richard Fox, on Henry VIII's accession, Wolsey gained a seat on the Council and was named King's Almoner and registrar of the Order of the Garter. He was also heavily involved in the English campaigns in France and in the subsequent peace negotiations.

The English occupation of Tournai had also made Wolsey bishop of that lucrative see in 1513, though there was a French rival appointed by the Pope himself. Wolsey was named Bishop of Lincoln in February 1514, being promoted to the archbishopric of York only a few months later. In 1515 Wolsey was created Lord Chancellor by Henry VIII and a Cardinal Priest by Leo X, with the title of Santa Cecilia in Trastevere – largely because the Pope needed English support against the French. Though there were attempts to secure his election as Pope in the conclaves of 1521 and 1522, it seems that Wolsey never visited Rome. Thus, Wolsey's great administrative ability, influential contacts and personal friendship with the King, allowed this 'butcher's cur' to become the most powerful statesman and prelate in England. Such power demanded, in Wolsey's estimation, an equal display of glory. Wolsey's gentleman-usher and biographer, George Cavendish, recorded that the new cardinal's red hat was

> . . . conveyed hither in the bag of a varlet, who seemed to all men to be but a person of small estimation. Whereof York, being advised of the baseness of the messenger and of the people's opinion and rumour, thought it for his honour meet that so high a jewel should not be conveyed by so simple a messenger. Wherefore he caused him to be stayed by the way, immediately after his arrival in England, where he was newly furnished in all manner of apparel with all kind of costly silks, which seemed decent for such a high ambassador. And that done, he was encountered upon Blackheath and there received with a great assembly of prelates and lusty gallant gentlemen, and from thence conducted and conveyed through London with great triumph. Then was great and speedy provision and preparation made in Westminster Abbey for the confirmation of the Cardinal's high dignity. This was executed by all the bishops and abbots nigh or about London, in rich mitres and copes and other costly ornaments. It was done in so solemn a wise as I have not seen the like, unless it had been at the coronation of a mighty prince or king.

Wolsey solemnly received the red hat on 18 November 1515. In the principal procession the cross was borne by the Bishop of Rochester, St John Fisher. The sermon was preached by the Dean of St Paul's Cathedral, John Colet, who recalled the virtues of Wolsey that had led to his 'high and joyous promotion' and the 'the great zeal and favour' that the Pope had shown to the King. Colet spoke of 'the high and great power of a cardinal' who 'representeth the order of seraphim, which continually burneth in love of the glorious Trinity', and is therefore 'metely appareled with red'.

As Archbishop of York, Wolsey accrued further titles – Bishop of Bath and Wells (1518-24), Durham (1524-29) and Winchester (1529), and Abbot of St Albans (1521). Most significantly he was named legate *a latere* by

Leo X in 1518, making him the Pope's permanent representative and easily outranking Archbishop Warham of Canterbury. Some have suggested that Wolsey's 'legatine despotism' over the bench of bishops actually prepared the way for Henry's 'imperial headship' over the Church of England in the 1530s. As Chancellor and supreme royal adviser, Wolsey had a virtual monopoly of power and access to the King – the nearest England has ever got to a Richelieu or a Mazarin. While the young King indulged in 'pastime with good company', the Cardinal spent hours at his desk and only consulted with the Council once he had discussed matters with Henry. Having described some kingly entertainment, the ever present (if sometimes misleading) George Cavendish perceptively observed:

> All this matter I have declared at length, because you shall understand what joy and delight the Cardinal had to see his prince and sovereign lord in his house so nobly entertained and pleased. This was always his only study, to devise things for His Majesty's comfort, not weighing the charges or expenses. It delighted him so much, to have the King's pleasant princely presence, that nothing was to him more delectable than to cheer his sovereign lord, to whom he owed so much obedience and loyalty – as reason required no less, all things well considered.

A clear demonstration of Wolsey's wealth and power is that two of his residences were turned into important royal palaces. Hampton Court was leased by Wolsey from the Knight Hospitallers in 1515 and rebuilt extensively. His terracotta coat of arms can still be seen on Anne Boleyn's Gatehouse. In 1525 he gave it to the King in exchange for Richmond Palace, which Henry seldom used. After Wolsey's downfall his London house, York Place, was forfeited to the Crown and grew into the great Palace of Whitehall. A F Pollard observed that: 'It is one of the ironies of Wolsey's career that he should not only have unconsciously done so much to build up the modern English state, but should also have unwittingly provided the habitat for its swelling bureaucracy.'

Less well known is his palace at Moor Park, near Rickmansworth, Hertfordshire, which he gained through his Abbacy of St Albans and subsequently enlarged. The future Cardinal du Bellay, who was French ambassador towards the end of Wolsey's life, thought that Moor Park was more splendid than Hampton Court, and it was here that the 'Treaty of the More' was signed between France and England on 30 August 1525. Moor Park is now better known for its golf course.

The Cardinal's power and wealth was also displayed in his public journeys.

Cavendish describes one such:

> Then marched he forward out of his own house at Westminster, passing through all London, over London Bridge, having before him of gentlemen a great number, three in a rank, in black velvet livery coats and the most part of them with great chains of gold about their necks. And all this yeomen, with noblemen's and gentlemen's servants, following him in French tawny livery coats, having embroidered upon their backs and breasts of the same coats these letters 𝕿 and 𝕮, under the Cardinal's hat. His sumpter mules, which were twenty in number and more, with his carts and other carriages of his train, were passed on before, conducted and guarded with a great number of bows and spears. He rode like a cardinal, very sumptuously, on a mule trapped with crimson velvet upon velvet, and his stirrups of copper and gilt; and his spare mule following him with like apparel. And before him he had his two great crosses of silver, two great pillars of silver, the great seal of England, his cardinal's hat, and a gentleman that carried his valaunce (otherwise called a cloak-bag) which was made altogether of fine scarlet cloth embroidered over and over with cloth of gold very richly, having in it a cloak of fine scarlet. Thus passed he through London and all the way of his journey, having his messengers passing before him to provide lodgings for his train.

Wolsey is often seen as an example of what a cardinal should not be – extravagant and the holder of many wealthy livings. He had a concubine, 'Mistress Lark', who bore him a daughter, Dorothy, who was quickly packed off to Shaftesbury Abbey, and a son, Thomas, who was publicly acknowledged as his nephew and spoilt rotten. Yet he did not completely neglect his devotions – he made pilgrimages to Walsingham, wore a hairshirt and after long hours of work 'he went to Mass . . . and then went straight into a garden, and after he had walked the space of an hour or more, and there said his evensong, he went to dinner'. He had a genuine concern for the wellbeing of the Church. Even Erasmus praised him as a champion of education as seen in his foundations at Ipswich and Oxford, though these were partly funded by the proceeds of Wolsey's dissolution of thirty religious houses in the 1520s – a decade before the more radical dissolutions under Cromwell. It seems that he wanted Cardinal's College (now Christ Church), Oxford, opened in 1525 on the site of the Augustinian priory of St Frideswide, to become a centre for Church reform, 'where scholars shall be brought up in virtue, and qualified for the priestly dignity'. John Foxe wrote that: 'If all the rest had been finished . . . it might well have excelled not only all colleges but also palaces of princes.' The college was endowed with a fine library and a choir of sixteen choristers and twelve 'clerkes skilled in polyphony'. Its first choirmaster was the composer, John Taverner, who produced many of his finest works while he was there, such as the *Missa Gloria tibi Trinitas*. Wolsey also showed an interest in visiting monastic houses and hoped to create thirteen new episcopal sees in England and to reorganise the Irish dioceses.

However, dark clouds were gathering, as Cavendish records:

> Then began other matters to brew and take place that occupied all men's heads with divers imaginations, whose stomachs were therewith full filled without any perfect digestion. The long hid and secret love between the King and Mistress Anne Boleyn began to break out into every man's ears.

Shakespeare had Wolsey in mind when he wrote the famous lines: 'O, how wretched is that poor man that hangs on princes favours!' The essential reason for the Cardinal's downfall was his failure to obtain for Henry the desired annulment of his marriage to Catherine of Aragon. Losing the King's favour meant that he quickly lost everything else – and there were many in both Church and State who welcomed his fall. As legate he had been caught in a trap of loyalty to his King and his Pope. Moreover, the office of legate left him highly vulnerable since the Statute of Praemunire (last revised in 1393) forbade deferring English legal or property matters to a foreign court and, as will be remembered, Beaufort was charged with a similar breech by his opponent, Humphrey of Gloucester. In the end the papal tribunal, which Wolsey headed together with Campeggio, had to refer the case to Rome once a stalemate was reached in the summer of 1529. That October Wolsey was dismissed, charged with Praemunire and sent off to York, where he watched with dismay the confiscation of much of his property. Henry's action not only punished his failed servant but sent a clear message to Clement VII – the King would not take 'no' for an answer.

Wolsey was pardoned in February 1530 and continued as Archbishop of York, complete with its huge income. His last months were not those of a doomed man. At his palace in Southwell 'he kept a noble house and plenty both of meat and drink for all comers, both for rich and poor'. He confirmed hundreds of children, and, on Maundy Thursday, washed the feet of fifty-nine poor men at Peterborough. But the King was getting increasingly suspicious and Wolsey was arrested for treason in November. Fever probably cheated the headsman of a job – he died en route to the Tower at Leicester Abbey, protesting his innocence and loyalty to the Crown. When he received the Last Rites he said, 'I pray God that that sacrament may be the damnation of my soul if ever I thought to do disservice to my King.'

Cavendish furnishes us with this account of Wolsey's obsequies:

> The body was taken out of the bed where he lay dead. Upon him, next his body, he had a shirt of hair, besides his other shirt which was of very fine linen Holland cloth. This shirt of hair was unknown to all his servants who continually attended upon him in his bedchamber, except to his chaplain, who was his ghostly father. In this he was buried, and laid in a coffin of boards, having upon his dead corpse all such vestures and ornaments as he had been professed in when he was consecrated bishop and archbishop, such as mitre, crozier, ring, and pall, with all other things belonging to his profession. And he lay thus all day in his coffin, open and barefaced, that all men might see him lie there dead without feigning. Then when the mayor, his brethren and all others had seen him, lying thus until four or five of the clock at night, he was carried so down into the church with great solemnity by the abbot and convent, with many torches alight, singing such service as is due for such funerals.
>
> And being in the church the corpse was set in Our Lady chapel, with many tapers of wax buring about the hearse, and divers poor men sitting about the same, holding lighted torches in their hands, who watched about the dead body all night, whilst the canons sang dirge and other devout orisons. And about four of the clock in the morning they sang Mass. And that done, and the body interred . . . by the time that all things and all ceremonies that to such a person were decent and convenient were finished, it was about six of the clock in the morning.

Rather than being the perfect essay in Renaissance corruption, it can at least be said of Wolsey that he was a devoted servant of the Crown, a skilled politician and a prominent patron of the arts. Ultimately, Wolsey realised that this was not enough. On his deathbed, he is said to have bemoaned:

> If I had served God as diligently as I have done the King, He would not have given me over in my grey hairs. Howbeit, this is the just reward that I must receive for my worldly diligence and the pains that I have taken to do the King service and to satisfy his vain pleasures, not regarding my godly duty.

For the entry on Santa Cecilia in Trastevere see p. 48.

GIULIO DE' MEDICI
1479 - 1534
CARDINAL DEACON OF SANTA MARIA IN DOMNICA (1513)
CARDINAL PRIEST OF SAN CLEMENTE (1517)
CARDINAL PRIEST OF SAN LORENZO IN DAMASO (1517)
POPE CLEMENT VII (1523)

The See of Worcester had a unique part to play in the English Reformation. Before his translation to Canterbury in 1583, John Whitgift was bishop, a keen enforcer of Anglican church order under Elizabeth I. Forty years previously, Hugh Latimer, a noted reformer who was to be killed during the reign of Queen Mary, had occupied the Worcester *cathedra*. On the eve of the break with Rome, the see was held by four Italians between 1497 and 1522, two of whom are included in this book: Giulio de' Medici and Girolamo Ghinucci. Medici later became Pope Clement VII, who commissioned Michelangelo's *Last Judgment* for the Sistine Chapel and excommunicated Henry VIII, declaring his divorce from Catherine of Aragon and marriage to Anne Boleyn null and void.

Cardinal de' Medici had been provided to Worcester *in commendam* on 7 June 1521. This was part of the Tudor policy of appointing foreigners to English dioceses who had proved (or would prove) useful to English interests. Medici was not only the Pope's closest adviser but also the Cardinal Protector of England (from 1513). He resigned in September 1522, shortly before his election as Pope, in favour of Ghinucci, but during his short period as Bishop of Worcester he participated in the conclave that elected Adrian VI. Needless to say, Medici never set foot in Worcester, which was part of a long list of rich benefices.

Giulio was the illegitimate son of Giuliano de' Medici and his mistress, Fioretta Gorini, but was brought up by his uncle, Lorenzo the Magnificent, following the murder of his father in the Pazzi Conspiracy shortly before his birth. Destined for the Church, he studied canon law at Pisa and became a Knight Hospitaller of St John of Jerusalem and Prior of Capua. He joined the household of his cousin, Cardinal Giovanni de' Medici, who was elected Pope Leo X in 1513. The new Pope soon followed the convention of using his new position to enrich his family. Leo's nephew, Lorenzo, became Duke of Urbino, and another nephew, Innocenzo Cibo, was created Cardinal Deacon of Santi Cosma e Damiano. At the same consistory, on 28 September 1513, Leo gave the red hat to Giulio, whom the new Pope had recently appointed Archbishop of Florence. Before the ceremony, Giulio was declared to be legitimate by a special commission, who conveniently discovered that his parents had secretly married at the time of his conception.

Medici came to be recognized as Leo's most able adviser and an excellent manager of the Pope's financial affairs. He was legate to the papal army in the 1515 campaign against Francis I, the War of Urbino (1517), the Marche campaign (1520) and the war in Lombardy (1521), and involved in the planned crusade against the Turks of 1517. Indeed, the historian, Francesco Guicciardini, commented that Giulio was more suited to arms than holy orders. As Leo's counsellor, the Cardinal was also heavily involved in the condemnation of Luther (1520) and the negotiation of an anti-French alliance with Charles V (1521).

Giulio was thus a strong candidate to succeed Leo at his death in December 1521 and attracted powerful support in the resulting conclave. However, there were also those who were unsurprisingly opposed to the idea of a second Medici Pope; a number of alternative candidates appeared, including Thomas Wolsey. The cardinals reached a stalemate that was broken when Giulio de' Medici declared that he was unworthy of mounting the Throne of Peter and voiced his support for Adrian Florensz Dedel, the Cardinal of Utrecht. Little known in Rome, Dedel was a deeply spiritual, ascetic Flemish scholar who had been tutor to Charles V and was the Emperor's favoured candidate. Giulio saw such a compromise candidate as the easiest solution and had obtained assurances that the reign would be short and that he would have imperial support at a future conclave. It was perhaps hoped that consideration of the unworldly Dedel would also highlight Medici's own suitability for the job. The Dutchman was duly elected and unusually kept his baptismal name, becoming Pope Adrian VI. Since he had not been present at the election, he was shipped to Civitavecchia by a fleet of fourteen imperial galleys. Adrian was unpopular with the Romans, surrounding himself with Flemish familiars, speaking Latin with a 'barbarous' accent, living on a florin a day and frowning on carnivals, festal celebrations and lucrative appointments. While his life was exemplary, it was economically disastrous for the many who depended on papal profligacy. The new Pope even ordered all the cardinals and bishops in Rome to take up residence in their own dioceses, many of which had not seen their bishop before.

Pope Adrian's reign was indeed short; he died on 14 September 1523 and remained the last non-Italian Pope until 1978, when Cardinal Wojtyla of Krakow was elected as John Paul II. The conclave that followed Adrian VI's death lasted fifty days, but Giulio de' Medici eventually triumphed, backed by the Holy Roman Emperor, the King of England and even the King of France.

Pope Clement VII began his reign with high expectations, especially given his experience in directing Leo X's policies, but his own Pontificate was to be a disappointment due to his over-subtle and indecisive diplomacy and the insurmontable challenges that faced him. The historian Leopold von Ranke would later call him the most disastrous of Popes and the Venetian Ambassador, Antonio Soriano, reported that 'he speaks well and sees into everything, but is very timid'. Lacking money and a clear vision, Clement continually shifted his support between France and the Empire in a delicate juggling act, which inevitably led to trouble.

Following the Imperial victory of Pavia in 1525, at which the King of France was captured, Clement sought the Emperor's protection and then entered an anti-Habsburg alliance with France, Venice, Florence and Milan (the League of Cognac, 1526). On 6 May 1527 the Imperial Army, composed of unpaid and poorly disciplined Lutheran *Landsknecht* mercenaries and Spanish Catholics, entered Rome and started a terrifying rampage through the city. Eight thousand people were killed on the first day and the surviving inhabitants had to endure several weeks of rape and pillage, mutilations and murder. Of the one hundred and eighty-nine Swiss Guards, only forty-two survived, the rest falling as they defended the Vatican. According to one eyewitness, 'Hell hath nothing to compare with the present state of Rome.' As Lutheran graffiti were added to Raphael's frescoes, papal tombs desecrated and the future Julius III hung up by his hair, the Pope was held a virtual prisoner in Castel Sant' Angelo.

The Sack of Rome left an indelible mark on the mind of Pope Clement. He had been completely humiliated. The kind of devastation that Rome had endured had not been known there for over a thousand years, leading Erasmus to remark: 'Truly, this is not the ruin of one city, but of the world.' The sack shocked Europe, and Charles V, who felt the obvious contradiction between being defender of the Church and sacker of the Eternal City, hurriedly commissioned a justification from the humanist Alfonso de Valdés, claiming that the incident was God's way of purifying and renewing the Roman Church.

Clement remained, for all intents and purposes, a prisoner within the walls of Castel Sant' Angelo until the early hours of 7 December 1527, when he was allowed to escape, disguised as a servant. He made his way to Umbria and the comparative safety of Orvieto.

It was during his sojourn in Orvieto that the Pope received a delegation from Henry VIII seeking dispensation for a divorce from his first wife, Catherine of Aragon. When the delegation returned to England they reported to the King the miserable circumstances in which they found the Pope amongst the roofless rooms of his palace. 'All things are in such scarcity and dearth as we think has not been seen in any place,' they reported, adding that 'for the Pope's bedchamber, all apparel in it was not worth twenty nobles, bed and all.'

Concerned with the survival of the relatively new Tudor dynasty, Henry urgently needed a son. He thus wanted to divorce Catherine of Aragon and marry a court lady, Anne Boleyn, whose sister had herself borne Henry a son in 1526. The Holy See was used to problems arising from royal marriages – indeed, Julius II had granted Henry a dispensation so that he could marry Catherine, his late brother's widow, in the first place. However, this new case proved to be a sticky one: not only was theological opinion more or less on the Queen's side, but the Pope knew himself to be at the mercy of Catherine's nephew, the Emperor. Clement procrastinated and delayed his final decision, but ultimately did not compromise in his defence of the marriage bond. The stalemate ended dramatically in 1533 when Henry VIII broke with Rome and declared himself head of the Church of England. On 11 July of that year the Pope proclaimed the excommunication of the English King.

In the summer of 1528 Rome was deemed safe enough for the Pope to return. In early 1529 he signed the Treaty of Barcelona with Charles V. The Emperor assisted the Pope in regaining most of his territory and the Medici's in reclaiming Florence, which had been declared a Republic by rebels around the time of the Sack of Rome, and this was achieved after a ten-month siege in 1530. Meanwhile, Clement recognized Charles as King of Naples and agreed to crown him as Holy Roman Emperor. This would be the last imperial coronation of a Habsburg by a Pope and took place not in Rome but Bologna, since Charles was pre-occupied with Turkish advances in Central Europe (including an unsuccessful siege of Vienna) and wished to be near his territories. The coronation took place amid much splendour at the church of San Petronio on 24 February 1530, which happened to be the Emperor's birthday and the anniversary of his victory at Pavia. As was customary on such occasions, the newly-crowned Emperor vested as a deacon at the Pontifical Mass that followed and he conducted himself 'in so seemly and devout a fashion, as one long accustomed to fulfil such services, that all standing around were filled with wonder and joy'. The occasion allowed lengthy talks between the two leaders at the Palazzo Pubblico. Italian politics had prevented them from concentrating on the threat of Lutheranism, and Clement agreed to call a General Council the following year, though this never materialized.

Clement's final year saw a dynastic triumph in the marriage of Caterina de' Medici to the Duke of Orléans, who later succeeded to the French Throne as Henry II (1547). Clement himself presided at the marriage ceremony at Marseilles on 28 October 1533 and provided for the lavish celebrations that continued for some days. The marriage disgusted the Emperor but fulfilled the Medici dream of marrying into a great royal dynasty; Caterina would mother three French monarchs (Francis II, Charles IX and Henry III) and remained an influential voice in European politics until her death in 1589.

Clement VII died on 25 September 1534 having suffered liver failure, increasing fraility and failing eyesight. Benvenuto Cellini visited the Pontiff shortly before his death:

> I found him in bed in a most deplorable condition. Nevertheless, he received me with the greatest kindness, and wished to inspect the medals and the dies. He sent for spectacles and lights, but was unable to see anything clearly. Then he began to fumble with his fingers at them, and having felt them a short while, he fetched a deep sigh, and said to his attendants that he was much concerned about me, but that if God gave him back his health he would make it all right. Three days afterwards the Pope died.

His passing was not mourned in Rome, on account of the horrors of the Sack of Rome, still vivid in the popular memory, and the heavy taxes recently imposed to pay for Caterina's wedding. Clement's tomb in St Peter's was soon desecrated with excrement and graffiti – *Clemens Pontifex Maximus* was changed to *Inclemens Pontifex Minimus*. His body was later moved to the choir of Santa Maria sopra Minerva, opposite the resting place of Leo X.

Pope Clement was survived by his only son, Alessandro, probably the fruit of a youthful liaison with a black serving girl in the Medici household,

Simonetta da Collavechio. Alessandro was Duke of Florence between 1532 and his assassination in 1537, and shortly before his death married the Emperor's illegitimate daughter, Margaret of Parma, thus sealing the Treaty of Barcelona and neatly balancing Caterina's marriage to the Duke of Orléans. Alessandro had 'a dusky skin, thick lips and matted hair' and was nicknamed *il Moro* ('the Moor'). Consequently, he has even been called 'the first black head of state in the modern western world'.

SANTA MARIA IN DOMNICA (PIAZZA NAVICELLA)

The *diaconia* of Cardinal de' Medici (1513-17) origin- ated as the house church of an early Christian lady, St Cyriaca. The present church was built by that great builder of basilicas, Pope St Paschal I (817-24), and restored by Leo X (1513-21), Cardinal de' Medici's cousin, who commissioned the fine portico of the church. Leo also had set in place the distinctive galley fountain that stands in front of the church. Before his election as Pope, Leo was the titular cardinal of this church. The twentieth century Jesuit theologian Henri de Lubac was also titular cardinal here.

Inside the church the apse is filled with a ninth century mosaic of the Virgin and Child enthroned in the lush garden of paradise amidst the choirs of angels. At the end of the right aisle is the tomb of Princess Antonia of Luxembourg († 1954), the second wife of Rupert of Bavaria, the Jacobite claimant to the British Throne.

SAN CLEMENTE (VIA LABICANA)

The *titulus* of Cardinals de' Medici (1517) and Ghinucci (1537-41) is one of the most famous in Rome. Few other Roman churches display so well the antiquity of the sites on which they are built. San Clemente is a twelfth century structure built over a fourth century basilica and, below, an even older *domus ecclesia* and pagan temple, all of which can be viewed to a greater or lesser extent. What can be seen here gives a good impression of what would be found under many Roman churches if they suffered the huge expense and disturbance of excavation.

The basilica may be entered via a small and tranquil courtyard which gives no sense of the glories that lie beyond in the church. Inside, there are antique columns, a stunning cosmatesque pavement and a beautiful sixth century choir area that was dismantled from the previous lower basilica and set up once again in its present position. There is also a stunning twelfth century mosaic of Christ upon a cross which has seemingly been plunged into the earth, out of which great roulades of foliage have sprung up, giving shade and protection to all manner of living creatures. Since 1667 the church has been in the hands of the Irish Dominicans, one of whom (Fr Joseph Mulooly) was responsible for excavating the lower levels. The basilica contains the bones of St Clement I, St Ignatius of Antioch and St Cyril, as well as Cardinal Ghinucci's tomb

SAN LORENZO IN DAMASO (PIAZZA DELLA CANCELLERIA)

Situated in the precincts of the Palazzo Cancelleria, the basilica was erected by Pope St Damasus (366-84), who is buried under the high altar, and rebuilt by Bramante in 1495. A subsequent redecoration of the interior of the church has given it something of the feel of a dark nineteenth century opera house. St Bridget of Sweden, who lived nearby, used to pray before the crucifix in the chapel opening from the right aisle. The church was the *titulus* of Cardinal de' Medici (1517-23) and held *in commendam* by the Cardinal Duke of York between 1763 and 1807. In the sacristy there is a fine white vestment with his coat of arms.

LORENZO CAMPEGGIO
1471/2 – 1539
CARDINAL PRIEST OF SAN TOMMASO IN PARIONE (1517)
CARDINAL PRIEST OF SANT' ANASTASIA (1519)
CARDINAL PRIEST OF SANTA MARIA IN TRASTEVERE (1528)
CARDINAL BISHOP OF ALBANO (1534)
CARDINAL BISHOP OF PALESTRINA (1535)
CARDINAL BISHOP OF SABINA (1537)

Born at Milan to a Bolognese family of notable lawyers, Lorenzo Campeggio was educated at Pavia and Bologna and won fame as Professor of Law at Pavia. He married Francesca Guastavillani and had five children, one of whom, Alessandro, later became Bishop of Bologna (1526) and Cardinal Priest of Santa Lucia in Silice (1551).

Upon his wife's death in 1509, Lorenzo decided to receive holy orders. He quickly rose to become Auditor of the Roman Rota (1511), the Church's supreme court of justice, and Bishop of Feltre in north-eastern Italy (1512). A trusted servant of the Church and celebrated lawyer, the rest of his life was largely spent on diplomatic missions, especially to Germany and England. While absent on a mission to the Emperor Maximilian in 1517, Leo X created him a Cardinal Priest with the title of San Tommaso in Parione. Campeggio was one of thirty-one cardinals created that day in one of the largest consistories in the Church's history. Also elevated to the sacred purple along with him was Adrian Florensz Dedel, who was to succeed Leo X as the ascetic reformer, Adrian VI.

The following year Campeggio was sent to England as legate in order to win Henry VIII's support in a proposed crusade against the Turks, but was delayed at Calais until Wolsey was appointed co-legate. However, he seems

BAINBRIDGE   1511 - 1514

Cardinal Christopher Bainbridge

THOMAS WOLSEY, CARDINAL ARCHBISHOP OF YORK.

ABOVE: *Cardinal Wolsey, as seen in a portrait at Christ Church, Oxford.*

OPPOSITE TOP LEFT: *A fresco from the Sala di Constantino in the Vatican Palace depicts the baptism of Constantine. Pope Silvester, performing the baptism, is portrayed with the features of Pope Clement VII – the former Cardinal Giulio de' Medici.*

OPPOSITE TOP RIGHT: *A statue of Pope Clement VII, which surmounts his tomb in the Basilica of Santa Maria Sopra Minerva.*

OPPOSITE BOTTOM: *Cardinal de' Medici's (Pope Clement VII's) coat of arms, carved on the Ponte Sant' Angelo.*

Against the King's divorce: Cardinals Campeggio (above),
and St John Fisher (facing page) in Hans Holbein's drawing.

R Episcopus de rofestez
factus fuit H Card Ann 1535

John   Fisher

The portrait of Cardinal Reginald Pole in Lambeth Palace, where the last Catholic Archbishop of Canterbury died in 1558.

Si decem millia Pædagogorum habeatis in Christo sed non multos
Patres nam in Christo Jesu per Euangelium ego vos genui. 1 Corint₄

TOP: *Cardinal Pole and his coat of arms.*

LEFT: *Cardinal William Allen in a portrait from the English College, which he helped to found in Rome in 1579.*

ABOVE: *The arms of Cardinal William Peto.*

EMINENTISSIMUS AC REVERENDISS. DNUS FRATER PHILIPPUS THOMAS HOWARD S.R.ECCL. CARDINALIS ORDE PRÆDICATO.

PATER THOMAS-
ANA-
CARDO ROMÆ APTUS

HOWARDUS CARDINA:
GRAMMA
IN ALTIS ARDUUS.

Cardinibus suffultæ suis sunt ostia ROMÆ.
CARDO novus THOMAS ARDUUS ALTA tenet
ALTA tenet fidei Monumenta, ducumque refulgens
stemmate Purpureis APTUS adesse Choris.

Ordo Dominici Natum, sed et Anglia vidit
tutorem fidei. nunc quoqs ROMA Patrem.
Urbis et Orbis amor tatem conservet Atlantem
quo tutus maneat Relligionis apex.

H Adlard sc.

An engraving (facing page) and portrait (above) of Cardinal Philip Howard.

CLOCKWISE FROM TOP LEFT: *Maria Clementina Sobieski, the mother of Cardinal Stuart; the young Henry Stuart, Duke of York; Canova's monument to the Stuarts in St Peter's, Rome; the Cardinal Duke of York.*

FACING PAGE: *'James III' receiving his son, Cardinal Stuart, at the Palazzo Muti in Rome. The Cardinal (in the foreground, to the right of centre) is wearing a black coat, red stockings and even red heels on his shoes.*

Cardinal Thomas Weld

CLOCKWISE FROM TOP LEFT: *Thomas Weld as Titular Bishop of Amycla; with his grandchildren; Mary Lucy Weld, the Cardinal's daughter; Lucy, wife of the Cardinal-to-be.*

FACING PAGE: *G Jones' painting of Cardinal Weld at the consistory at which he received the red hat. Around the Pope's throne are gathered the papal court, and in the top right-hand can be seen the Cardinal's daughter and her family, discreetly positioned behind a curtain.*

ABOVE: *Cardinal Acton as Pope Gregory XVI's counsellor. He is seen standing between Tsar Nicholas I and the Pope.*

Cardinal Charles Acton

to have made a favourable impression, for the King gave him what is now the Palazzo Torlonia in Rome, and in 1523 he became Cardinal Protector of England, replacing the recently elected Clement VII.

In 1524 Campeggio was named Bishop of Salisbury although he never actually resided there, and at the same time held the archbishopric of Bologna and several smaller Italian bishoprics. Despite such pluralism, Campeggio's voice was that of a staunch reformer, especially during the short pontificate of Adrian VI, calling the officials of the *Dataria* (one of the papal curial offices) 'blood-suckers' and complaining about the excessive granting of indulgences, such as those connected to the rebuilding of St Peter's.

In 1528 he was in England again to hear the divorce suit of King Henry against Catherine of Aragon, though he was suffering from gout and had to be carried in a litter. Here he found himself in a highly delicate position. The vacillating Pope Clement had privately told him to move slowly and refer any final decisions to Rome. He failed to reconcile the couple or even induce the Queen to retire into a convent; moreover, to declare the marriage invalid was to question Julius II's bull of 1503 that had dispensed the couple from all impediments. The case was withdrawn and Campeggio left for his summer vacation, although his luggage was searched for imperial bribes and papal bulls at the port, a clear sign of Henry's suspicions that Campeggio had sympathies with the Emperor (Queen Catherine's nephew). The whole debacle is supposed to have led to the Duke of Suffolk's exclamation: 'By the Mass, now I see that the old saw is true, that there was never legate nor cardinal that did good in England.' In 1534 Campeggio was deprived of the See of Salisbury since he was a foreigner and an absentee.

Elsewhere he was involved with the growing Lutheran threat in Germany, and he took a leading part at the Diets of Nuremberg (1524) and Augsburg (1530). He died in Rome of gout and fever on 25 July 1539 and was buried in the portico of Santa Maria in Trastevere. In 1554 his son, Cardinal Alessandro, was buried in the same tomb. It is thought that, in 1571, at least some of Cardinal Campeggio's bones were transferred to the church of Santi Marta e Bernardino, a church that Campeggio had built in Bologna.

SAN TOMMASO IN PARIONE (VIA PARIONE)

From 1517 to 1519 Cardinal Campeggio was the first cardinal of this *titulus*. The little church was made a titular church by Pope Leo X in order to be able to give a title to each of the thirty-one cardinals that he created in July 1517.

This small church, which is of ancient origins, is in the region of Rome called *Parione*. The first written records of its existence are of the consecration of a new church on the site by Pope Innocent II in 1139. St Philip Neri, the second 'Apostle of Rome', was ordained priest there on 23 May 1551, some thirty years before the church was rebuilt once again. In 1937, due to the poor condition of the church, the *titulus* was transferred to the

nearby Chiesa Nuova. Today San Tommaso is the Ethiopian church in Rome, where the Coptic Rite is regularly celebrated.

For the entry on Sant'Anastasia see p. 75.

For the entry on San Giorgio in Velabro see p. 172.

For the entry on Santa Maria in Campitelli see p. 133.

SANTA MARIA IN TRASTEVERE
(PIAZZA SANTA MARIA IN TRASTEVERE)

The oldest Marian church in Rome, this was the location of a miraculous spring of oil at the time of Christ's birth – hence the words *Fons Olei* above the door of a house (No. 26) next to the basilica. The church was the *titulus* of Cardinal Campeggio (from 1528), and also of Cardinal Stuart (1759-61), whose coat of arms can be seen above the entrance, on the choir stalls, and on the altar of the *Capella della Strada Cupa* (bottom of the right aisle). He is also mentioned in a Latin inscription located in the corridor leading to the sacristy. Near the basilica is the Palazzo San Callisto, the home for many years of Cardinal Gasquet.

The basilica itself is one of the most glorious in Rome that is not designated as a Papal Basilica. For any cardinal of any time this would have been and is a highly prized *titulus*. The church is set in a large piazza that is the heart of the Trastevere area of Rome. At the latest, a church was built on this site during the pontificate of Pope St Julius I (337-52). The structure that can be seen today is the result of the commission of Pope Innocent II (1130-43).

The interior of the church surpasses in beauty and dignity even that which is promised by the exterior's mosaics, frescos and Romanesque campanile. Resplendent in the twelfth century apse mosaic is the enthroned Lord Jesus Christ sharing His throne with the Blessed Virgin Mary; thirteenth century mosaics by Pietro Cavallini depict scenes from the life of the Virgin; a fine cosmatesque pavement and a stunning gilded ceiling carry the eye down the church to the raised sanctuary and the high altar.

The inscription on the tomb of Cardinal Campeggio.

St John Fisher
c. 1459 – 1535
Cardinal Priest of San Vitale (1535)

Cardinals wear crimson robes to show that, like the early martyrs of Rome, they are prepared to witness to Christ, even to the point of shedding their own blood. Among the English cardinals, only Fisher has been allowed to exemplify this greatest love; among the English bishops of his generation, only Fisher firmly opposed Henry VIII's divorce and break with Rome.

Fisher was born and educated in the market town of Beverley in the East Riding of Yorkshire, eight miles northwest of Hull. Buried in the town's minster was the eighth-century Archbishop of York, St John of Beverley, to whom Fisher had a great devotion.

Fisher's father, Robert, was a mercer, and after his death in 1477 his widow, Agnes, married William White. Fisher's half-sister, Elizabeth White, entered the Dominican convent at Dartford. Fisher wrote two treatises on the religious life for her from his cell at the Tower, *A Spirituall Consolation* and *The Wayes to Perfect Religion*, and she ended her days in exile in Antwerp.

The young Fisher studied at Michaelhouse, Cambridge (later merged with King's Hall to form Trinity College), and was ordained at York on 17 December 1491, aged twenty-two, gaining the benefice of Northallerton in North Yorkshire. Academically brilliant, he rose quickly, becoming a Fellow of Michaelhouse (1491), Senior Proctor (1494), Master of his college (1496/7) and Vice Chancellor (1501).

From around 1498 Fisher started acting as chaplain and confessor to the mother of Henry VII, Lady Margaret Beaufort (the great-niece of Cardinal Beaufort). The two worked together to build up the University: through Fisher's encouragement she established the Lady Margaret Professorship of Divinity (1502) and enlarged Christ's College (1505). Thanks to Fisher, money from her estate was posthumously used to found St John's College in 1511. He himself was the first holder of the Professorship of Divinity.

In 1504 Fisher was appointed to the See of Rochester. This was a poor diocese, with revenues amounting to only £300 a year, and seen as a stepping-stone to higher office. However, Fisher chose to remain there for over thirty years and turned down translation to the richer dioceses of Lincoln (1514 and 1521) and Ely (1515). He is reputed to have said that he would not change his poor old wife for the richest widow in England. Such a blatant disregard for careerism made him a model for St Charles Borromeo, the reforming Archbishop of Milan, who placed portraits of St Ambrose and the Bishop of Rochester in his study. Fisher was a dedicated pastor, a popular preacher and a man of great prayerfulness and personal asceticism. An early biographer has left us detailed accounts of these attributes:

> And first, because there is small hope of health in the members of that body where the head is sick, he began his visitation at his head church of Rochester, calling before him the priors and monks exhorting them to obedience, chastity and true observation of their monastical vows; and where any fault was tried, he caused it to be amended. After that he carefully visited the rest of the parish churches within his diocese in his own person: and sequestrating all such as he found unworthy to occupy that high function, he placed other fitter in their rooms; and all such as were accused of any crime, he put to their purgation, not sparing the punishment of simony and heresy with other crimes and abuses. And by the way he omitted neither preaching to the people, nor confirming of children, nor relieving of needy and indigent persons; so that by all means he observed a due comeliness in the house of God.

Fisher did not forget his beloved Cambridge and after his move to Rochester was elected Chancellor, a post which was confirmed for life in 1514. He befriended Desiderius Erasmus and encouraged him to teach Greek at Cambridge and to accept the Lady Margaret Professorship of Divinity (1511-14). As a guest at Queens' College, Erasmus prepared his Greek edition of the New Testament, which was eventually published at Basle in 1516 and has been described by a recent writer, Michael Macklem, as 'in a sense the crowning achievement of Fisher's years at Cambridge'.

Fisher was famed not only as a scholar but also as a preacher and he delivered the sermons at the obsequies of Henry VII and Lady Margaret Beaufort in 1509. He was assiduous in promoting good preaching by others. In his own sermons he made much use of Sacred Scripture and images that his audience could readily understand:

> If a table be foul and filthy by a long continuance, first we rase [scrape] it, after when it is rased we wash it, and last after the washing we wipe and make it clean. Our soul is compared unto a table wherein nothing was painted, nevertheless with many misdoings and spots of sin we have defouled and made it deform in the sight of God. Therefore it is needful that it be rased, washed and wiped. It shall be rased by the inward sorrow and compunction of the heart when we are sorry for our sin. It shall be washed with the tears of our eyes when we [ac]knowledge and confess our sin. And last it shall be wiped and made clean when that we be about for to make amends and do satisfaction by good deeds for our sins. These three things that we have spoken of cometh without doubt of the gracious pity of God. Thou art sorry for thy sin, it is a gift of Almighty God. Thou makest knowledge of thy sin weeping and wailing for it, it is a gift of Almighty God. Thou art busy in good works to do satisfaction, which is also a gift of Almighty God.

Bishop Fisher's pastoral solicitude and powerful preaching were rooted in and nourished by his life of prayer:

> He never omitted so much as one collect of his daily service, and that he used to say commonly to himself alone without the help of any chaplain, not in such speed or hasty manner to be at an end as many will do but in most reverent and devout manner so distinctly and treatably [deliberately] pronouncing every word that he seemed a very devourer of heavenly food, never satiated nor filled therewith. In so much as talking on a time with a Carthusian monk who much commended his zeal and diligent pains in compiling his book against Luther, he answered again saying that he wished that time of writing had been spent in prayer, thinking that prayer would have done more good and was of more merit. . . .
>
> When he himself would say Mass, as many times he used to do, if he were not letted [prevented] by some urgent or great cause, ye might then perceive in him such earnest devotion that many times the tears would fall from his cheeks. And lest that the memory of death might slip from his mind, he always accustomed to set upon one end of the altar a dead man's skull which was also set before him at his table as he dined or supped, and in all his prayers and other talk he used continually a special reverence and devotion to the name of Jesus. Now to those his prayers he adjoined two wings, which were alms and fasting by the help whereof they might mount speedier to heaven.

The very quality of John Fisher's outward appearance has been left to posterity in the famous sketch by Hans Holbein. The Bishop is seen in his later years, the crisis of the Henrician storm breaking over him. Yet there is a quite extraordinary luminous quality about the sketch. In it we see something of the man of prayer, something of the man of resolve and something of the physical results of his life of asceticism:

> And when he had no strangers, his order was now and then to sit with his chaplains, which were commonly grave and learned men, among whom he would put some great question of learning, not only to provoke them to better consideration and deep search of the mysteries of religion but also to spend the times of repast in such talk that might be (as it was indeed) pleasant, profitable and comfortable to the waiters and standers by. And yet was he so dainty and spare of time that he would never bestow fully one hour at any meal. His diet at table was for all such as thither resorted, plentiful and good, but for himself very mean. For upon such eating days as were not fasted, although he would for his health use a larger diet than at other times, yet was it with such temperance that commonly he was wont to eat and drink by weight and measure. And the most of his sustenance was thin pottage, sodden with flesh, eating of the flesh itself very sparingly. . . .
>
> The ordinary fasts of the Church he kept very soundly and to them joined many other particular fasts of his own devotion, as appeared well by his thin and weak body, whereupon though much flesh was not left, yet would he punish the very skin and bones upon his back. He wore most commonly a shirt of hair and many times he would whip himself in most secret wise. When night was come, which commonly brings rest to all creatures, then would he many times dispatch away his servants and fall to his prayers a long space. And after he had ended the same, he laid him down upon a poor hard couch of straw and mats (for other bed he had none) . . . he never rested above four hours at one time but straightways rose and ended the rest of his devout prayers.

The 1520s saw a new phase in Fisher's life as he was drawn into religious controversy, first with reformers such as Luther and Oecolampadius. When the papal bull that denounced Luther, *Exsurge Domine* (1520), was promulgated in England by Cardinal Wolsey outside St Paul's Cathedral, Fisher was chosen to be the preacher. The sermon was a synthesis of a theological tract that he was composing at the time against the Lutheran heresy. This work, *Assertionis Lutheranae confutatio*, became one of the most widely known and circulated of the confutations of Lutheranism. Two further works followed that also confronted Luther's writings: *Defensio regiae assertionis*, a defence of King Henry VIII's own attempts at religious controversy, and *Sacri sacerdotii defensio*, a defence of the Catholic understanding of the priesthood.

On another front Fisher countered the attacks of a Swiss–based writer, Johannes Oecolampadius, who had argued against the doctrine of Christ's Real Presence in the Eucharist. Fisher's response, *De veritate corporis et sanguinis Christi in eucharistia* (1527) was highly regarded by the Fathers of Trent as a cogent and perceptive argument in defence of Catholic Eucharistic doctrine.

From 1527 the matter of King Henry's Divorce was to be the most pressing matter for Fisher. This was to bring him both the red hat and public death on a London scaffold. He became Catherine of Aragon's chief supporter and may have written as many as eight works on the subject. At the Blackfriars Trial of 1529 he daringly compared his prophetic defence of the sanctity of the marriage bond to that of John the Baptist, whose feast day was to be held shortly after. This implied that Henry had some affinity with the adulterous Herod Agrippa, with Anne Boleyn as his Salome.

The King continued to pursue his goals but with greater determination. Fisher, meanwhile, became stronger in his public refutation of the King's desires. Thus it was Fisher who led the resistance to Henry VIII's claim to be Supreme Head of the Church in England and it may have been Fisher who suggested the insertion of the clause 'as far as the law of Christ allows', which qualified the acceptance of the King's headship of the Church in the document to be signed by the clergy.

Such strength on the part of the Bishop of Rochester caused some to try to find a way to rid themselves of this turbulent priest. In February 1531 someone attempted to murder Fisher by poisoning his porridge. Two died – a gentleman of his household and a poor woman begging for alms; many others were taken ill, although the Bishop escaped since he had not touched his food. The King swiftly passed a law condemning poisoners to the gruesome punishment of being boiled alive and this was the fate of Fisher's unfortunate cook, Richard Roose. On another occasion the roof of Fisher's London house was damaged by gunshot, which seemed to come from the Earl of Wiltshire's residence nearby and resulted in the Bishop's speedy departure for Rochester. Fisher's early biographers suggest that the King was at least partially responsible for both these incidents, although the truth will never be fully known.

By the 1530s Fisher's health was beginning to fail. In April 1533 Thomas Cranmer, the new Archbishop of Canterbury, decreed that Henry's first marriage was null and void and in June Anne Boleyn was crowned Queen. That September, Fisher appealed for help to the Emperor Charles V (nephew of Catherine of Aragon), hinting that any assistance given would be as agreeable to God as fighting the Turks. However, it is not clear what exactly Fisher had in mind and, throughout his opposition to the King, there is little evidence of the Bishop recruiting followers or planning conspiracies. Fisher had little experience of international power politics and his letter to the Emperor was probably no more than a desperate cry for help.

Time was obviously running out for Fisher. It was his involvement with the Kentish visionary, Elizabeth Barton, which finally led to his arrest and the confiscation of his possessions. Popularly known as 'the Holy Maid of Kent', Barton openly prophesied doom for Henry, Anne and England should he pursue his desired divorce. Fisher heard her inflammatory predictions in person and it was for this – even though she said nothing to him that she did not say publicly – that Fisher was arrested, after Barton confessed that her message was fraudulent.

After payment of a fine he regained his possessions only to lose them and his liberty for the rest of his life when in April 1534 he and Thomas More refused to take the oath which confirmed the Act of Succession. They were seized and sent to the Tower, where Fisher was kept in an upper storey of the Bell Tower for fourteen months.

In January 1535 Fisher was deprived of his bishopric. He was badly treated in captivity and appealed to Cromwell that 'I have neither shirt nor sheet nor yet other clothes that are necessary for me to wear but that be ragged and rent too shamefully.' Meanwhile, Pope Paul III, who had succeeded the prevaricating Clement VII, unexpectedly declared Fisher Cardinal Priest of San Vitale on 20 May 1535. It has been suggested that the Pope hoped the King would feel obliged to set a cardinal free. The red hat was subsequently sent in the direction of England only for it to be stopped, by order of the King, at Calais. Henry sent Cromwell to question Fisher about whether he would accept the hat if it were offered him. Fisher's biographer reported what ensued:

> "Sir," said [Fisher], "I know myself far unworthy of any such dignity, that I think of nothing less than such matters; but if he do send it me, assure yourself I will work with it by all means I can to benefit the Church of Christ, and in that respect I will receive it on my knees." Mr Cromwell making report afterward of this answer to the King, the King said again with great indignation and spite, "Yea, is he yet so lusty? Well, let the Pope send him a hat when he will; but I will provide that whensoever it cometh, he shall wear it on his shoulders, for head he shall have none to set it on."

According to the Imperial Ambassador, the King threatened to send Fisher's head to the Pope in order to receive the red hat.

At Westminster Hall on 17 June Fisher was found guilty of high treason for not submitting to the King as head of the Church in England. Originally sentenced to be hanged, drawn and quartered, the sentence was commuted to beheading. Sentence was carried on Tuesday 22 June, the feast of England's protomartyr, St Alban. Such was his weakness that he was carried to Tower Hill on a chair. He had been ordered to 'use as little speech as may be', and on the scaffold he said:

> Christian people, I am come hither to die for the faith of Christ's holy Catholic Church, and I thank God hitherto my stomach hath served me very well thereunto, so that yet I have not feared death; wherefore I do deserve you all to help and assist me with your prayers, that at the very point and instant of death's stroke, I may in that very moment stand steadfast without fainting in any one point of the Catholic faith, free from any fear. And I beseech Almighty God of His infinite goodness to save the King and this realm, and that it may please Him to hold His holy hand over it, and send the King good counsel.

Then he knelt down, recited the *Te Deum* and other prayers, and laid his head on the block. His head was severed with one stroke of the axe and the crowd were amazed to see such a quantity of blood produced by his lean and slender body. His headless body was left lying naked on the scaffold until dusk, from whence it was thrown into a grave next to the nearby church of All Hallows. According to one dubious tradition that echoes the story of St John the Baptist, the Cardinal's head was brought to Anne Boleyn. She struck the mouth, saying 'Is this the head that so often exclaimed against me?' and is said to have cut her hand on one of Fisher's teeth, leaving a scar that remained for the rest of her short life.

We can be more certain that his boiled head was impaled on a pole on London Bridge; after a fortnight it was reported that the head 'grew daily fresher and fresher, so that in his lifetime he never looked so well'. It was soon thrown into the Thames and replaced by the head of St Thomas More. Fisher's grave became a site of veneration and his body was translated to the privacy of the Chapel of St Peter ad Vincula within the Tower, where it remains to this day.

The execution of 'the saintliest bishop in Christendom', together with that of More, Reynolds and the Carthusians, caused a great outcry in England and overseas. Many blamed the poor harvests of 1535 on the martyrdoms. The exiled Reginald Pole wrote in his *De Unitate* (1536):

> What other have you, or have you had for centuries, to compare with Rochester in holiness, in learning, in prudence, and in episcopal zeal? You may be, indeed, proud of him, for, were you to search through all the nations of Christendom

in our days, you would not easily find one who was such a model of episcopal virtues. If you doubt this, consult your merchants who have travelled in many lands; consult your ambassadors; and let them tell you whether they have anywhere heard of any bishop who has such a love for his flock as never to leave the care of it, ever feeding it by word and example; against whose life not even a rash word could be spoken; one who was conspicuous, not only for holiness and learning, but for love of country.

Devotion to Fisher continued within the Catholic community and, together with More, he was beatified by Leo XIII in 1886 and canonised by Pius XI in 1935. Their feast is kept on 22 June.

SAN VITALE (VIA NAZIONALE)

From the busy Via Nazionale one descends a large and wide flight of steps to enter the ancient portico of this simple basilica. The church dates from the early fifth century and is dedicated to St Vitalis and his family, all martyred in the first century. The church has been rebuilt several times, most notably by Pope Sixtus IV before the Jubilee Year of 1475. There are no columned aisles or outstanding artistic achievements in this quite large church, but there is a great sense of peace and restrained beauty.

GIROLAMO GHINUCCI
(1480 – 1541)
CARDINAL PRIEST OF SANTA BALBINA (1535)
CARDINAL PRIEST OF SAN CLEMENTE (1537)

Despite Henry VIII's break with Rome, St John Fisher was not the only English cardinal created by Pope Paul III on 20 May 1535. Uniquely, two English diocesan bishops, both deprived of their office by the King, were elevated to the sacred purple that day – the soon-to-be-martyred Bishop of Rochester, and the absentee Bishop of Worcester, Girolamo Ghinucci.

Born in Siena in 1480, Ghinucci began his ecclesiastic career as a canon of Siena Cathedral. He held various offices in Rome under Julius II and was a key figure in organising the Fifth Lateran Council (1512-17) and encouraging English participation so as to counter Louis XII's rival council at Pisa. He was named Bishop of Ascoli Pisceno on 16 October 1512, which he later resigned in 1518.

Sent to England as Leo X's nuncio, he won the favour of Henry VIII and acted as his counsellor and representative in Spain. He tirelessly acted as a mediator between Henry and Rome, following a foreign policy that tried to ensure the ongoing enmity between France and England, thus serving papal interests in the Italian peninsular. In 1521 Ghinucci helped arrange the granting of the title *Christianae Fidei Defensor* to Henry as a reward for his loyalty and orthodoxy, as expressed in his *Assertio* (a defence of the Church's sacramental theology against Luther).

The diplomat, Bishop Gigli of Worcester, died in Rome in 1521 and Giulio de' Medici was appointed to the vacant see by the Pope, with the King's approval. Ghinucci eventually persuaded de' Medici, who already had a string of rich benefices, to resign in favour of him. On 26 September 1522 Ghinucci was named Bishop of Worcester. Like his predecessor, Ghinucci never took possession of Worcester and was enthroned by proxy on 2 March 1523. Also that year he was named Apostolic Administrator of Malta, a post he held until 1538.

Ghinucci was obviously given the bishopric of Worcester as a reward for past assistance and a platform for future loyalty. The Tudors relied upon allies like him in the absence of a stronger power base in Rome. From 1528 King Henry and Wolsey tried to secure a red hat for Ghinucci to further his usefulness. In 1526 he helped Wolsey gain Italian scholars and books for the new Cardinal's College, Oxford, and soon became embroiled in the matter of the King's divorce, seeking to persuade the Pope to be favourable to King Henry's cause. However, despite his best efforts, the Italian prelate, like Wolsey, soon lost favour.

The King expelled him from the See of Worcester in 1534, but Ghinucci continued to use the title until his death in 1541 and, in Rome, became a supporter of the declining English Hospice. By this time he had been created Cardinal of Santa Balbina (21 May 1535), helped organise the Council of Trent, acted as legate in the peace negotiations between Francis I and Charles V (1538) and administered the Sees of Cavaillon (1537–40) and Tropea (1538–41). The Pope even gave him the administration of the Welsh See of St David's in 1537, following the death of Bishop Rawlings, although the appointment was meaningless and Henry meanwhile elevated William Barlow to the see. Ghinucci died on 3 July 1541 and was buried in the ancient basilica of San Clemente, which had been his *titulus* since 1537.

For the entry on Santa Balbina see p. 66.

For the entry on San Clemente see p. 94.

Cardinal Ghinucci's coat of arms surmounts his memorial plaque in the Basilica of San Clemente.

REGINALD POLE
1500 – 1558

CARDINAL DEACON OF SANTI NEREO E ACHILLEO (1536)
CARDINAL DEACON OF SANTI VITO E MODESTO (1540)
CARDINAL DEACON OF SANTA MARIA IN COSMEDIN (1540)
CARDINAL PRIEST OF SANTA MARIA IN COSMEDIN (1555)

'Be as cunning as serpents and as innocent as doves.' When Margaret, Countess of Salisbury, gave birth to her third son in March 1500 she could never have guessed how quickly and dramatically the times were about to change, rendering so naturally apposite the future motto of Cardinal Pole.

Born at Stourton Castle in Staffordshire, Reginald Pole was the younger son of Sir Richard Pole and Lady Margaret Plantagenet, the daughter of the Duke of Clarence and niece of Edward IV. Educated at the Sheen Charterhouse, Oxford and Padua, the fact that his cousin, Henry VIII, financially supported these studies suggests that a high–flying career was in store for the young Reginald. It seems that Catherine of Aragon saw Pole as a possible suitor for Princess Mary, but he instead followed an ecclesiastical career. While still a layman, Pole was appointed Dean of Wimbourne (1518) and Dean of Exeter (1527). His big chance came when the King asked him to consult the University of Paris over the matter of the desired divorce. Paris gave a favourable opinion but the 'King's great matter' was beginning to trouble Pole. After Wolsey's death in November 1530, Henry offered him the prestigious See of York, and also that of Winchester, but Pole refused because he saw such appointments as inevitably involving explicit support for the King's policy.

He obtained Henry's permission to continue his studies overseas, while still receiving the revenues from his English benefices. He immersed himself in academia and declined the King's summons to return to England and declare his learned opinion on the divorce. To help him in this he was sent copies of Stephen Gardiner's *Of True Obedience* and Richard Sampson's *Oratio de Dignitate et Potestate Regis*, both supporting the King's position and attacking papal primacy. Pole wrote a treatise to explain his position, *De Unitate* (1536), meant for the King's eyes only. He warned the King of the dangers both to his soul and his Kingdom, writing that his subjects 'cannot be quieted with these innovations touching opinions in religion', and exhorted him to return to the unity of the Church. Pole compared Henry to Nero and Domitian, boldly calling him a greater enemy to Christendom than the Turk, and attacked the recent executions of Fisher, More, Reynolds, and the Carthusians:

> Is it possible? Could you slay men like these, who by your own judgment in former days, and by the judgment of all, were held in the highest esteem for innocence, virtue and learning, and that for no other reason than they would not violate their conscience by assenting to your impious laws?

The King was less than pleased with the work and invited Pole to court to discuss the matter further. Unsurprisingly, Pole remained in Italy. Around the same time the Pope, Paul III, invited him to participate in a commission headed by Cardinal Contarini concerning the reform of the Church. Pole hesitated, since a move to Rome would mean a further breakdown in his relations with his kingly cousin, but eventually joined the papal court. He became heavily involved with the *spirituali*, a group strongly in favour of reform and reconciliation with the Protestants. Pole received tonsure, the minor orders and the diaconate and was created a Cardinal Deacon on 22 December 1536, the same day as two future Popes, Julius III and his successor Paul IV. In 1538 the Pope appointed him as warden of the English Hospice in Rome to ensure its loyalty to Rome. Twenty years later Cardinal Allen transformed this fourteenth century institution into the English College, a seminary for the training of English priests.

Meanwhile in England the Pilgrimage of Grace (1536) was brutally squashed and the ransacking and dissolution of the monasteries began. The Pope appointed Pole as legate *a latere* to England. He was sent to Flanders to meet any representative that Henry might send and he also probably tried to raise support from Francis I and Charles V to overthrow the King. Henry countered this by persuading the King of France and the Regent of Flanders to expel Pole from their territory; men were despatched to kidnap or poison him. Henry wrote to Sir Francis Bacon: 'We would be very glad to have the said Pole by some means trussed up and conveyed to Calais.' Pole was declared a traitor and deprived of his benefices. Suspicion fell on his family and at the end of 1538 the Cardinal's mother (the Countess of Salisbury), his brothers Lord Montagu and Sir Geoffrey Pole, and kinsman Henry Courtenay, Marquess of Exeter, were all arrested.

Lord Montagu was beheaded on Tower Hill on 9 December 1538; Courtenay, convicted because he had been in a correspondence with the Cardinal, met a similar fate on 9 January 1539. Margaret Pole was eventually condemned to death – a silk tunic embroidered with the Five Precious Wounds found in her possessions was supposed to link her with a recent rising in the north – but the King was reluctant to kill one of his closest kin. She was kept in the Tower for two years, 'tormented by the severity of the weather and insufficient clothing'. After the Yorkshire Rebellion of 1541, the venerable lady was beheaded in private on Tower Green on 27 May. She was only given one hour's notice. Tradition has it that she refused to lay her proud Plantagenet head on the block and that consequently the executioner had to chase her round the scaffold, swinging his axe. Though it might make a colourful story for Beefeaters to tell impressionable tourists, the truth is that Lady Margaret died with dignity despite the fact that the novice headsman 'hacked her head and shoulders almost to pieces'. Leo XIII beatified her in 1886.

Pole wrote that: 'Until now I had thought God had given me the grace of being the son of the best and most honoured ladies in England . . . but now he has vouchsafed to honour me still more by making me the son of a martyr.'

Meanwhile, Pole was involved in peace negotiations between the Empire and France (1539) and entrusted with the Patrimony of St Peter, a crucial administrative office (1541). Based in Viterbo, he became closely connected to the likes of Michelangelo, Vittoria Colonna and Marcantonio Flaminio. He was sent as one of three papal legates to the Council of Trent, where he preached a strong sermon blaming the ills of the Church on the laxity of the clergy.

At the 1549 conclave, Pole was one of the leading *papabile* and some bankers put his odds at ninety-five per cent. In the end he was not elected, lacking only a single vote, presumably because he refused to campaign and spent the time writing a dialogue, *De Summo Pontifice*, which claimed that the only true candidate for the Throne of the Fisherman was one who did not seek such honour.

Pole was sent to negotiate a settlement between Rome and England at the accession of Edward VI. By 1553 the young King was dead and the goddaughter of Margaret Pole, Mary Tudor, ascended the throne. Pole was appointed legate to England. The Emperor delayed Pole's journey to England since the latter, still only a deacon, was perceived once again as a potential suitor to the Queen, and thus a rival to Philip of Spain. Pole therefore only reached the English shores once this unpopular marriage had been finalised. On 30 November 1554 he reconciled England to the Holy See. He told Parliament that he aimed 'not to pull down but to build; to reconcile, not to censure; to invite but without compulsion'. Peace was his by-word and he called himself the 'Pole Star'. He organised a legatine synod in 1555 and passed many reforms, though he refused help from St Ignatius Loyola and his Society of Jesus. One of the Cardinal's great interests was clerical education – not only was he Chancellor of both Oxford and Cambridge (from 1556) but was one of the first reformers in the Catholic world to suggest the establishment of diocesan seminaries. The Synod's eleventh decree demanded: 'That in cathedrals there be educated a certain number of beginners, from which, as from a seed bed [*tanquam ex seminario*], priests may be chosen who can worthily be placed in charge of the churches.' The idea was later picked up by the Council of Trent, though seminaries would not reach English soil until the nineteenth century.

At the end of 1555 Pole became a Cardinal Priest and his *diaconia* of Santa Maria in Cosmedin was raised *pro illa vice* to that of a *titulus*. On 20 March 1556 he was ordained a priest, and consecrated Archbishop of Canterbury two days later at the Observant Franciscan friary in Greenwich. His predecessor, Thomas Cranmer, had just been burned at the stake in Oxford. Pole received the pallium at St Mary-le-Bow on Lady Day that year.

Those who see Pole as Mary's henchman in her harsh anti-Protestant policy, which sent nearly three hundred to the stake, often forget that Pole himself fell foul of the Inquisition, especially over his suspected 'pro-Protestant' views concerning justification by faith. He was protected by Julius III but, with the election of Paul IV in 1555, became a suspect again. The new Pope, who had campaigned against Pole in the 1549 conclave, withdrew Pole's legatine powers and summoned him to trial for heresy in Rome. Pole was eager to clear his name but the Queen's representative in Rome, Sir Edward Carne, warned him that he would probably be locked away in the prisons of the Inquisition. He thus remained in England, protected by the Queen, and wrote an *apologia*. Meanwhile, much to the Queen's anger, the Pope appointed a new legate, the aged William Peto. In the end, the charges against Pole came to nothing, although Roman gossip held that Mary Tudor might renew her father's break with Rome over the matter.

Pole died of the flu, twelve hours after Queen Mary, at Lambeth Palace on 17 February 1558 and left his work of Catholic Restoration unfinished. He was buried in the Corona chapel at Canterbury Cathedral, near the former shrine of St Thomas – a prominent position

The tomb of Cardinal Pole in Canterbury Cathedral.

for the last Catholic Archbishop of Canterbury. According to the seventeenth century historian, John Strype, he also narrowly missed out on becoming King: there may well have been enough support for his claim to the throne had he not died within hours of his cousin, Queen Mary.

For the entry on Santi Nereo e Achilleo see p. 50.

SANTI VITO E MODESTO (VIA CARLO ALBERTO)

Cardinal Pole was briefly Cardinal Deacon of this church in 1540. Situated next to one of the arches of the Porta Esquilina, it is dedicated to two martyrs who suffered in 303. A church is first recorded as standing on this site during the reign of Pope

Leo III (795–816). The present church, which is usually closed, is the result of the rebuilding ordered by Pope Sixtus IV.

SANTA MARIA IN COSMEDIN (PIAZZA DELLA VERITÀ)

Cardinal Pole's church (1540–58), with its distinctive twelfth century campanile was built in the sixth century to serve the Greek community in Rome, and now serves Romans of the Melkite tradition. After rebuilding in the eighth century, the church commissioned through the centuries a fine ensemble of cosmatesque pavement, choir and paschal candlestick, adding in the thirteenth century a fine baldacchino above the high altar.

The church is included on most tourist itineraries because of the *Bocca della Verità* (Mouth of Truth), placed in the portico in 1632. This is a marble drain cover, sculpted into a grotesque face and dating from around 100 BC. Those who were accused of lying placed their hand into the mouth and were told that it would be bitten off if they did not tell the truth. The church also possesses the skull of St Valentine, which is crowned with roses every 14 February.

WILLIAM PETO OFM
C. 1478 – 1558
CARDINAL PRIEST – NO TITULUS (1557)

William Peto (or Peyto) was probably born sometime after 1478, the son of Edward Peto of Chesterton, Warwickshire, and Goditha Throckmorton of Coughton. He joined the Observant Franciscans, studied at both Oxford and Cambridge and rose to become Father Provincial. Since his friary at Greenwich was near the royal palace, he sometimes preached before the royal family and acted as confessor to Catherine of Aragon and the Princess Mary.

On Easter Sunday 1532, as 'the King's great matter' was approaching crisis point, Peto preached a court sermon which condemned the proposed royal divorce and prophesied that black dogs would lick the blood of Henry, like King Ahab. This was supposedly fulfilled fifteen years later as the King's body was taken to Windsor. According to the evidence of Sir George Throckmorton, Peto believed that the King could not annul his marriage unless it was proven that Catherine had consummated her previous marriage to Prince Arthur. He also held that Anne Boleyn was herself out of bounds since Henry had 'meddled with the mother and the sister'. With such strong opinions, it is little wonder that an agent of Cromwell's called him 'a tiger clad in a sheepskin, a perilous knave'.

Shortly afterwards, after refusing to recant his position, Peto was imprisoned in Lambeth Tower together with the warden of the Greenwich friary, Henry Elston. On their release they were sent into exile overseas. Peto printed a book at Lüneberg that defended the Queen's cause, *The Glass of Truth* (1533), and maintained close links with other members of the opposition. Based in Antwerp, he continued to write and distribute books. Peto was perhaps fortunate to escape to the Low Countries; another

Observant friar, Blessed John Forest, was later convicted of treason and burned at Smithfield (1538).

In 1539 Peto was included in a Bill of Attainder against the Pole family and their associates. He eventually went to Italy and in March 1543 Paul III appointed him to the See of Salisbury, which had been offered to Pole four years previously. Not surprisingly, Henry did not recognise the appointment and Peto never took possession. Based in Rome, he alternated with Bishop Goldwell of St Asaph's as *locum tenens* of the English Hospice, Rome.

At Mary Tudor's accession, Peto returned to England and took up residence in the re-established friary at Greenwich, where he expected to live his final years in peace and seclusion. He was also appointed the Queen's confessor. However, completely unexpectedly, he was created Cardinal Priest, without a titular church, on 14 June 1557. Paul IV, who like Peto was in his eighties, had befriended the English friar during his sojourn in Rome. Pole had recently been removed from his legateship, on suspicion of heresy, and the Pope wished to replace him with the frail Peto. The Queen was not amused and refused to allow the envoy carrying the Pope's briefs into the country. Friar William himself declined the elevation on the grounds of age and poor health, but the Pope refused to back down. The resulting deadlock between Pope and Queen was ended by the new cardinal's death at Greenwich in April 1558.

Peto's great-nephew, George Napier (or Napper), one of the Douai priests, was martyred at Oxford on 9 November 1610 and beatified in 1987.

WILLIAM ALLEN
1532 – 1594
CARDINAL PRIEST OF SAN MARTINO AI MONTI (1587)

William Allen was a complex and controversial figure – his red hat was linked to the Spanish Armada – but without doubt he did more than any other to ensure the survival of English Catholicism through the long reign of Elizabeth I.

He was born in 1532 at Rossall in Lancashire, one of the strongholds of the old Faith, and educated at Oriel College, Oxford, where he took his BA in 1550. Six years later, during the reign of Mary I, he became Principal of St Mary's Hall (merged with Oriel College in 1902), and, from 1558, held a canonry at York. However, he resigned his post after Elizabeth's accession, together with many other Catholic Heads of College, and in 1561 took up residence overseas. Although he returned to Lancashire after a serious illness in 1562, he left England for the last time three years later. Memories of mid-century Lancashire and Oxford, both highly conservative and resilient to the new religion, would colour his image of England for the rest of his life.

In exile Allen was ordained a priest (1565) and wrote a series of controversial tracts, such as *Certain Brief Reasons concerning the Catholick Faith* (1564), treatises defending purgatory and confession, and *De Sacramentis* (1565). Allen was part of a large exiled community of English Catholic scholars that clustered together in the university towns of Louvain and Douai. Between 1558 and 1568 over a hundred senior members of Oxford alone had left for reasons of conscience and joined this diaspora. An English printing press was set up at Louvain, as well as, for a brief time, two houses of studies nicknamed 'Oxford' and 'Cambridge'. To provide order among these scattered exiles, Allen founded the English College at Douai in 1568 with the help of John Vendeville, a local professor and future Bishop of Tournai.

Douai was an ideal centre: it was not far from the English Channel and its University had recently been founded by Paul IV, with the support of Philip II, for the special purpose of combating the Protestant heresy. The first Chancellor was Richard Smith, who had formerly been appointed by Henry VIII as the first Regius Professor of Divinity at Oxford. The scholarly atmosphere at Douai resulted in an English translation of the Latin Vulgate Bible, known as the Douai-Rheims Version, which was produced by Gregory Martin (formerly of St John's, Oxford) and partly edited by Allen. In 1582 the New Testament was published, predating the King James Version by nearly thirty years. Thus Douai became a sort of surrogate Oxbridge, fostering scholarship in defense of the truth while the exiles waited for the opportune moment to return to England.

The English College provided an orthodox education and produced fresh blood for the English Church in the form of the 'seminary priests'. Allen was clear that personal excellence was the primary aim of his college: 'Our students, intended for the English harvest,' he wrote, 'are not required to excel or be great proficients in theological science . . . but they must abound in zeal for God's house, charity and thirst for souls.' Allen also left his students in little doubt as to the hardships they would face when returning to England: 'I could reckon unto you the miseries they suffer in night journeys in the worst weather that can be picked, peril of thieves, of waters, of watches, of false brethren.'

Already by 1580 a hundred priests had been sent on the Mission, including the first of the college's one hundred and sixty martyrs, St Cuthbert Mayne († 1577). Douai ensured that Catholicism never died out in England, as it had in parts of northern Europe. St Robert Southwell spoke for his brother students when he wrote that it had now become their duty,

> . . . by the gentleness of [their] manners, the fire of [their] charity, by innocence
> of life and an example of all virtues, so to shine upon the world as to lift up the
> Res Christiana that now droops so sadly, and to build up again from the ruins
> what others by their vices have brought so low.

However, Douai did not prove to be a stable base for the exiles. The college transferred to Rheims in 1578, where the New Testament was published (1582). This move from Spanish to French territory was necessitated by the Eighty Years' War (Dutch Revolt) and the growing anti-English feelings in Douai, since the exiles were seen as close allies of the Spanish Crown. Nor was Rheims an ideal home (due to the French Wars of Religion), and the college returned to Douai in 1593. In the meantime Allen transformed the moribund English Hospice in Rome into the Venerable College of St Thomas de Urbe, established by papal bull in 1579.

Founding these colleges presented many problems. Financially they were a drain, especially since there were no dioceses to support the students as Trent envisaged. Douai largely depended on the Spanish Crown, and Rome on the revenues of the old Hospice. English donations and papal grants (cut back by Sixtus V in 1585) were also important. Problems of identity added to the situation. Douai was both a school and a seminary; Rome was primarily a seminary (despite the presence of a handful of lay students). The early history of the colleges was overshadowed by debates about whether its alumni should return home as part of a missionary offensive or wait for a change in regime – a discussion that soon developed into an ongoing feud between the Jesuits and the secular clergy. In Rome the dissensions led to the resignation of the first Rector, Dr Morus Clynnog. Little wonder that Allen wrote in May 1582:

> I know for certain from experience that it would be easier to guide to salvation a thousand souls in England than a hundred in this exile, which of itself breeds murmurings, complaining, contradictions and discontent. When Moses leads the peoples through the desert, he suffers much.

In 1581 Allen was named 'Prefect of the English Mission', making him in effect the ecclesiastical superior of the English clergy. Allen hoped to convert England through the clergy trained in his colleges, but he was not afraid to use the temporal arm. His ideal was to restore a Catholic to the throne, and with his in mind he co-operated with the powers of Catholic Europe, in particular Spain.

He got himself involved in various plots to overthrow the Queen from as early as 1572, and in 1583 was named Bishop of Durham and legate in the event of the success of the Duc de Guise's proposed invasion. On 7 August 1587 he was named a cardinal and, at the end of the month, received the red hat. Allen's elevation to the sacred purple, at Philip II's insistence, was closely linked to the Armada, which hoped to invade Protestant England and leave Allen as Archbishop of Canterbury. His *Admonition to the Nobility and People of England* called on them to join the Spaniards and depose Elizabeth, that 'sacrilegious heretic' and 'incestuously begotten bastard'. It was little surprise that the Elizabethan regime considered Allen and his seminaries overseas as such dangerous threats. An English spy, closely watching his movements, left us the following description of Allen as he appeared in 1580:

> Tall of stature and slender; his beard cut short and somewhat red in colour. His face full of wrinkles; under his right eye a mole, not very big. Longhanded, the nails of his fingers long and growing up.

After the failure of the Armada, Philip II tried to gain for Allen the archbishopric of Malines but he never took possession of the see. Though only a cardinal for seven years, he participated in the conclaves that elected Urban VII, Gregory XIV, Innocent IX and Clement VIII. Gregory XIV named him Prefect of the Vatican Library and, remembering perhaps his work on the Douai-Rheims Bible, asked him to help prepare a revision of the Vulgate.

Energetic and devout, though at times politically imprudent, Allen inspired generations of priests and the legacy of his seminaries overseas continues to this day. He achieved much, but misjudged the attitude of his fellow countrymen and died a venerable but disappointed man at the English College, Rome, on 16 October 1594, aged sixty-two. As he lay dying, he told the Spanish Ambassador that: 'The greatest pain he suffered was to see that after God had given him the grace that by his persuasion so many had borne imprisonments, persecutions and martyrdom in England, he had deserved by his sins to end his life on that bed.' The 'Cardinal of England' was buried at the college, where his monument can still be seen although his tomb was ransacked by French troops at the close of the eighteenth century. The Cardinal's vestments were bequeathed to a church near Rossall 'if the Kingdom of England should have returned to the Catholic faith'.

For the entry on San Martino ai Monti see p. 17.

Philip Thomas Howard OP
1629 – 1694
Cardinal Priest of Santa Cecilia in Trastevere (1675)
Cardinal Priest of Santa Maria sopra Minerva (1679)

The best part of a century passed between the death of Cardinal Allen and the creation of the next English cardinal. This was hardly surprising given the underground nature of the English Catholic Church and the disagreements within the community itself about leadership – indeed, between 1631 and 1685 there was no active bishop in the country. It seems, however, that in a vain effort at reunion, an unknown agent offered the red hat to William Laud, the Archbishop of Canterbury, in 1633. Needless to say, Laud declined the invitation. Around the same time there were rumours that George Con, a Scotsman attached to the household of Cardinal Barberini who served as papal agent in London, was to be created a cardinal but this never materialised. In the end, the only English cardinal of the seventeenth century was a scion of the House of Norfolk.

Philip Thomas Howard, the 'Cardinal of Norfolk', belonged to a family of martyrs. His great-grandfather, St Philip Howard, Earl of Arundel, died in the Tower after a decade of imprisonment for the Faith, and his uncle, Blessed William Stafford, was beheaded on Tower Hill in 1680 during the hysteria following the Popish Plot.

The first of the Howard cardinals was born on 21 September 1629 at Arundel House in the Strand, London, the third son of Henry Frederick Howard (then Lord Maltravers and, from 1646, third Earl of Arundel) and Elizabeth Stuart (daughter of the Duke of Lennox). Educated at Cambridge, Utrecht and Antwerp, he was only sixteen when he entered the Dominican house at Cremona against his family's wishes. When John Evelyn breakfasted with Philip's grandfather on Easter Monday 1646 it was reported that the Earl was 'in tears on some private discourse of crosses that had befall'n his illustrious family, particularly the Undutifullnesse of his Grandson Philip's turning Dominican Frier'. Philip's father appealed to Rome to intervene, as he feared that pressure had been brought to bear on his son to make him enter the Order, but when Pope Innocent X interviewed the young man he established beyond his satisfaction that there had been no foul play. Philip, who had now moved to Rome, was professed at the Basilica of San Clemente on 19 October 1646, taking the name 'Thomas' in honour of the 'Angelic Doctor', and ordained priest in Rennes in 1652.

In 1657 he returned to England to raise funds for the establishment of a Dominican friary and school at Bornhem in Flanders. This was set up at the end of the year, with Howard as prior and novice master. The priory was limited to thirteen members and a daughter foundation soon became a necessity. Howard unsuccessfully tried to open a house at Dieppe and, in 1665, accepted an old priory at Tangiers (now in Morocco), a city that was part of Catherine of Braganza's dowry. In 1660 Howard opened a convent for Dominican nuns at Vilvorde, which later moved to Brussels and became a centre of the Jacobite diaspora. The Order of Preachers was the chosen order of the Norfolks: Antonia, Frances, Catherine, Mary Delphina, Mary and Elizabeth Howard all became nuns at Vilvorde, while Philip's brother Francis (Fr Dominic) was also admitted into the Order.

During the exile of Charles II, Philip became a trusted confidant of the King, sometimes running secret missions for him to England. After the Restoration, Howard took an active part in the negotiations that preceded Charles' marriage to the Catholic Catherine of Braganza at Winchester. He became the new Queen's chaplain (1662) and Grand Almoner (1665), being accorded the singular privilege, for Catholic clergy of the time, of publicly wearing clerical dress (though not his habit) and using chambers at Whitehall.

Meeting the Dominican in 1666, Samuel Pepys described him as a 'good natured gentleman' with whom he 'discussed much of the goodness of the musique in Rome; and of the great buildings which the Pope (whom in mirth to us, he calls Anti-Christ) hath done in his time'. There were various moves to make Howard a bishop – in 1672 he was even secretly appointed Titular Bishop of Helenopolis, with a view to making him Vicar Apostolic. He was never consecrated due to the opposition of the English Chapter, which demanded either a bishop with ordinary jurisdiction or no superior at all. This was a real problem because there had been no active English bishop since the resignation of Richard Smith (Titular Bishop of Chalcedon) in 1631 and, besides, according to the Royal Marriage Settlement, the Queen's Grand Almoner was supposed to have bishop's orders.

As a prominent member of the 'Catholic Party' at court, Howard had his enemies, especially after the unpopular Declaration of Indulgence (1672), which attempted to introduce a degree of religious liberty and seemed to threaten the Anglican Establishment. Howard was forced to leave England after it was claimed that his book, *The Method of Saying the Rosary . . . as it is said in Her Majesty's Chapple at St James* (1669), contained illegal copies of papal bulls.

He returned to Bornhem, where he was still prior, and on 9 June 1675 was unexpectedly visited by a papal messenger and told that Clement X, in what was to be his last consistory, had named him a cardinal on 27 May. It is thought that the Pope had been encouraged by his Irish Dominican confessor, John Baptist Hackett, who had taught Howard in the novitiate. The new cardinal was given the title of Santa Cecilia in Trastevere, although after the death of Cardinal de Retz (1679) the title changed to the beautiful Dominican church of Santa Maria sopra Minerva. Henceforth Howard lived in Rome and was never to set foot in England again. In this he was perhaps fortunate, for in 1678 Titus Oates mentioned Howard in his wild allegations, contending that the Popish Plot hoped to leave him as Archbishop of Canterbury. As mentioned above, this alleged plot led to the execution of the Cardinal's uncle.

Nevertheless, at the request of Charles II, the Pope nominated the new cardinal as Cardinal Protector of England and Scotland in 1679. He was conscientious in his promotion of his native Church, assisting in the establishment of the feast of St Edward the Confessor for universal observance in the Roman Calendar, raising funds for and granting faculties to the secular clergy, and overseeing the various colleges scattered across the continent.

Howard's name is especially honoured at the English College in Rome, where he was Cardinal Protector from 1680. He changed the house language from Latin to English, 'because these youths were beginning to forget their mother tongue', and banned the admission of commoners (non-church students). In 1685 the Cardinal built a *palazzo* next door, on the site of the notorious Corte Savelli prison, and rebuilt the college itself, though this caused anxiety for the Rector who lost rents through the demolition of houses and was never sure exactly how much of the work the Cardinal was actually paying for. Nevertheless the English community could be proud of the new complex on what is now the Via di Monserrato. The magnificent frescoes of Andrea Pozzo still survive in the college refectory and Martyrs' chapel – a powerful sign in the middle of Baroque Rome that England was truly part of the universal Church.

Howard continued to support Dominican endeavours – he put much energy into the foundation of St Thomas' College, Louvain (which only opened in 1697), restored the Basilica of Santi Giovanni e Paolo on the Celian (briefly an English Dominican priory) and oversaw the refoundation of the English Dominican Province in 1694, three weeks before his death.

He also championed an 'Institute of Clerics Living in Common' which had been founded by a Bavarian mystic and priest, Bartholomew Holzhauser, and hoped to introduce this into England as a way of combating idleness, sexual temptation and the uncontrolled administration of property among the clergy. He may even have tried to impose their rule of life upon the English College. Sensible though it was, this plan failed to win over the English seculars, suspicious of any hint of monasticism.

Howard's *palazzo* was the focus of celebrations surrounding the accession of the Catholic James II and for three days a fountain outside flowed with wine. However, Howard was a 'gradualist' in relation to James II's religious policy and was often frustrated in his attempts at moderation. Howard treated James' headstrong ambassador in Rome, the Earl of Castlemaine, with caution. He was also dismayed at the King's attempt to gain a red hat for the Queen's youngest uncle, Rinaldo d'Este, and make him joint Cardinal Protector of England and Scotland. Rinaldo was created Cardinal Deacon in 1686, despite not having minor orders, and later received the *diaconia* of Santa Maria della Scala. Although he never became Co-Protector, the King tended to use his services and neglected those of Howard. D'Este resigned in 1695 having succeeded his father as Duke of Modena, and shortly afterwards married Charlotte Felicitas of Braunschweig-Lüneberg. Despite his ill-treatment at the hands of the King, Howard was unceasingly loyal to the House of Stuart. On the occasion of the birth of the Prince of Wales, he provided 'an ox roasted whole, stuffed with lambs, fowls and other provisions of all kinds [which] stirred up the wonder and gladdened the hearts of the common people of the city'. The event was preserved for posterity in an engraving called *Il Bue Arrostito* (The Roasted Ox).

Howard was instrumental in the division of England into four Apostolic Vicariates, ratified by Blessed Innocent XI in 1688. His former secretary and auditor, Dr John Leyburn, who had been appointed Vicar Apostolic of England in 1685, now became the first Vicar Apostolic of the London District. The first Vicar Apostolic of the Western District, Philip Michael Ellis, later served as Howard's secretary after the Revolution of 1688, which necessitated his exile.

Cardinal Howard also acted as Archpriest of the Basilica of Santa Maria Maggiore and participated in the conclaves that elected Blessed Innocent XI (1676), Alexander VIII (1689) and Innocent XII (1691). He sat on a number of congregations, including that of the Holy Relics. Gilbert Burnet, who was one day to become the Anglican Bishop of Salisbury, met the Cardinal during his visit to Rome, as he recalled in *The History of my own Times* (1723):

> Two French Gentlemen desired a note from me to introduce them to him. Their design was to be furnished with Reliques; for he was then the cardinal that looked after that matter. One evening I came in to him as he was very busy in giving them some Reliques. So I was called in to see them: And I whispered to him in English, that it was somewhat odd, that a priest of the Church of England should be at Rome, helping them off with the ware of Babylon. He was so pleased with this, that he repeated it to the others in French; and told the Frenchmen, that they should tell their countrymen, how bold the hereticks, and how mild the cardinals were at Rome.

Howard's generosity to the poor was matched by his own simple mode of living among his brother Dominicans at Santa Sabina, dressed in his Dominican habit and a scarlet zucchetto. The 'Cardinal of Norfolk' died on 17 June 1694 and was buried in a simply marked tomb in the choir of Santa Maria sopra Minerva, not far from the tomb of Pope Clement VII, sometime Bishop of Worcester. He left provision for two thousand Masses to be said for the repose of his soul and instructions that his grave be marked only by a flat stone devoid of the usually found praises to be found on such a memorial. The inscription runs:

> To Philip Thomas Howard of Norfolk and Arundel, Cardinal Priest of S Sopra Minerva of the Holy Roman Church, of the saintly family of the Order of Preachers, Archpriest of S Maria Maggiore, Protector of Great Britain, Grand Almoner of England, father of his country and of the poor. His sons of the English Province of the same Order, being named his heirs, placed this tablet in mourning for their most excellent father and restorer, with the approval of the eminent cardinals of the Holy Roman Church, Paulutius of Altieri, Francis of

Nerli, Galeatius Marescottus and Fabrutius Spada, the executors of his will. He died on 20 June in the year of our salvation 1694 at the age of 64.

For the entry on Santa Cecilia in Trastevere see p. 48.

SANTA MARIA SOPRA MINERVA (PIAZZA DELLA MINERVA)

Only from 24 March 1557 has this church served as a *titulus* of the Roman cardinals being awarded by Pope Paul IV (1555-9) first of all to the Dominican cardinal who was to succeed him as Pope Pius V, Cardinal Antonio Michele Ghislieri. Located near the Pantheon, the Minerva was the *titulus* of Cardinals Howard (1679-94) and Murphy-O'Connor (2001–). The church owes its name to the fact that it was built, in 1280, over the ruins of the ancient Roman Temple of Minerva. The basilica is run by the Dominicans and contains the bodies of St Catherine of Siena, Patron of Europe and of Italy, and Blessed Giovanni da Fiesole (Fra Angelico).

Although it is known as Rome's only gothic church there is little suggestion of this on the outside, the church's severe Renaissance façade having been built in 1453. The church has been richly endowed with artistic treasures over the centuries with artistic masterpieces, including Michelangelo's *The Risen Christ* and Filippino Lippi's Carafa chapel. Among the many noble families buried in its vaults lie two English cardinals – Giulio de' Medici (later Clement VII) and Philip Howard, both buried behind the high altar.

HENRY BENEDICT STUART
DUKE OF YORK
1725 – 1807
CARDINAL DEACON OF SANTA MARIA IN CAMPITELLI (1747)
CARDINAL PRIEST OF SANTA MARIA IN CAMPITELLI (1748)
CARDINAL PRIEST OF SANTI APOSTOLI (1752)[1]
CARDINAL PRIEST OF SANTA MARIA IN TRASTEVERE (1759)[2]
CARDINAL BISHOP OF FRASCATI (1761)[3]
CARDINAL BISHOP OF OSTIA AND VELLETRI (1803)

Cardinal York, the grandson of James II and brother of 'Bonnie Prince Charlie', has left his mark in and around Rome more than any of the other cardinals in this book. His coat of arms can be found in Santa Maria in Trastevere and his monument stands proudly at the back of St Peter's. There is a 'Largo Duca di York' in Frascati and a 'Via di Cardinal di York' near a villa that still bears his name in the Riserva Naturale della Valle dei Casali, to the west of Rome. Throughout the Castelli area there are numerous plaques in churches and on streets witnessing to his munificent patronage. In the little town of Monte Porzio, for example, there is a tablet on the Via Giuseppe Verdi recording the school he established in 1773 for 'the education of young girls in piety and the useful arts'. A stone's throw away, in the *duomo* of San Gregorio Magno, inscriptions recall the dedication ceremonies at which he pontificated in 1766 and the translation of the

---

[1] He continued to hold S Maria in Campitelli *in commendam* until 1759.

[2] He continued to hold Ss Apostoli *in commendam* until 1762.

[3] As well as being Cardinal Bishop, he retained *in commendam* the title of S Maria in Trastevere, 'because of his devotion to the Mother of God', until 1763. He then held S Lorenzo in Damaso *in commendam* until his death.

relics of the martyr, St Laconilla, which he organised in 1783. The Cardinal is indeed remembered as the *benemerito Cardinale Tuscolano* ('well-loved Cardinal of Frascati').

Henry Benedict Thomas Edward Maria Clement Francis Xavier Stuart was born in the Palazzo Muti (now the Palazzo Balestra) in Rome on 6 March 1725. As the second son of 'James III' and Maria Clementina Sobieska, he was baptised by Benedict XIII and proclaimed Duke of York. As a child, he was noted for his handsomeness, charm, love of music and piety. The Marquis d'Argenson wrote that 'he never passes before a crucifix or an altar without genuflecting like a sacristan' and the Duc de Richelieu would later tell him: 'Your Royal Highness may perhaps win the Kingdom of Heaven by your prayers, but never the Kingdom of Great Britain.' Henry's interest in religion was hardly surprising given the religiosity of his parents: his father's piety was intense and austere, while there were plans to open the cause for his mother's beatification after her early death in 1735.

Although placed in nominal charge of a French-supported invasion force based at Dunkirk during the campaign of 1745, Henry never showed the military flare of his brother, 'Bonnie Prince Charlie'. Indeed, Charles Edward partly blamed Henry's indecision for the failure of this expeditionary force to land in Scotland. Henry lingered on in Flanders, where the War of the Austrian Succession was in full flow, and spent a brief period on the staff of the Comte de Clermont. The future cardinal saw his only active service at the Siege of Antwerp, where the normally critical d'Argenson commented: 'He behaved with a valour which was at once natural and hereditary.'

Henry's military career did not last long and he soon decided to pursue an ecclesiastical one instead. On 30 June 1747 he was tonsured by Benedict XIV and four days later created Cardinal Deacon with the title of Santa Maria in Campitelli, despite not holding major orders. Of course, this was not unusual at the time and remaining in minor orders had the advantage of flexibility, since a dispensation could be granted in case political necessity demanded an advantageous marriage in the future.

However, on 1 September 1748 Henry was ordained priest. At the end of the year, on the feast of the Holy Innocents, Henry celebrated his first *Missa Cantata* in the Sistine Chapel, in the presence of his father and twenty-two cardinals. For his brother, having the second in line to the throne as an unmarriageable Catholic cardinal was an untold disaster and relations between them never fully recovered. Indeed, Charles' feelings on the matter partly explain his temporary conversion to Anglicanism during a trip to London in 1750 in an effort to win support. There were even rumours that Louis XV's minister, Cardinal Tencin, and James' minister, Daniel O'Brien (Earl of Lismore), had been bribed by the British Government to gain the red hat for Henry, such was the damage it would cause to the Jacobites. However, the Duke's move from throne to altar could be seen as a result of personal discernment and political realism – after all, his new status as cardinal guaranteed prestige, influence and a handsome income, which the Jacobite cause needed badly.

Cardinal Stuart quickly crept up the ecclesiastical ladder. He was made Protector of the Carthusians in Rome (1748), Archpriest of St Peter's (1751), Titular Archbishop of Corinth (1758), Cardinal Bishop of Frascati (1761) and Vice Chancellor (1763), which gave him the use of the magnificent Palazzo Cancelleria. He was also granted various benefices abroad, including the rich Flemish abbeys of Auchin (1748) and Saint-Amand (1752), both held *in commendam*. As a royal prince, Henry was given precedence over the rest of the Sacred College with the exception of the Cardinal Dean, wore ermine on his robes, and was allowed to sit on a cushioned chair in the Pope's presence. The Cardinal lived in princely splendour, commissioning leading composers like Porpora, keeping a large stable and entertaining lavishly. This did not prevent Benedict XIV from exclaiming: 'If all the Stuarts were as boring as he, no wonder the English drove them out.'

As Bishop of Frascati he played the role of shepherd with much pastoral zeal. He rebuilt the seminary, established the *Biblioteca Eboracense* (with some twelve thousand volumes), called diocesan synods in 1763 and 1776 and did much work for the poor. Less happy was his building of a Passionist *convento* on the summit of Monte Cavo, which involved the destruction of the well-preserved Roman Temple of Jupiter Latialis. When Nicholas Wiseman arrived as a student in Rome a decade after York's death he found that Frascati was full of memories of the Cardinal:

> Of that prettily-situated city, successor of Tusculum, from which the bishop yet derives his title, the Cardinal is still considered the great benefactor. Whatever else may have been wanting for his title, to a royal heart he was no pretender. His charities were without bounds; poverty and distress were unknown in his see. . . . The Diocese of Frascati was full, when the author first knew it, of recollections of that Cardinal Duke, all demonstrative of his singular goodness and simplicity of character.

The Cardinal was an elegant figure, with a 'smooth, ruddy [face], without a wrinkle'. According to his biographer, Brian Fothergill:

> In the privacy of his palace at Frascati the Cardinal would sometimes wear a purple coat laced with gold with a plain gold episcopal cross on his breast, or else a black coat lined with scarlet silk, a scarlet waistcoat, breeches of black velvet with scarlet stockings, and black shoes with scarlet heels.

Society gossips sometimes queried his taste for handsome young men and Mrs Piozzi declared in 1794 that he was keeping 'a catamite publicly at Rome'. It seems clear, however, that the Cardinal Duke was innocent of these grave accusations and that he had a horror of all impropriety. Interestingly, his young protégés included two future cardinals: Charles Erskine, the son of Jacobite exiles whose studies at the Scots College between 1748 and 1753 were sponsored by the Cardinal Duke, and Ercole Consalvi, who was educated at the Frascati seminary between 1771 and 1776.

The death of 'James III' on New Year's Day 1766 resulted in a further slump in Jacobite fortunes. Clement XIII had no wish to offend King George's Government and endanger the British Catholic community and so refused to acknowledge the accession of 'Charles III'. Henry was reprimanded for his open defiance of this papal policy, especially when he was seen in his carriage with his brother seated to his right, a position reserved for crowned sovereigns. At the same time, the Rectors of the English and Scots Colleges, together with the superiors of the Irish Dominicans and Franciscans, were banished from Rome on account of their support for the new 'King'. This did not prevent Henry from celebrating his own accession after his brother's death in 1788. He struck medals with the famous words *Non Desideriis Hominum sed Voluntate Dei* ('not accepted by men but chosen by the will of God') and was addressed as Majesty by his own household. He replaced the ducal coronet with a royal crown on his coat of arms and styled himself 'Cardinal *called* Duke of York'.

Like the other Stuart pretenders, 'Henry IX' continued the royal custom of touching with medals for scrofula, the 'King's Evil'. The story even abounded that the Cardinal touched the Duke of Gloucester, George III's delinquent brother, who was present at one of the ceremonies, although he pretended not to notice. As late as 1901 a handkerchief stained with Henry's blood kept in Ireland was still thought to have miraculous powers.

The new 'King over the water' was seen as a charming and harmless relic of an unfortunate dynasty and no one could seriously imagine a venerable

Roman cardinal becoming King of Great Britain and Head of the Church of England. The new 'reign' coincided with a period of revolutionary change. In 1798 Henry lost much of his revenues after the French invasion of Italy and took refuge first at Naples and then, after brief stays at Messina and Corfu, settled in Venice, where he took lodgings near the Rialto. Curiously, it was Lord Nelson's flagship, HMS Vanguard, which evacuated him to Sicily, affording the 'Cardinal King' his first and only opportunity of setting foot on British territory. He participated in the conclave of 1800, held in Venice under Austrian protection at the monastery of San Giorgio. Soon afterwards Henry had the pleasure of seeing the appointment of his protégé, Ercole Consalvi, as Cardinal Secretary of State to the newly elected Pius VII.

The revolutionary period brought the old elites together and saw a thawing of the enmity between the Houses of Stuart and Hanover. Through the representations of Stefano Cardinal Borgia, Mgr Erskine and Sir John Coxe-Hippisley, the Cardinal King was actually granted an annual pension by his third cousin twice removed, George III. On Henry's return to Rome it was reported that he often met with the Duke of Sussex, who spent a long period in the Eternal City, and that they amused themselves by their habit of 'Royal-Highnessing each other incessantly'.

In 1803 Henry became Dean of the College of Cardinals and, *ex officio*, Bishop of Ostia and Velletri. However, given his age and frailty, he was allowed to reside at Frascati. Here, one of his favoured companions was a stray dog that had attached itself to him at St Peter's – an occurrence that was interpreted as recognition of his royal blood since the dog, being a King Charles spaniel, had an instinctive attachment to the Stuarts.

The 'Cardinal King' died at Frascati on 13 July 1807, the forty-sixth anniversary of his translation to that diocese and the twenty-first year of his 'reign'. The *de jure* British Crown passed to his second cousin twice

The façade of Frascati Cathedral.

removed, Charles Emmanuel IV of Savoy, who was noted for his piety and ended his days in a Jesuit novitiate. After lying in state at the Palazzo Cancelleria, 'Henry IX' was buried at St Peter's with his father and brother. They are celebrated in Antonio Canova's monument (dating from 1819), near the entrance of the basilica, which was paid for partly by the Prince Regent. The bodies were placed in the crypt and moved slightly to the east in 1938 to make way for the eventual tomb of Pius XI. A new sarcophagus was commissioned and paid for by George VI; the old tombstones (calling the Cardinal 'Henricus IX') were deposited at the Pontifical Scots College. The Cardinal Duke now rests next to another English cardinal, Raphael Merry del Val.

The Cardinal Duke of York never visited Great Britain but he remains the most intriguing – and perhaps the most Roman – of England's cardinals. He is also the longest serving, having been cardinal for sixty years and ten days, and participating in the conclaves that elected Clement XIII (1758), Clement XIV (1769), Pius VI (1775) and Pius VII (1800).

SANTA MARIA IN CAMPITELLI
(PIAZZA DI CAMPITELLI)

Sometimes known as Santa Maria in Portico, the church was built in fulfilment of a vow made to Our Lady for the cessation of the plague in 1656. The tiny miraculous image of the Madonna above the high altar is much older, dating back to the sixth century. The church also contains the tomb of St John Leonardi, founder of the Congregation of the Mother of God. The church was the *titulus* of Cardinals Stuart (1747-52) and Gasquet (1915-29). The father of the former, James III ('the Old Pretender'), established a 'perpetual intercession for the conversion of England' here in 1766.

SANTI APOSTOLI (PIAZZA DEI SANTI APOSTOLI)

The present building dates from 1702, but the foundation goes back to the sixth century, and is now looked after by the Conventual Franciscans. A number of relics can be found in the *confessio* or crypt (made to resemble the catacombs in 1873), including those of the Apostles, Ss Philip and James. The basilica was the *titulus* of Cardinal Stuart (1752-59), who was consecrated bishop here on 19 November 1758. The exiled Royal Family lived in the nearby Palazzo Muti and both James III and Queen Clementina lay in state in the church. A monument to the Cardinal's mother can be found in the right aisle.

For the entry on Santa Maria in Trastevere see p. 98.

THOMAS WELD
1773 – 1837
CARDINAL PRIEST OF SAN MARCELLO AL CORSO (1830)

The Weld family, based at Lulworth Castle in Dorset, was of crucial importance to the English Catholic Church on the eve of emancipation. Most striking was their support for those religious driven out of France by the storms of Revolution, providing a house for the exiled English Jesuits at Stonyhurst and a community of Trappists at Lulworth. They also protected the exiled Poor Clares of Gravelines, who found sanctuary at Plymouth, and the Visitation nuns of Shepton Mallet and later Westbury (where Cardinal Weld's sister became Mother Superior). Despite their strongly Catholic pedigree, the family remained on good terms with George III who visited Lulworth four times and is said to have given permission for the family to build a mausoleum in the grounds and furnish it inside as they wished. This was a coded consent for them to build a Catholic chapel which acted as a sort of proto-cathedral, seeing various episcopal consecrations, including that of Bishop John Carroll of Baltimore, the first American bishop and founder of Georgetown University, on 15 August 1790.

Thomas Weld, the future cardinal, was born on 22 January 1773, the eldest of fifteen children. His father, Thomas, inherited Lulworth in 1775 following the death of his elder brother Edward, who had been the first husband of the famous Mrs Fitzherbert (later secretly married to the Prince Regent).

Thomas was educated privately by Fr Charles Plowden, a prolific writer and future Rector of Stonyhurst and Jesuit Provincial, and probably spent a brief time at the Jesuit College in Liège. In 1796 Thomas married Lucy Clifford, by whom he had a daughter, Mary Lucy. In 1810 he succeeded his father as Squire of Lulworth but was widowed five years later. In 1818, after his daughter had married her cousin, Hugh, the seventh Lord Clifford, Weld felt at liberty to offer himself for the priesthood despite (by the standards of the time) his mature age. As Wiseman later commented,: 'What life could have been less considered the way to ecclesiastical honours than this of a Dorsetshire country squire, in the field, or at his board?'

Lulworth was passed over to his brother, Joseph, who was a great yachting enthusiast, and Thomas went to Paris to be trained under the Abbé Carron, a holy priest who had opened the church of St Aloysius at Somers Town in 1808. On 7 April 1821 Weld was ordained by Archbishop Quelen of Paris, and the Vicar Apostolic of the London District, Bishop Poynter, sent him to the mission of St Mary's, Cadogan Street, which had partly been built by the Weld family. Here the new priest assisted another émigré priest, the Abbé Voyaux de Franous.

In 1826 Weld was appointed coadjutor to Bishop MacDonnell, Vicar Apostolic of Upper Canada, and consecrated Titular Bishop of Amycla by Poynter at St Edmund's College, Ware on 6 August. He is thus regarded as the first Canadian cardinal, although poor health meant that he never reached Canada and, in the meantime, resided in Hammersmith. He then travelled to Rome with his daughter, herself an invalid, and helped prepare the way for the Catholic Relief Act (1829). On 15 March 1830 Weld received the red hat from Pius VIII, so that the newly emancipated English Church would have a cardinal – the first since Philip Howard. The Prime Minister, the Duke of Wellington, had in fact recommended Weld as Bishop of Waterford and, although the Pope did not follow this suggestion, a mark of recognition following Catholic emancipation (1829) had been hinted at by Rome. The consistory at which Weld was created Cardinal Priest of San Marcello al Corso was watched by his daughter from behind a curtain. Curiously, there was another member of her family in the Sacred College – the then Bishop of Imola, Giacomo Giustiniani, who was related on his mother's side to the Clifford's.

Shortly after his elevation, Pope Pius died and Weld participated in the conclave that elected Gregory XVI. His splendid apartments in the Palazzo Odescalchi became a magnet for the many English Catholics who came to Rome, and it was here that Wiseman gave public lectures on such topics as 'The Connexion between Science and Revealed Religion'. In 1834 Weld became Cardinal Protector of the English College, though not without controversy. John Lingard feared that 'Both he and his son-in-law, Lord Clifford, are Jesuits to the backbone, and an incapable Rector may open to them a door for the reintroduction of the Jesuits.' The college had only recently passed from centuries of Jesuit control into the hands of English seculars, and it was thought that Weld's appointment would re-open this ancient tension.

Weld was also involved in matters arising in the colonies and the United States. He summoned the young William Ullathorne, future Bishop of Birmingham, to Rome to give an account of his pioneering work in Australia. Despite having been appointed Vicar Apostolic of Upper Canada, Weld never left Europe and his lack of knowledge of the situation across the Atlantic could lead to confusion. On 13 April 1833, Wiseman wrote to the Archbishop of Baltimore: 'The cardinals of the Congregation place the most complete confidence in Cardinal Weld for all business regarding England and America, though necessarily his previous choice of life can in no ways have qualified him for the slightest acquaintance with the ecclesiastical affairs of either.' An 'extraordinary blunder' occurred during a discussion regarding diocesan divisions in the United States:

> The map used upon the occasion not having room for the prolonged tract of Florida without enlarging the size of the sheet, this province was detached and represented separately in a small frame in some vacant corner of the map. Now Your Grace must know that geography is not a branch of education in Italy, and in consequence their Eminences considering that the real place of Florida, decided that the proposed demarcation could not be adopted as it united Florida in jurisdiction with Louisiana, I think, from which it was separated by such a vast tract of ocean.

Weld became a distinctive figure in the Eternal City, often seen in the company of his grandchildren. It is recounted that on one occasion, as he was driving in Rome, there was a violent storm and Weld used his ceremonial umbrella (found in all cardinal's carriages) to shelter his granddaughter from the rain. An almost certainly apocryphal story told by the family recounted how the Cardinal was in conclave when one of his grandchildren was born. Since he could not leave the elective assembly, the newborn child was put into the turn and swung into the conclave to meet its grandfather and, perhaps, other members of the Sacred College. Weld became affectionately known as 'the Cardinal of the Seven Sacraments'.

Weld died unexpectedly on 19 April 1837 of chronic bronchitis and fever, having blessed his grandchildren who knelt around his deathbed. He was buried at his *titulus* of San Marcello, alongside his daughter and son-in-law, where a monument to the Cardinal can still be seen. Ullathorne was present at a Requiem celebrated for him at San Carlo in Corso, where he witnessed a somewhat unedifying scene:

> The music was the celebrated *Requiem* of Mozart, performed by the best singers with instrumentation. But Mozart is rarely heard in Roman churches, and it attracted the artists and musicians. But when the thrilling tones of Mozart had become interrupted for a long time by the monotonous reading of Dr, later Cardinal, Wiseman in the harsh sounding English language . . . the Italians could stand it no longer, but set up a hissing all through the church. After a few moments Dr Wiseman got a hearing, and by a few words of grave and dignified rebuke restored silence until the lecture was completed.

Of the Cardinal's grandchildren, William became Bishop of Clifton (1857–93) and took part in the First Vatican Council, Walter was also ordained, Eleonora became a nun and Henry was awarded the Victoria Cross for his gallantry in the Crimea at the Battle of Inkerman (1854).

In his *Recollections of the Four Last Popes*, Wiseman paid tribute to Thomas Weld:

> It could not be expected that, at the mature age that Cardinal Weld had reached [when elevated to the Sacred College of Cardinals], he would master a new language, or perfectly learn the ways of transacting high ecclesiastical business; nor had the occupations of his life, nor even his brief studies, been calculated to make him equal those who from youth had been devoted to legal and theological pursuits. . . .
>
> As his share, the Cardinal brought into his council sterling good sense and businesslike habits, thorough uprightness and sincere humility; and soon acquired considerable influence in the congregations or departments of ecclesiastical affairs to which he was attached. At the same time he was genuinely courteous, hospitable and obliging. His apartments in the Odescalchi Palace were splendidly furnished and periodically filled with the aristocracy of Rome, native and foreign, and with the multitudes of his countrymen, all of whom always found him ready to render them any service. Indeed if he has a fault, it was the excessiveness of his kindness, too often undiscriminating in to objects, and liable to be imposed on by the designing or the unworthy. But surely if one must look back at life's close upon some past frailty, it would not be this defect that would beget most remorse. . . . Seldom has a stranger been more deeply and feelingly regretted by the inhabitants of a city, than was this holy man by the poor of Rome.

San Marcello al Corso (Piazza di San Marcello)

Dating back to the fourth century, this was the *titulus* of Cardinal Weld, who is buried in the third chapel on the right. Cardinal Consalvi, Secretary of State under Pius VII and a protégé of the Cardinal Duke of York, is also buried in this Baroque church. The church, which may have been built on the site where St Marcellus lived, is attached to the Generalate of the Servite Order.

The most famous treasure of this church is a much-venerated crucifix that was recovered undamaged in 1519 from the ashes of the previous church that had stood here. The great crucifix is a focus of devotion by the Roman faithful who have carried it in procession at times of great intercession for the city and the Church.

CHARLES JANUARIUS ACTON
1803 – 1847
CARDINAL PRIEST OF SANTA MARIA DELLA PACE (1842)
CARDINAL PRIEST OF SAN MARCO (1846)

Cardinal Acton's family, with its country seat at Aldenham Hall in Shropshire, had long been involved in European politics. The Cardinal's great uncle, John, commanded the fleet of the Grand Duke of Tuscany, and his father, Sir John Francis Edward Acton (sixth Baronet), was Prime Minister to King Ferdinand IV of Naples between 1780 and 1804. His closeness to the Neapolitan Royal Family led to rumours of an affair with Queen Maria Carolina, the daughter of Maria-Theresa and sister of Marie-Antoinette.

Charles Januarius Acton was born in Naples on 6 March 1803 and was baptized in the Royal Chapel, with the Queen herself acting as godmother. Rather unusually, Charles' mother was his father's niece, the daughter of his brother, Joseph Edward, who was a General in the Neapolitan Army. At the time of the wedding in 1800, the bride was aged fourteen and the bridegroom sixty-four, causing a great sensation in aristocratic circles. The marriage, which was only possible through a papal dispensation, was solemnized at a Catholic service in Palermo and (for reasons of English law) an Anglican service aboard Nelson's ship, HMS Foudroyant, which was then lying in Palermo harbour. The famous Lady Hamilton, Nelson's mistress, was one of the witnesses.

The future cardinal spent most of his early years in Sicily. In 1811 his father died and was buried, after a state funeral, at the Church of the Cruciferi in Palermo. The bereaved family moved back to England, setting up home in London (44 Montagu Square and then 71 Pall Mall) and Aldenham. Charles, who had received his first lessons from a future Bishop of Marseilles, the Abbé De Masnod, continued his studies at the Academy run by an émigré priest, the Abbé Quequet, in Parsons Green. The Actons' Catholicism made education at Westminster School impossible and Charles briefly attended a school at Isleworth and was then tutored privately by an Anglican minister in Kent. He went up to Magdalene College, Cambridge but, as a Catholic, was banned from taking his degree.

The young Charles had discerned a call to the priesthood on the day of his First Communion at Richmond. After leaving Cambridge he decided to pursue this calling further and in 1823 entered the elite *Accademia degli Nobili Ecclesiastici* in Rome. Here he had private tuition with the future Cardinal Fornari and soon caught the attention of the Secretary of State, Cardinal della Somaglia.

Upon ordination he was made a domestic prelate by Leo XII. He immediately began his diplomatic career, being sent as secretary to the nuncio in Paris, the future Cardinal Luigi Lambruschini, and then, in 1829, was appointed vice legate (or governor) in Bologna by the short-lived Pius VIII. After several curial jobs, he became in 1837 Auditor of the Roman Rota.

On 24 January 1842 Gregory XVI, to whom Acton was particularly close, named him Cardinal Priest of Santa Maria della Pace, though it seems that he had first been created *in pectore* three years earlier. The new cardinal was known for his unassuming manner, good nature and sharp wit, and was generous to the poor, even selling his silver candlesticks in order to redeem somebody imprisoned for debt. Indeed, this generosity resulted in huge debts. The Cardinal's sister, Lady Throckmorton, reluctantly sold a valuable necklace to raise funds for him, much to her husband's horror.

Acton instructed many converts, including the future Oratorian priest and hymn writer, Edward Caswall (1847). His secretary for many years was Thomas Grant, later Rector of the *Venerabile* and first Bishop of Southwark, who died in the odour of sanctity during the First Vatican Council.

As the senior English cleric, Cardinal Acton showed great interest in events across the Channel. In 1840, before his elevation to the sacred purple, he had been influential in increasing the number of Apostolic Vicariates from four to eight, although he resisted plans for the restoration of the Hierarchy since he thought the time was not yet right. The English, he thought, 'throughout their history had been factious, and opposed to authority, and were not to be entrusted with more and more independent power'. Pope Gregory shared this view for, as a former Prefect of Propaganda, he had had a sometimes difficult relationship with the Vicars Apostolic.

As Cardinal, Acton was Protector of the Venerable English College

(1842–47) and encouraged the Passionist mission to England, led by Blessed Dominic Barberi.

Acton had a great devotion to Our Lady of Good Counsel, whose shrine is near Rome at Genazzano. On one occasion in the autumn of 1845 he was travelling there from Palestrina accompanied by members of his household and three students of the English College, when the carriage spun out of control and was thrown off the road down a twenty-foot bank. Amazingly there were no serious injuries and even the carriage survived intact. The Cardinal attributed this fortunate escape to the intercession of the Blessed Virgin and, on finally reaching the shrine, chanted the *Te Deum*. He ordered an *ex voto* of the scene to be painted in thanksgiving.

However, despite this miraculous intervention on the road to Genazzano, the Cardinal was not long for this world. Still only in his forties, many expected Acton to rise even higher in the Church – there were strong rumours that he would be appointed Archbishop of Naples and at the 1846 conclave he is supposed to have received nine votes. He was a trusted adviser to Gregory XVI, who said that he never had to read anything of his twice over. The Cardinal was the sole witness and interpreter at the historic interview in 1845 between that Pope and Tsar Nicholas I, who was no friend to the Catholics under his rule. Acton kept the memorandum of what was said on this occasion a close secret until his death, although the audience undoubtedly prepared the way for the Concordat of 1847.

In December 1846 Acton was named Prefect of Indulgences and Relics and given the new titular church of San Marco. However, poor health necessitated his premature retirement, first to Palermo and then to Naples. He died of consumption at the Jesuit house in Naples on 23 June 1847 and was buried in the vaults of Naples Cathedral.

His nephew, Sir John Emerich Edward Dalberg Acton, the First Lord Acton, succeeded Newman as editor of *The Rambler* and won fame as a notable historian. The Cardinal showed great interest in his nephew and Lord Acton later made an abortive effort to bring his uncle's remains home to Aldenham – he wrote that 'it would be an act of respect which I owe to his memory'.

SANTA MARIA DELLA PACE (PIAZZA SANTA MARIA DELLA PACE)

Built by Sixtus IV (1471–84) and situated near the Piazza Navona, this was the titular church of Cardinal Acton (1842–46). The bodies of Ss Basilissa and Anastasia, disciples of St Peter and martyrs, lie beneath the high altar.

The outside of the church is particularly fine with a semi–circular porch. Attached to the church is a beautiful cloister designed by Bramante. Inside the church Carlo Maderno designed the high altar in 1614. Above this altar is enshrined an ancient painting of the Madonna. Tradition relates that a drunken soldier pierced the painting with his sword whereupon blood spurted forth. Pope Sixtus IV was brought to see the picture and made a vow to build a church dedicated to the Blessed Virgin if she brought peace in a war being waged with Florence at that time. Peace came and hence the church's dedication to St Mary of Peace.

San Marco Evangelista (Piazza San Marco)

This ninth century basilica, on the site of a church founded by Pope St Mark, is at the back of the Palazzo di Venezia. Its façade is a splendid Renaissance portico and, inside the church, there is a striking ninth century apse mosaic. The church was briefly the titular church of Cardinal Acton (1846-47) and also Albino Luciani (later John Paul I). Amongst the church's many relics is a finger of St Patrick.

NICHOLAS WISEMAN
1802 – 1865
CARDINAL PRIEST OF SANTA PUDENZIANA (1850)

Nicholas Patrick Stephen Wiseman was born in Seville on 2 August 1802, the son of the merchant James Wiseman and his second wife, Xaviera (née Strange), who shortly afterwards laid the infant on the Lady altar of Seville Cathedral and consecrated him to the service of the Church. The street on which he was born was later named the *Calle del Cardenal Wiseman*. Like Cardinal Merry del Val, Wiseman's family had settled in Seville from Waterford due to the many opportunities afforded by trade. Nicholas had an older brother, James, and a sister, Frasquita ('Fanny'), who later married into Italian nobility and became the Countess Gabrielli of Fano. At the age of three, his father died and the family left Seville for Waterford, where Nicholas began to learn English.

In 1809 Nicholas and his brother went to Ushaw College (again, like Merry del Val), where his studious interests were noticed by the Vice President, John Lingard (see Appendix II), and the Professor of Syntax, Charles Newsham. Wilfrid Ward described the young Wiseman: 'A somewhat gawky youth, with limbs all knit together, betokening the absence of all aptitude for athletics, sauntering about with a book under his arm, oftener alone than in company.' However, in later life Wiseman had a great love for Ushaw, and wrote a play, *The Hidden Gem*, for the college's jubilee of 1858. It was at Ushaw that the future cardinal decided to go forward for the priesthood. A cottage near the college was often shown as the place where the momentous decision was made, while Nicholas was sheltering from a storm.

In 1818 he entered the English College in Rome. The sea journey from Liverpool to Leghorn was arduous and full of adventure:

> During this period a fortnight was spent in beating up from Savona to Genoa, another week in running from Genoa to Livorno; a man fell overboard and was drowned off Cape St Vincent; a dog went raving mad on board from want of fresh water, and luckily, after clearing the decks jumped or slipped into the sea; the vessel was once at least on fire; and all the passengers were nearly lost in a sudden squall in Ramsay Bay, into which they had been driven by stress of weather, and where they of course landed: and the reader, who may now make the whole journey in four days, will indulgently understand how pleasing must have been to those early travellers' ears the usual indication, by voice and outstretched whip, embodied in the well-known exclamation of every *vetturino*, *Ecco Roma!*

The English College had recently been re-established by Robert Gradwell after the ravages of the French occupation and Wiseman was part of the first batch of students. 'One felt at once at home,' Wiseman later wrote, 'it was English ground, a part of the fatherland, a restored inheritance.' Within a few days, Wiseman and five companions found themselves in audience with Pius VII, who exhorted them, 'I hope you will do honour both to Rome, and to your own country.' Wiseman subsequently rose to the top of his class and took his degree as Doctor of Divinity by public disputation on 7 July 1824, in the presence of Cardinal Zurla and many other dignitaries:

> When the time comes, the respondent finds himself, he hardly knows how, seated behind a table at the end of an immense hall, which it requires a sustained voice to fill, supported by his professors, who may edge in a word at his ear, in case of possible straits. A huge oval chain of chairs stretches down the room, on either side, and soon begins to be occupied by professors, doctors, and learned men, of whom he has heard perhaps only in awe; each of whom receives a copy of the thesis, and cons it over, as if to find the weak point between the plates of mail, into which he will later try to thrust his spear. I remember well, in the particular instance before my eye, that a monk clothed in white glided in, and sat down in the inner circle, but though a special messenger was despatched to him by the professors, he shook his head, and declined becoming an assailant. He had been sent to listen and report. It was Fr Cappellari, who in less than six years was Pope Gregory XVI. Not far from him was seated the Abbé de Lamennais, whose works he so justly and so witheringly condemned. Probably it was the only time that they were ever seated together, listening to an English youth vindicating the Faith, of which one would become the oracle, and the other the bitter foe.

Wiseman was ordained priest on 10 March 1825. Continuing his studies, he specialised in oriental languages and published his *Horae Syriacae* in 1827 to critical acclaim. The following year he was named Professor in Hebrew and Syro-Chaldaic at the Sapienza University.

By this time Wiseman was also Vice Rector of the English College and special preacher for the English in Rome. When Gradwell was raised to the episcopate in 1828, Wiseman took over as Rector (with George Errington as Vice Rector) and Roman Agent of the English Vicars Apostolic, aged just twenty-five. The young Rector was popular with the students, taking them on expeditions to archaeological sites, and made the college a centre of intellectual and social life. During the period he received the likes of Newman, Gladstone and Macaulay as guests. Throughout his whole life, Wiseman maintained his deep love and devotion to Rome as the see of St Peter's successor. In his later life he wrote:

> St Peter's is itself only when the Pope is at the high altar . . . on the very spot which becomes him, the one living link in a chain, the first ring of which is riveted to the shrine of the Apostle below.

By the mid-1830s Wiseman's thoughts increasingly turned to England, where it seemed the Oxford Movement would soon lead to England's conversion. In 1835 Wiseman embarked on a lecture tour in London and, the following year, co-founded *The Dublin Review* (which in 1961 was re-named *The Wiseman Review*), aiming 'to depict both for English Catholics themselves and for an inquiring age the "genius of Christianity" in its Catholic form'. Despite the undoubted benefits of these visits, eyebrows were being increasingly raised in Rome that the Rector was spending so much time away from his college.

In 1840, when Gregory XVI increased the number of Vicars Apostolic from four to eight, Wiseman became Coadjutor Vicar Apostolic of the new Central District and President of Oscott. On 8 June (Whit Monday) he was consecrated Titular Bishop of Melipotamus by Cardinal Fransoni at the English College, in the presence of his mother. Shortly afterwards, he left Rome after a residence of some twenty-two years. Not surprisingly, many in England felt he was too 'Roman', especially the 'old Catholics', who were suspicious of any change after centuries of caution and compromise.

In 1847 Wiseman became Pro-Vicar Apostolic of the London District (succeeding Bishop Walsh as Vicar Apostolic in 1849) and was involved in negotiations with Rome over the possibility of re-establishing the Hierarchy. Blessed Pius IX was in favour, but the clouds of revolution intervened. Then, in the spring of 1850, Wiseman heard that he was to be created Cardinal Priest of Santa Pudenziana, and assumed this would entail a curial post. He even made plans to buy a property in the sleepy Castelli town of Monte Porzio, where the English College owned a villa. However, on arriving in Rome, he found out that he was to be Archbishop of Westminster at the helm of a new Hierarchy, and issued a triumphant pastoral letter on 7 October, titled *Extra Portam Flaminiam* ('Out of the Flaminian Gate'), proclaiming that, by papal brief: 'We govern and shall continue to govern, the counties of Middlesex, Hertford and Essex, as Ordinary thereof, and those of Surrey, Sussex, Kent, Berkshire, and Hampshire, with the islands annexed, as Administrator with ordinary jurisdiction.' Wiseman concluded:

> The great work, then, is complete; what you have long desired and prayed for is granted. Your beloved country has received a place among the fair Churches, which, normally constituted, form the splendid aggregate of Catholic Communion; Catholic England has been restored to its orbit in the ecclesiastical firmament, from which its light had long vanished, and begins now anew its course of regularly adjusted action round the centre of unity, the source of jurisdiction, of light, and of vigour. How wonderfully all this has been brought about, how clearly the hand of God has been shown in every step.

This caused uproar back home – Queen Victoria, perhaps somewhat understandably, asked: 'Am I Queen of England or am I not?' and Lord Winchilsea even urged the declaration of war on an aggressive Pope. The furore led to the sensational conversion of the Duke of Norfolk to Anglicanism and the passing of the Ecclesiastical Titles Act (1851), prohibiting the Catholic assumption of territorial titles.

Wiseman's years at Westminster were marked by numerous disputes with the other bishops and even his own coadjutor, Vicar General and chapter, especially over the ultramontane direction which was seen behind many of his decisions. It seemed to his brother bishops that Wiseman acted as if he was Primate of England, when in reality he was only the Metropolitan Archbishop. The restoration of the Hierarchy meant that many contentious issues had to be faced regarding administration and government. The Cardinal presided over the Provincial Synods of 1852, 1855 and 1859, which defined the status of cathedrals, chapters and missions (there were no parishes until 1918).

The question of seminary education caused the most tension, especially Wiseman's much-publicised disagreement with George Errington

(Titular Archbishop of Trebizond), who served as coadjutor with right of succession from 1855. The so-called 'Battle of Westminster' involved a clash over the appointments of W G Ward (a married lay man and convert) and members of the new Oblates of St Charles (including Herbert Vaughan) to the staff of St Edmund's, Ware. Although the Oblates eventually left the college, Errington was removed as coadjutor and Wiseman began to rely increasingly on converts such as Henry Manning, John Morris and also the young Vaughan, all of whom appeared more sympathetic than the cautious 'old Catholics'. Indeed, one of Wiseman's great qualities was his recognition of the potential of the Oxford converts – without the support of Wiseman, it is unlikely that Manning would be included in a book of English cardinals.

Wiseman was responsible for overseeing the establishment of a newly confident Catholic presence in England. These were years of great growth – in London alone, the number of churches increased from twenty-four in 1826 to one hundred and two in 1863, and the number of priests from one hundred and thirteen to two hundred and fifteen. He promoted Catholic education and energetically supported the Catholic Poor School Committee, which distributed school funding and set up a teachers' training college at Brook Green. Wiseman welcomed many religious communities to London, including the Oratorians, Redemptorists, Passionists, Rosminians and Marists, and encouraged the spread of popular devotions such as Vespers and Benediction or the annual *Quarant'Ore*.

He remained 'ultramontane' in his attitude towards Italian politics, supporting the temporal power of the Pope and opposing Garibaldi's visit to London in 1864. In the words of W Meyer: 'Wiseman saw Rome as the heavenly Jerusalem, "the capital of spiritual Christianity".' A hymn that he penned, at one time extremely popular, celebrated this vision of Rome:

Full in the panting heart of Rome,
Beneath the Apostle's crowning dome,
From pilgrims' lips that kiss the ground,
Breathes in all tongues one only sound:
"God Bless our Pope, the great, the good."

The Cardinal remained a prolific and internationally respected writer – an occupation that he found 'a recreation, and often a solace and a sedative'. Perhaps his most popular work was the novel *Fabiola: or, The Church of the Catacombs* (1855), later translated into ten languages. His *Recollections of the Last Four Popes and of Rome in Their Times* was produced in 1858 and looked back with nostalgia to his youth in the Rome of Pius VII, Leo XII, Pius VIII and Gregory XVI. He even wrote parlour plays for friends, such as his *Strawberries and Cream* and *The Woman of Business*, now kept in the Westminster Diocesan Archives. His concern for scholarship led to the foundation, in 1861, of the Academia of the Catholic Religion, based on a similar society in Rome and aiming to foster the English Catholic intelligentsia. He was a gifted (though rather long-winded) speaker on a variety of subjects; at the time of his death, he was preparing a Royal Institution lecture on William Shakespeare.

Wiseman was a temperamental character, although he could be genial company and clearly enjoyed his food – an Irish servant used to refer to him as 'his immense'. 'Newman's disciples', claimed Lytton Strachey, 'were astounded and grieved to find that [Wiseman] sat down to four courses of fish during Lent. "I am sorry to say", remarked one of them afterwards, "that there is a lobster salad side to the Cardinal." '

By November 1864 it was clear that Cardinal Wiseman was dying. The end finally came on 15 February 1865, but his last illness allowed him to plan his funeral rites to the last detail. 'See that everything is done quite right,' he told Canon Morris, 'do not let a rubric be broken.'

In the event, the funeral ceremonies attracted huge crowds and almost as much attention at that of the Duke of Wellington in 1852. The Cardinal lay in state in the grand drawing room of his York Place residence, vested in pontifical vestments and an alb that had been made by the Orphanage of the Faithful Virgin in Norwood, with the inscription 'Father of Orphans, pray for them.' The Requiem took place on 23 February at the Pro-Cathedral of St Mary Moorfields, which was covered in funereal black, as the *Telegraph* reported:

> The columns of the aisles were swathed from capital to plinth in inky black, relieved by diagonal bands of amber marking the princely rank of the illustrious dead. The high altar was one huge black sarcophagus, but the intensity of its gloom was relieved by its six towering candlesticks of silver. Achievements of the cardinal's arms and sable banners, emblazoned with crosses, were displayed in various parts of the church, from the body of which the daylight was entirely excluded.

After the Mass, at which Manning peached, a long procession of carriages made their way to Kensal Green Cemetery. A brass band played Handel's Funeral March as the entourage moved along the Euston Road and the vast crowds, which, according to *The Tablet*, numbered as many as a million, had much to admire. Carriages contained the English and Welsh Hierarchy, the clergy, various charities and embassies, and even a representative of Queen Marie-Amelie, the widow of Louis Philippe of France. In their midst was the coffin, covered by a magnificent pall and escorted by twelve attendants wearing crape armlets with the Cardinal's monogram. This was preceded by a carriage and four containing the Cardinal's hat, carried on a gold cushion. Wiseman was finally interred at Kensal Green although, forty-two years to the day after his death, his body was translated to the crypt of Westminster Cathedral.

Despite the obvious flaws in Wiseman's personality, English Catholics will always be indebted to him. Wilfrid Ward famously wrote: 'He found them a persecuted sect, he left them a church.' It was indeed appropriate that the text Manning chose for his panegyric of Wiseman was 'Let Nehemias be a long time remembered, who raised up for us our walls that were cast down, and set up the gates and the bars, who rebuilt our houses' (Sir 49: 13).

SANTA PUDENZIANA (VIA URBANA)

This ancient basilica honours a first century Christian, St Pudentiana, who was thought to have been the daughter of Pudens and Claudia (hosts of St Peter) and who, together with her sister, St Praxedes, hid the bodies of the early martyrs. Tradition has it that their mother, Claudia Britannica, was a Briton – hence it was appropriate that this church was the *titulus* of Cardinals Wiseman and Bourne. It was also the *titulus* of Luciano Cardinal Bonaparte (great-nephew of the Emperor Napoleon) and is today the Filipino church in Rome.

The church itself was originally part of a second century complex of baths. These were converted into a church by Pope St Siricius (384-99). The mosaic of Christ and the Apostles that decorates the apse is one of the most ancient in Rome, perhaps dating from the fifth century.

HENRY EDWARD MANNING
1808 – 1892
CARDINAL PRIEST OF SANTI ANDREA E GREGORIO MAGNO (1875)

Henry Edward Manning, 'the Poor Man's Cardinal' and Archbishop of Westminster for some twenty-seven years, was one of the most prominent figures of the nineteenth century. He even had the dubious honour of being included in Lytton Strachey's *Eminent Victorians* (1918) alongside Florence Nightingale, Dr Arnold and General Gordon, although the Cardinal is presented as a bigot, representing all that was wrong with the Victorian Age. In the 'tall gaunt figure, with the face of smiling asceticism, the robes, and the biretta, as it passed in triumph from High Mass at the Oratory to philanthropic gatherings at Exeter Hall, from Strike Committees at the Docks to Mayfair drawing-rooms where fashionable ladies knelt to the Prince of the Church', it seemed to Strachey as if the deference and superstition of the Middle Ages truly lived on.

Manning was born at Copped Hall in Totteridge, Hertfordshire on 15 July 1808. The house has since been demolished but visitors to the local Nature Reserve can still see the ornamental Darlands Lake, the brainchild of the Cardinal's mother and originally part of their extensive grounds. His father, a wealthy sugar merchant, rose to become Governor of the Bank of England, Lord Mayor of London and MP for Evesham. Henry Edward was educated at a private school in Totteridge, before moving on to Harrow. His years at this famous school formed in him a regular prayer life, but there was little indication of Manning's future career. His greatest distinction at Harrow was playing in the cricket eleven, including two matches against Eton at Lords. During one inter-house match in around 1823 two future archbishops (Manning and Trenchard of Dublin) and three bishops (Wordsworth, Oxenden and Terry) all played. Manning, we are told, was also a dandy (or 'buck') and even sported Hessian top-boots with tassells – a contrast to the soiled biretta and faded scarlet cassock of later years.

In 1827 Manning went up to Balliol College, Oxford and became a renowned debater (and eventually President) at the Union. He spoke 'at every meeting, on all subjects, with unfailing fluency and propriety of expression'; indeed, such were his unequivocal opinions on all things that he earned the nickname of 'the Pope'. William Ewart Gladstone even described him as 'one of the three handsomest men at Oxford, not at all religious'. Little did he suspect that over forty years later Manning would attend the Union's jubilee banquet (1873) as Archbishop of Westminster.

Manning took a first class degree in 1830 and spent a brief period working at the Colonial Office. In 1831 the Manning family business collapsed and his father died, events which were to spark off a religious conversion. In 1832 Henry took up a fellowship at Merton College and was ordained an Anglican minister. He served his first curacy at Lavington-with-Graffham in Sussex. Shortly afterwards the rector, Rev John Sargent, died and Manning succeeded him. He married Sargent's beautiful young daughter, Caroline, on 7 November 1833, the ceremony being performed by the bride's brother-in-law, Samuel Wilberforce (future Bishop of Oxford and Winchester). His wife's family would later prove influential in his conversion to Rome – two sisters-in-law, Mrs Henry Wilberforce and Mrs George Ryder, would eventually be received into the Church with their husbands and children. Meanwhile Manning concentrated on his Sussex parish, where he first came face-to-face with widespread poverty. His concern for the underdog would mark the rest of his life.

Within four years Manning's wife was dead of consumption, leaving her husband (now rural Dean of Midhurst) a childless widower who often wrote his sermons beside her tomb. After his appointment as Archdeacon of Chichester in 1841, Manning erected a stained glass window in the cathedral in her memory. Years later, as Manning lay dying, he entrusted a volume of his wife's prayers and thoughts, which he kept under his pillow, to Herbert Vaughan, saying: 'Not a day has passed since her death on which I have not prayed and meditated from that book. All the good I may have done, all the good I may have been, I owe to her.' Despite his austere appearance, Manning clearly had a very human heart.

As Archdeacon of Chichester, Manning embarked on visitations of all the parishes in the diocese and published four volumes of his sermons. Having commenced his ecclesiastical career with evangelical leanings, by this time he had swung round to become a prominent member of the Oxford Movement. It was the acceptance on the part of the Privy Council of the Rev G C Gorham and his unsound doctrines on baptismal regeneration that caused Manning finally to reconsider his position within the Anglican Communion. On 6 April 1851 he was received into the Catholic Church at Farm Street. Manning received minor orders from Cardinal Wiseman the following Sunday and was ordained a priest on 14 June. For the ensuing three years he studied at the *Accademia* in Rome, at the same time as his successor at Westminster, Herbert Vaughan, and another future Cardinal, Edward Howard. He also developed a close relationship with Blessed Pius IX.

After gaining his doctorate in theology, he returned to England and founded, with the encouragement of Cardinal Wiseman, the Oblates of St Charles, a community of secular priests, inspired by St Charles Borromeo and based in Bayswater, then one of the most destitute parts of London. He also became Provost of the Metropolitan Chapter of Westminster and a Domestic Prelate. Understandably, Manning's background and meteoric rise led to resentment in some quarters. Nor were the Oblates universally appreciated, especially by the Chapter and Wiseman's coadjutor, Archbishop Errington. Their presence in the seminary – Herbert Vaughan, an Oblate, becoming its Vice Rector at the age of twenty-three – was a bitter area of contention that was only resolved by their withdrawal. Errington himself also became a casualty and was dismissed as coadjutor with right of succession, therefore making Manning's appointment to Westminster possible.

However, on the death of Cardinal Wiseman in 1865, Manning was not included on the *terna* of three names sent to Rome. Instead, the Chapter selected Errington (now retired to Prior Park), Clifford (the grandson of Cardinal Weld) and Grant (of Southwark) and it was said that the canons would rather have elected Beelzebub than Provost Manning. When Grant and Clifford removed their names in the hope that Errington would be appointed, the Pope was displeased and eventually settled on Manning, who was the favoured candidate of Mgr Talbot (the Pope's trusted English confidant).

Manning was duly consecrated Archbishop of Westminster by Bishop Ullathorne at St Mary Moorfields on 8 June 1865, travelling to Rome to receive the pallium from the Pope on 29 September. It had taken him just fourteen years to make the journey from being an Anglican archdeacon to a Catholic archbishop.

At the First Vatican Council (1869-70) he had became one of the chief proponents of the doctrine of papal infallibility, lobbying for support and even delivering a rousing speech that lasted nearly two hours. This was one of the reasons for Manning's rift with Newman, who advised moderation. In the end, the 'ultramontanes' won convincingly and the dogma was duly defined *ex cathedra* on 18 July 1870, just days before outbreak of war between France and Germany prorogued the Council. On 15 March 1875 Manning was created cardinal with the titular church of Santi Andrea e Gregorio Magno on the Coelian Hill. So strong an impression had he made in Rome that he received a handful of votes at the 1878 conclave.

As archbishop, Manning presided over the Fourth Provincial Council of Westminster (1873) and opened forty churches, including the Pro-Cathedral of Our Lady of Victories in Kensington. He supported the building of Westminster Cathedral as a memorial to Wiseman but his priority was education – 'Could I leave twenty thousand children without education and drain my friends and my flock to pile up stones and bricks?' Believing that: 'The care of children is the first duty after, and even with, the salvation of our own soul,' Manning set up the Westminster Diocesan Education Fund in 1866. He was particularly concerned with the 'rescue' of Catholic children from workhouses and the homes of Dr Barnardo (who was antagonistic to the idea of Catholic education for children), and the opening of Poor Law Schools and orphanages. Manning also supported the emigration of poor children to Canada, where they faced a brighter future, and supported the Canadian Catholic Emigration Society, founded by one of his secretaries, Fr Thomas Seddon.

Manning was convinced that Oxford and Cambridge were unsuitable places of study for Catholics and a formal prohibition was obtained from Rome. This again brought him into conflict with Newman, who hoped to establish an Oratory in Oxford that could look after the needs of Catholic undergraduates. The Cardinal eventually opened a Catholic University College in Kensington in 1875, though financial difficulties led to its closure in 1882. He also established a diocesan seminary in Hammersmith, dedicated to St Thomas.

If Manning was ecclesiologically an ultramontane, he was seen as a political liberal. In 1884 he served on a Royal Commission that investigated the condition of working-class housing. He endorsed trade unionism, believed that every citizen had a right to work and became a popular hero after mediating in the London Dock Strike of 1889 – in the May Day parades of 1890, his image appeared on banners alongside Karl Marx. His active involvement with the poor and marginalized even led to accusations that the Cardinal was a rampant socialist; Manning preferred to see himself as a 'Mosaic Radical', following the likes of Moses and Jesus – 'People call it socialism,' he once said, 'I call it Christianity.' He showed a great concern for the Irish community, although he condemned their political radicalism – 'Show me an Irishman who has lost the Faith,' he said in his Birmingham Town Hall speech of 1867, 'and I will show you a Fenian.' However, this identification of the Church with the poor and the Irish horrified some of the older Catholic families.

Further afield he campaigned against the African slave trade and the persecution of the Jews in Russia. Earlier, he had arranged for nuns to care for the Catholic wounded in the Crimea and became a close friend of Florence Nightingale. Indeed, such was his concern for social issues that he was one of the cardinals who called upon Leo XIII to give a clear lead on such matters. The result was the groundbreaking Encyclical, *Rerum Novarum* (1891).

Manning's personality was a great contrast to that of Wiseman. He was a disciple of the temperance movement and in 1867 promoted a 'Truce of St Patrick', gaining from Rome an indulgence for all those who abstained from drink on the eve and feast of the saint. From 1872 he keenly supported the Total Abstinence League of the Cross. It is indeed ironic that Manning's face appears on the sign for *The Cardinal* pub behind Westminster Cathedral. He was a disciplinarian and therefore not always popular with his clergy – one canon of Westminster remarked that the death of Mrs Manning was the greatest misfortune that had ever befallen the Catholic Church in England. Yet, despite his austerity, Manning was a charismatic figure. Looking back to his first audience with the Cardinal, Francis MacNutt – an American Papal Chamberlain – wrote that,

> . . . while his photographs, liberally displayed in shop windows, had made his features familiar to me, I was none the less impressed by the ascetic cast of his countenance, a something no camera ever caught, and by his beautifully modulated voice. It seemed to me that I had never heard our language so faultlessly spoken. The shabbiness of his dress was conspicuous. The several cardinals I had known in Rome were sufficiently gorgeous, and I took this for granted. Here, I beheld the most illustrious of them all, with the red silk of his sleeves actually frayed, and a biretta, faded into a dull pink tone, set carelessly on his head.

Manning died of pneumonia on 14 January 1892, leading the Pope to comment: 'A great light of the Church has gone out.' Thousands lined the streets along the route from the Oratory – which until the opening of the cathedral was used for many important occasions – to Kensal Green Cemetery on 21 January. His remains were exhumed on 15 February 1907 and re-interred in the crypt chapel of St Edmund under the high altar of Westminster Cathedral. As Strachey put it:

> He who descends into the crypt of that cathedral which Manning never lived to see, will observe, in the quiet niche with the sepulchral monument, that the dust lies thick on the strange, the incongruous, the almost impossible object which, with its elaborations of dependent tassels, hangs down from the dim vault like some forlorn and forgotten trophy – the Hat.

SANTI ANDREA E GREGORIO MAGNO AL CELIO
(PIAZZA SAN GREGORIO)

Situated on the Coelian Hill and normally referred to as 'San Gregorio', this church is intimately linked to the conversion of England. Originally the home of St Gregory the Great, he converted it into a monastery over which he was abbot. As Pope he sent a group from the monastery to Kent in 597. A list of these missionaries is preserved near the entrance to the church, including Ss Augustine, Laurence, Mellitus, Paulinus, Justus and Honorius. The church, which is now run by the Camaldolese Order, only became a *titulus* in 1839, thanks to Gregory XVI. It was therefore available to serve as the title of three Archbishops of Westminster – Cardinals Manning, Vaughan and Griffin.

EDWARD HENRY HOWARD
1829 – 1892
CARDINAL PRIEST OF SANTI GIOVANNI E PAOLO (1877)
CARDINAL BISHOP OF FRASCATI (1884)

On 18 November 1852 dense crowds gathered on the streets of London to bid farewell to the Duke of Wellington, victor of Waterloo (1815) and Prime Minister in the late 1820s. The leader of the squadron of Life Guards in the funeral procession that day, Colonel Edward Henry Howard, was also bidding a farewell – to army life, as he prepared to train for the priesthood.

Born in Nottingham on 13 February 1829 to Edward Gyles Howard and Frances Anne Henage, the future cardinal was educated at Oscott during the rectorship of Nicholas Wiseman. It is said that the young Edward used to joke that one day he would be a Prince of the Church. However, any embryonic priestly vocation was initially put to one side when, after several years studying in Edinburgh, he joined the 2nd Life Guards. Edward became a prominent figure on the social scene – he was a keen dancer and once famously performed the feat of emptying the 'Standard of Hesleyside', a goblet that held a whole bottle of claret. However, a period of illness in 1851 led him to discern his vocation more seriously and, shortly after Wellington's funeral, he resigned his Army Commission and sent his uniforms and clothes to Nazareth House, Hammersmith, where the gold lace was used for making vestments.

Howard went to the Academy of Noble Ecclesiastics on the Piazza Minerva in Rome, the so-called 'purple' seminary since it was a traditional nursery of prelates. Unlike other seminaries of the time, students lived in elegantly furnished rooms and were waited on by servants. After two years here, where he regularly served the early morning Mass of his fellow student, Henry Edward Manning, he was ordained at the English College by Cardinal Wiseman at four in the morning of 8 December 1854, the day on which

Blessed Pius IX defined the dogma of the Immaculate Conception.

Like Wiseman, Howard was a gifted linguist and, encouraged by the desire to work in the Orient, he became fluent in Arabic, Coptic, Hindustani and Russian. He never did become a missionary but devoted his life to Propaganda Fide, specialising in the Oriental Rites. He went to India to arrange the 1857 Concordat that partially relieved the 'Indo-Portuguese Schism', a dispute over territorial jurisdiction.

Howard was consecrated as Titular Archbishop of Neo-Caesarea at St Peter's in 1872 and, shortly afterwards, became Coadjutor Bishop of Frascati. In 1877 he was created a Cardinal Priest, with the title of Santi Giovanni e Paolo.

Despite his Oriental expertise, Howard showed a keen interest in the English-speaking Church. In 1878 he became Cardinal Protector of the English College, to which he later bequeathed his extensive library. He was also involved in the negotiations surrounding the restoration of the Scottish Hierarchy and the foundation of the Canadian College, Rome, and the Catholic University in Washington.

In 1881 Leo XIII appointed him Archpriest of St Peter's and in 1884 Cardinal Bishop of Frascati, positions both previously held by the Cardinal Duke of York. 'Cardinale Ovardi', as the Italians pronounced his name, became a familiarly eccentric figure around Rome, with his military posture and his passion for all things equestrian. According to Abbot Hunter-Blair:

> His English Eminence went about quite unconcernedly, often on foot; and the Romans would gaze after his tall and stalwart figure with amazed admiration as he swung homewards through the narrow streets, after visiting, perhaps, the Station of the day, or the *Quarant' Ore* – a most conspicuous and commanding figure with his red-trimmed overcoat, silver-buckled shoes, and gold-and-scarlet-tasselled hat, and his liveried footman following him, bearing the cardinalitial prayer-books and other implements of devotion.

He took a great interest in the paraphernalia connected to his position – jewels belonging to his mother were placed in his mitre and one visitor to Rome declared him to be 'as vain as a peacock'. Despite his elegant appearance and the magnificence of his home, the Villa Negroni, Howard exhibited a genuine pastoral concern for the poor. According to his obituary in *The Tablet*, 'Whenever he could hear of a house in which a child lay dying he would start off with the Holy Oils, and the Romans were accustomed to seeing the tall English prelate hurrying along the streets and climbing up the rickety stairs six or seven storeys high to find some sick child to be confirmed.'

Serious illness forced him to return to England in April 1888 and he took up residence at Brighton, finally settling down in a villa at nearby Hatch Beauchamp. Here he was tended by his devoted Italian servant, Gaetano della Donne, and the rector of St Joseph's, Brighton, Fr du Plerny, who acted as his chaplain. He died on 16 September 1892. When news reached the Vatican, the bells of St Peter's tolled. Since this honour was reserved only to the Archpriest of the Basilica and the Pope, many Romans assumed that the eighty-two year old Pope Leo had himself died. The remains of the second Howard cardinal were placed in a coffin that was seven feet six inches long and laid to rest in the Fitzalan chapel in Arundel. Archbishop Vaughan of Westminster celebrated the Requiem Mass and the Life Guards sent a wreath of lilies, jasmine and chrysanthemums.

SANTI GIOVANNI E PAOLO (PIAZZA SANTI GIOVANNI E PAOLO)

Built over the remains of Ss John and Paul, martyrs during the reign of Julian the Apostate, this fourth century foundation has connections with several cardinals of England. The portico was erected by the English Pope, Adrian IV (Breakspear). Under Philip Cardinal Howard it was briefly a house of English Dominicans. Today it is a house of the Passionist Order and contains the shrine of St Paul of the Cross, who prayed so fervently for the conversion of England. Blessed Dominic Barberi, the priest who received John Henry Newman into the Catholic Church, lived here in the nineteenth century. It was the titular church of Edward Cardinal Howard (1877-84) and also of Eugenio Pacelli (later Pius XII).

Whilst the exterior of the church promises antiquity, the interior, like so many in Rome, is the result of Baroque workmanship.

VEN. JOHN HENRY NEWMAN
CONG. ORAT.
1801 – 1890
CARDINAL DEACON OF SAN GIORGIO IN VELABRO (1879)

Perhaps England's most famous and learned cardinal, John Henry Newman, was born at 80 Old Broad Street in the City of London on 21 February 1801. Shortly afterwards, on 9 April, he was baptised in the Wren church of St Benet Fink on Threadneedle Street, which was subsequently demolished. He was the eldest of the six children of John Newman, a London banker, and Jemima Fourdrinier, of old Huguenot stock, whose sister later became the grandmother of the popular comic writer P G Wodehouse.

The family experienced growing prosperity, moving to what is now Southampton Place in Bloomsbury (1802) and between 1804 and 1807 owning a country residence (Grey Court House) at Ham in Surrey. Newman loved this house and later wrote that 'it has ever been in my dreams' – it was here that he learned billiards and watched the celebrations following the battle of Trafalgar.

Newman was sent to Dr George Nicholas' renowned school at Ealing in 1808, where he met his first Catholic cleric, an émigré priest. More importantly, the school at Ealing provided the context for his first conversion, which left him a committed Calvinist and a sense that he was called to the celibate life. Rather like Manning's evangelical conversion, Newman's was partly occasioned by the failure of his father's bank in March 1816.

At the end of that eventful year of 1816 Newman was matriculated at Trinity College, Oxford (having failed to get a place at Exeter College) and took up residence the following June. The University was, in the words of Sheridan Gilley, 'somewhere between a semi-secular monastery and a gentleman's dining-club', and the young student, though overawed by the beauty of the dreaming spires, was shocked by the behaviour of many of

Cardinal Nicholas Wiseman

Yours faithfully, &c.

N. Wiseman

FACING PAGE: *An engraving of Cardinal Wiseman.*

ABOVE: *Wiseman aged 48, from an oil painting at Oscott.*

The funeral of Cardinal Wiseman at St Mary Moorfields.

A sketch of Cardinal Manning in old age.

ABOVE: *Manning as Archbishop of Westminster: a contemporary coloured print.*

FACING PAGE: *An 1871* Vanity Fair *cartoon of Manning, with the caption, 'The next Pope'.*

THIS PAGE AND FACING PAGE: *Cardinal Edward Howard and his coat of arms.*

a Sketch from St Mary's

COR AD COR LOQUITUR

THIS PAGE CLOCKWISE FROM TOP LEFT: *Newman as a cardinal; in younger days as vicar of St Mary the Virgin, Oxford; Newman's arms and motto; in Oratorian habit.*

FACING PAGE CLOCKWISE FROM TOP LEFT: *Newman's study at the Birmingham Oratory; the desk in the Birmingham Oratory library at which Newman wrote (standing up) his* Apologia pro vita sua; *Newman's red hat - the galero.*

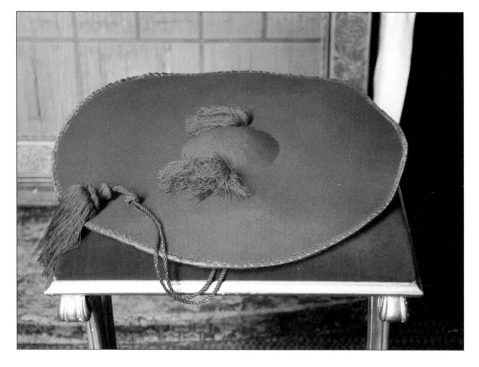

ABOVE: *Cardinal Herbert Vaughan*

FACING PAGE CLOCKWISE FROM TOP: *Vaughan as Bishop of Salford; Vaughan was the only English Ordinary to be Cardinal Protector of the* Venerabile, *and his coat of arms still hangs in the college refectory; Vaughan's red hat above his tomb in Westminster Cathedral.*

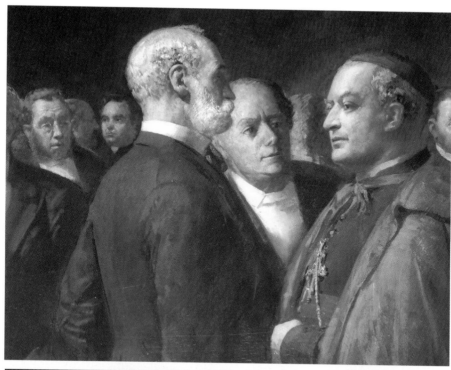

ABOVE: *Cardinal Raphael Merry del Val, from a picture to mark the 1917 Pio-Benedictine Codification of Canon Law.*

FACING PAGE: *Cardinal Merry del Val (left) at the episcopal consecration of Mgr Arthur Hinsley (centre) in the chapel of the English College, Rome on 30 November 1926.*

Three English cardinals – actual or prospective – are pictured together in the library of the English College after Hinsley's episcopal consecration. Hinsley himself is second from left, Cardinal Francis Gasquet is third from left, and Cardinal Merry del Val (the principle consecrator) is in the centre.

his fellow students – 'If anyone should ask me what qualifications were necessary for Trinity College, I should say there was one – drink, drink, drink.' Despite winning a scholarship in April 1818, a breakdown in health meant a poor performance in Finals and he took what was the equivalent of a pass degree in mathematics and a third in classics.

On 1 November 1821 his father was declared bankrupt and shortly afterwards sold their Bloomsbury house. Domestic decline coincided with success for Newman as he unexpectedly won a prestigious fellowship at Oriel. Not only did this mark Newman's academic coming-of-age but the Oriel Senior Common Room boasted the likes of Richard Hurrell Froude, Edward Hawkins, William James, John Keble, Edward Pusey and Blanco White (an apostate Catholic priest), all key figures in Newman's intellectual and spiritual development. On Whit Sunday 1825 Newman was ordained an Anglican priest, by which time he had began pastoral ministry at the rundown church of St Clement's and was acting as Vice Principal of St Alban's Hall (later purchased by Merton). In 1828 he was appointed Vicar of the University Church of St Mary's and his famous sermons were later published in the six volume *Parochial Sermons*. As Matthew Arnold reminisced: 'Who can forget the charm of that spiritual apparition, gliding through the dim afternoon light of St Mary's, rising into the pulpit, and then breaking the silence with a spiritual music, subtle, sweet, mournful?'

Newman had his first full encounter with Catholicism when he travelled to the Continent with Froude in December 1832. Visiting the Eternal City the following Spring, they met the Rector of the English College, Dr Wiseman, but still viewed Rome with suspicion – Newman was shocked by the custom of kissing the Pope's foot and referred to the clergy as 'wretched Tridentines'. However, like many others of his day, he was becoming increasingly alarmed by the reforming movements within the Anglican Communion. The plan to suppress ten Irish bishoprics evoked John Keble, then Professor of Poetry, to preach a sermon *On National Apostasy* on 14 July 1833. This came to be seen, at least by Newman, as the beginning of the 'Oxford Movement', which aimed to restore High Church principles, especially the idea of the Anglican Communion being of divine institution and acting as a *via media* between the Roman Catholic Church and Protestantism. Between 1833 and 1841 Newman, Keble and Pusey among others wrote the *Tracts for the Times*. As a leading Tractarian, Newman was never far from controversy and it was the furore aroused by his Tract No. 90, which interpreted the Thirty-Nine Articles in keeping with the Council of Trent, which brought the series to a close and led to his withdrawal from public life and his eventual resignation from St Mary's.

Newman took refuge at Littlemore (a chapelry attached to St Mary's) in 1842. Joined by disciples such as John Dalgairns, William Lockhart, Richard Stanton and Ambrose St John, he lived an almost monastic life and retreated within himself to study, write works such as *An Essay on the Development of Christian Doctrine* and seek the truth. The road gradually led to Rome – he preached his last Anglican sermon, *The Parting of Friends*, at Littlemore on 25 September 1843 and was finally received into the Catholic Church on 9 October 1845 at the hands of Blessed Dominic Barberi, an Italian Passionist. Soon afterwards, Newman went to the Propaganda College in Rome to study for the priesthood. There he became increasingly attracted by the Congregation of the Oratory of St Philip Neri, partly because 'it seemed more adapted than any other for Oxford and Cambridge men'. He undertook his Oratorian novitiate at S Croce and on 27 November 1847 received the papal brief for the foundation of the English Oratory. Returning home, he lived briefly at Maryvale and St Wilfrid's, Cotton, before moving to a former gin distillery on Alcester Street, Birmingham (1849) and finally planting his Oratory at Edgbaston (1852).

Having just founded the English Oratory, Newman was appointed in November 1851 as the first Rector of a new Catholic University in Ireland (the present University College Dublin). In Dublin his discourses on higher education were later published as *The Idea of a University*. Several other projects that he took up, including a magazine for educated Catholics (*Catholic University Gazette*), an Oratory and Catholic College at Oxford, and a new translation of the Bible, met with rejection or failure.

His writings are unrivalled in their quality and scope from the logical treatise *A Grammar of Assent* to the poetry of *The Dream of Gerontius*, later set to music by Elgar. Perhaps it has only been towards the end of the last century that the vision of his writings has been more fully appreciated.

With the amount of interest that his life has attracted, it is little surprise that the 'behind the scenes' negotiations which won the red hat for Newman have been carefully recorded. This presents a fascinating sidelight into the process by which a person might be considered worthy to become a member of the Sacred College – at least in the nineteenth century – and how easily the possibility of such an honour might evaporate.

In July 1878 the Duke of Norfolk (whose cousin, Edward Henry

Howard, had been created a curial cardinal in 1877), the Marquis of Ripon and Lord Petre asked Manning to request the red hat for Newman from the recently elected Pope Leo XIII. Manning entrusted a letter to Cardinal Howard, who was then in London, to be carried to the Cardinal Secretary of State. Manning's draft of the letter was fulsome, praising

> ...the singular and unequalled services rendered by Dr Newman to the Catholic faith ... His submission to the Church has alone done more to awaken the mind of Englishmen to the Catholic religion....The veneration for his powers, his learning, and his life of singular piety and integrity is almost as deeply felt by the non Catholic population of this country as by the members of the Catholic Church....There remains therefore only one mark of confidence of the Holy See to so distinguished a priest. And no greater gratification to the Catholics of England could be given than by the elevation of Dr Newman into the Sacred College.

Months passed without the letter reaching its destination, Cardinal Howard remaining in England for longer than was expected. By early December 1878 the Duke himself was kneeling at the feet of Pope Leo making his request in person. The Duke reported that the Pope 'seemed willing to consider' the request. It would seem from later remarks, however, that the Pope needed little encouragement in this enterprise: 'My Cardinal, it was not easy, it was not easy. They said he was too liberal, but I had determined to honour the Church in honouring Newman. I always had a cult for him. I am proud that I was able to honour such a man.' This last remark of the Pope illuminates his response to a close friend, the Commendatore de Rossi, shortly after being elected Bishop of Rome. The Commendatore had asked, 'What, Holy Father, will be your policy as Pope?', to which the Pope replied: 'Wait till you see my first cardinal; that will show you what will be typical of my reign.'

It would seem that significant voices were raised in Rome against the idea of elevating Newman to the Sacred College. At home in England, Newman's cause would have been more efficiently served if Manning was not the chief protagonist. Despite the letter he dispatched with Howard, it is certain that he personally held a different opinion of the achievements of John Henry Newman than many of his co-religionists. J E C Bailey recounted a conversation he once had with Manning:

> "From an observation you made," [Manning] said, "I gather that you are under the impression that Doctor Newman is a good Catholic." I replied that such was my vague belief. He retorted: "Either you are ignorant of the Catholic

doctrine, or of the works of Doctor Newman" – he always said "Doctor Newman" in Oxford fashion, and never gave him the title of Cardinal. After asking me which of Newman's books I had read, he proceeded to tick off on his tapering fingers, in his usual way, ten distinct heresies to be found in the most widely-read works of Dr Newman. This seemed to me, at the time, on a par with Voltaire's discovery of a series of heresies in the Lord's Prayer.

Pope Leo, however, was not to be deterred. At the beginning of 1879 Lorenzo Cardinal Nina, the Secretary of State, wrote to Manning requesting that he would, with the utmost discretion, discover whether Newman would actually accept the honour of being created a cardinal if he were to be offered it. Manning forwarded the letter to Ullathorne who asked Newman to come to him. Since both were unwell at the time Ullathorne entrusted the news to Fr Thomas Pope, a priest of the Oratory. Thus on 31 January, 1879, Newman was acquainted with the Holy Father's desire to bestow upon him the red hat.

On 3 February, Newman met Ullathorne at Oscott to discuss his foreboding about accepting the red hat. The principal concern for Newman was that he would be obliged to reside in Rome, as was usually expected of cardinals who were not diocesan bishops. Newman cited both his age and the responsibility that he had for the novices of the Oratory as reasons for declining the Pope's favour – he did not feel that he could accept and seek seemingly to bargain with the Pope about where he would live afterwards.

Ullathorne had no doubt that Newman should accept the Pope's offer. Thus it was agreed that Newman would write to the Secretary of State expressing his profound gratitude for the honour that Pope Leo wished to bestow on him yet stating his desire to complete his life in the company of his Oratorian community. Bishop Ullathorne undertook to write a covering letter that would leave the Holy See in no doubt as to Newman's acceptance of the dignity but with the clear request that this would not mean his having to leave England. Taken together, the meaning of the two letters was clear.

But Manning sent only Newman's letter to Rome. Travelling to Rome he wrote to the Duke of Norfolk from Paris that 'Dr Newman declined the offer for many reasons of age, health, habits, etc, etc, and wrote a letter fully detailing his reasons to the Bishop: to be sent to Rome: which has been done.' Ullathorne was informed of Manning's letter and on 11 February he wrote to Cardinal Nina himself with an accurate account of the meaning of Newman's letter. On 18 February 1879 *The Times* published the news that Newman had declined the sacred purple and in the following days Herbert Vaughan had directed that a notice to the same effect should be published in *The Tablet*.

An exasperated Newman wrote to the Duke of Norfolk on 20 February telling him that he had not refused to be made a cardinal:

> Of course it implies that an offer has been made to me, and that I have sent my answer to it. Now I have ever understood that it is a point of propriety and honour to consider such communications *sacred*. The statement therefore cannot come from me. Nor could it come from Rome. It could only come from someone who not only read my letter, but, instead of leaving the Pope to interpret it, took upon himself to put an interpretation upon it, and published that interpretation to the world . . . if so high an honour was offered me, I should not answer it by a blunt refusal.

Clearly, Newman believed Manning to have been the instigator of the news of Newman's refusal of the red hat.

Upon receiving this news, the Duke of Norfolk wrote to Manning in Rome, enclosing a copy of Newman's letter and strongly suggested to him that he should tell the Pope that Newman was not refusing the Pope's offer of the red hat. Manning immediately arranged to see the Pope and, having done so, he wrote to the Duke to assure him: 'The Holy Father gave me leave to write and say that Dr Newman need not change his way of life nor leave the Oratory.' On 1 March all doubt was dispersed when Ullathorne brought Newman the news that the Pope understood precisely the import of Newman's letter and that there were no further obstacles to his being raised to the Sacred College. 'The cloud is lifted from me forever,' declared Newman. On 15 March in a letter from Cardinal Nina, Newman received the formal offer of the red hat. Upon the publication of the news Newman was deluged with letters of congratulation.

Manning wrote to both Newman and the Duke professing his miscomprehension of Newman's real intent until he had received the Duke's letter in Rome. Newman also wrote to the Duke concerning the faltering series of events which, happily, eventually resulted in comprehension on the part of the Pope regarding Newman's reaction to the offer of the red hat. Newman wrote of the affair, 'I wish it all swept out of every one's mind and my own.'

Newman set off for Rome on 16 April, arriving in the Eternal City on 24 April, being warmly received by Pope Leo XIII three days later. On the morning of Monday 12 May the secret consistory was held in which Pope Leo named Newman a cardinal. Hours later, just after noon, at Cardinal Edward Howard's apartments in the Palazzo della Pigna, a messenger presented to Newman the *biglietto* from the Cardinal Secretary of State which officially announced Newman's elevation. Having opened the document himself, Newman handed it to Bishop Clifford of Clifton who read to the large assembly of nobles and ecclesiastics that crowded Howard's appartment. The messenger then proceeded to announce that the Holy Father would receive Newman at ten the next morning in order to confer the red biretta upon him. The response of a new cardinal to such news has frequently been in centuries past a short speech of some significance. Such a speech from one like John Henry Cardinal Newman was bound to have been of the highest order and has been known ever since as the '*Biglietto* Speech'. Newman began with a few words of thanks in Italian before proceeding in English:

Vi ringrazio, Monsignore, per la participazione che m'avete fatto dell' alto onore che il Santo Padre si è degnato conferire sulla mia umile persona –

And, if I ask your permission to continue my address to you, not in your musical language, but in my own dear mother tongue, it is because in the latter I can better express my feelings on this most gracious announcement which you have brought to me than if I attempted what is above me.

First of all then, I am led to speak of the wonder and profound gratitude which came upon me, and which is upon me still, at the condescension and love towards me of the Holy Father in singling me out for so immense an honour. It was a great surprise. Such an elevation had never come into my thoughts, and seemed to be out of keeping with all my antecedents. I had passed through many trials, but they were over; and now the end of all things had almost come to me, and I was at peace. And was it possible that after all I had lived through so many years for this?

Nor is it easy to see how I could have borne so great a shock, had not the Holy Father resolved on a second act of condescension towards me, which tempered it, and was to all who heard of it a touching evidence of his kindly and generous nature. He felt for me, and he told me the reasons why he raised me to this high position. Besides other words of encouragement, he said his act was a recognition of my zeal and good service for so many years in the Catholic cause; moreover, he judged it would give pleasure to English Catholics, and even to Protestant England, if I received some mark of his favour. After such gracious words from his Holiness, I should have been insensible and heartless if I had had scruples any longer.

This is what he had the kindness to say to me, and what could I want more? In a long course of years I have made many mistakes. I have nothing of that high perfection which belongs to the writings of saints, viz., that error cannot be found in them; but what I trust that I may claim all through what I have written, is this, — an honest intention, an absence of private ends, a temper of obedience, a willingness to be corrected, a dread of error, a desire to serve Holy Church, and, through divine mercy, a fair measure of success. And, I rejoice to say, to one great mischief I have from the first opposed myself. For thirty, forty, fifty years I have resisted to the best of my powers the spirit of liberalism in religion. Never did Holy Church need champions against it more sorely than now, when, alas! it is an error overspreading, as a snare, the whole earth; and on this great occasion, when it is natural for one who is in my place to look out upon the world, and upon Holy Church as in it, and upon her future, it will not, I hope, be considered out of place, if I renew the protest against it which I have made so often.

Liberalism in religion is the doctrine that there is no positive truth in religion, but that one creed is as good as another, and this is the teaching which is gaining substance and force daily. It is inconsistent with any recognition of any religion, as *true*. It teaches that all are to be tolerated, for all are matters of opinion. Revealed religion is not a truth, but a sentiment and a taste; not an objective fact, not miraculous; and it is the right of each individual to make it say just what strikes his fancy. Devotion is not necessarily founded on faith. Men may go to Protestant churches and to Catholic, may get good from both and belong to neither. They may fraternise together in spiritual thoughts and feelings, without having any views at all of doctrine in common, or seeing the need of them. Since, then, religion is so personal a peculiarity and so private a possession, we must of necessity ignore it in the intercourse of man with man. If a man puts on a new religion every morning, what is that to you? It is as impertinent to think about a man's religion as about his sources of income or his management of his family. Religion is in no sense the bond of society.

Hitherto the civil power has been Christian. Even in countries separated from the Church, as in my own, the dictum was in force, when I was young, that: "Christianity was the law of the land." Now, everywhere that goodly framework of society, which is the creation of Christianity, is throwing off Christianity. The dictum to which I have referred, with a hundred others which followed upon it, is gone, or is going everywhere; and, by the end of the century, unless the Almighty interferes, it will be forgotten. Hitherto, it has been considered that religion alone, with its supernatural sanctions, was strong enough to secure submission of the masses of our population to law and order; now the philosophers and politicians are bent on satisfying this problem without the aid of Christianity. Instead of the Church's authority and teaching, they would substitute first of all a universal and a thoroughly secular education, calculated to bring home to every individual that to be orderly, industrious, and sober, is his personal interest. Then, for great working principles to take the place of religion, for the use of the masses thus carefully educated, it provides – the broad fundamental ethical truths, of justice, benevolence, veracity, and the like; proved experience; and those natural laws which exist and act spontaneously in society, and in social matters, whether physical or psychological; for instance, in government, trade, finance, sanitary experiments, and the intercourse of nations. As to religion, it is a private luxury, which a man may have if he will; but which of course he must pay for, and which he must not obtrude upon others, or indulge in to their annoyance.

The general character of this great *apostasia* is one and the same everywhere; but in detail, and in character, it varies in different countries. For myself, I would rather speak of it in my own country, which I know. There, I think it threatens to have a formidable success; though it is not easy to see what will be its ultimate issue. At first sight it might be thought that Englishmen are too religious for a movement which, on the continent, seems to be founded on infidelity; but the misfortune with us is, that, though it ends in infidelity as in other places, it does not necessarily arise out of infidelity. It must be recollected that the religious sects, which sprang up in England three centuries ago, and which are so powerful now, have ever been fiercely opposed to the union of Church and State, and would advocate the un-Christianising of the monarchy and all that belongs to it, under the notion that such a catastrophe would make Christianity much more pure and much more powerful. Next the liberal principle is forced on us from the necessity of the case. Consider what follows from the very fact of these many sects. They constitute the religion, it is supposed, of half the population; and, recollect, our mode of government is popular. Every dozen men taken at random whom you meet in the streets has a share in political power, – when you inquire into their forms of belief, perhaps they represent one or other of as many as seven religions; how can they possibly act together in municipal or in national matters, if each insists on the recognition of his own religious denomination? All action would be at a deadlock unless the subject of religion was ignored. We cannot help ourselves. And, thirdly, it must be borne in mind, that there is much in the liberalistic theory which is good and true; for example, not to say more, the precepts of justice, truthfulness, sobriety, self-command, benevolence, which, as I have already noted, are among its avowed principles, and the natural laws of society. It is not till we find that this array of principles is intended to supersede, to block out, religion, that we pronounce it to be evil. There never was a device of the Enemy so cleverly framed and with such promise of success. And already it has answered to the expectations which have been formed of it. It is sweeping into its own ranks great numbers of able, earnest, virtuous men, elderly men of approved antecedents, young men with a career before them.

Such is the state of things in England, and it is well that it should be realised by all of us; but it must not be supposed for a moment that I am afraid of it. I lament it deeply, because I foresee that it may be the ruin of many souls; but I have no fear at all that it really can do aught of serious harm to the Word of God, to Holy Church, to our Almighty King, the Lion of the Tribe of Judah, faithful and true, or to his Vicar on Earth. Christianity has been too often in what seemed deadly peril, that we should fear for it any new trial now. So far is certain; on the other hand, what is uncertain, and in these great contests commonly is uncertain, and what is commonly a great surprise, when it is witnessed, is the particular mode by which, in the event, Providence rescues and saves his elect inheritance. Sometimes our enemy is turned into a friend; sometimes he is despoiled of that special virulence of evil which was so threatening; sometimes he falls to pieces of himself; sometimes he does just so much as is beneficial, and then is removed. Commonly the Church has nothing more to do than to go on in her own proper duties, in confidence and peace; to stand still and to see the salvation of God.

Mansueti hereditabunt terram,
Et delectabuntur in multitudine pacis.

The following morning at the Vatican, Newman received his red biretta from the hands of Pope Leo XIII. The next day, Wednesday, he was received at the English College to be presented with a complete set of vestments and other necessary cardinalatial accoutrements given by the English-speaking community in Rome. Lady Herbert Lea made a short address on behalf of those present:

My Lord Cardinal,

We, your devoted English, Scotch, Irish, and American children at present residing in Rome, earnestly wishing to testify our deep and affectionate veneration for your Eminence's person and character, together with our hearty joy at your elevation to the sacred purple, venture to lay this humble offering at your feet. We feel that in making you a cardinal the Holy Father has not only given public testimony of his appreciation of your great merits and of the value of your admirable writings in defence of God and his Church, but has also conferred the greatest possible honour on all English-speaking Catholics, who have long looked up to you as their spiritual father and their guide in the paths of holiness. We hope your Eminence will excuse the shortness and simplicity of this address, which is but the expression of the feeling contained in your Eminence's motto, "Heart speaking to Heart", for your Eminence has long won the first place in the hearts of all. That God may greatly prolong the years which have been so devoted to his service in the cause of truth is the earnest prayer of your Eminence's faithful and loving children.

Newman replied to this greeting with suitably gracious words:

My dear friends,

Your affectionate address, introductory to so beautiful a present, I accept as one of those strange favours of divine providence which are granted to few. Most men if they do any good die without knowing it; but I call it strange that I should be kept to my present age – an age beyond the age of most men – as if in order that, in this great city, where I am personally almost unknown, I might find kind friends to meet me with an affectionate welcome and to claim me as their spiritual benefactor. The tender condescension to me of the Holy Father has elicited in my behalf, in sympathy with him, a loving acclamation from his faithful children. My dear friends, your present, which while God gives me strength I shall avail myself of in my daily Mass, will be a continual memento in his sight both of your persons and your several intentions. When my strength fails me for that great action, then in turn I know well that I may rely on your taking up the duty and privilege of intercession, and praying for me that, with the aid of the Blessed Virgin and all saints, I may persevere in faith, hope, and charity, and in all that grace which is the life of the soul till the end comes.

On Thursday 15 May Cardinal Newman received the red hat from Pope Leo XIII in a public consistory along with nine other members of the Sacred College of Cardinals, including the Pope's brother. It is thought that Pope Leo desired to make Newman the Cardinal Priest of San Nicolò in Carcere, but both the last vacancy amongst the cardinal presbyters and San Nicolò were claimed by others. Newman was thus offered Sant'Adriano in Foro Romano but thanks to the offices of the British in Rome, the ancient church of San Giorgio in Velabro was finally granted to the Cardinal.

For the rest of the year Newman found himself responding to the delight of his friends and the great and the good of Britain at the award of the red hat. Hundreds of letters, dinners and receptions were to occupy much of his time but there were also formal niceties to be observed with regards his new position. In the words of Sheridan Gilley:

> On 25 November 1879, he sent out according to the forms prescribed from Rome, letters in Italian to his brethren in the Sacred College and to his new cousins, the Catholic Kings and Queens and the Emperor and Empress of Brazil. He had enjoyed a kind of apotheosis into an international Amanach de Gotha, and the sort of adulation more usually reserved for obituaries.

The creation of Newman as cardinal meant that there were three English cardinals in the Sacred College, even if only for a short time – a reflection of the political importance of Great Britain and the success of the 'Second Spring'. Dispensed from having to spend his remaining years in Rome, Newman lived at his beloved Oratory in Birmingham, where he was still known as 'the Father' and wore his Oratorian habit with a red skullcap and biretta. As he approached his ninetieth birthday, Newman grew increasingly frail, and said his last Mass on Christmas Day 1889. He finally died of pneumonia on the evening of 11 August 1890. After a Requiem in the church of the Birmingham Oratory he was buried at Rednal, in the same grave as his close friend, Ambrose St John. Newman chose the inscription for his gravestone himself – *Ex umbris et imaginibus in veritatem*, 'From the shadows and reflections, into the truth.'

In 1958 the cause for Newman's beatification was opened but the process has seemed to many to be a very long one. On 22 January 1991 John Paul II signed the document that proclaimed his heroic virtue and declared him 'Venerable'. Yet, as Newman himself once wrote, 'Great saints . . . like the everlasting mountains, grow as we recede from them.' Indeed, 'Time is necessary, as the proof of things.'

Much has been written about the uneasy relationship of the two great cardinals, Manning and Newman, but it would seem that few have understood so well as Newman himself that the Spirit gives different gifts to those called to serve. These gifts are not in competition with each other but rather serve to build up the Church. David Newsome captures the essence of this reality in his conclusion to *The Convert Cardinals*. He points out that for Newman there were two kinds of saints. There were those like St Ambrose and St Athanasius, who were, according to Newman,

> . . . men of acute and ready mind, with accurate knowledge of human nature and large plans, and persuasive and attractive bearing, genial, sociable, and popular, endowed with prudence, patience, instinctive tact and decision in conducting matters, as well as boldness and zeal.

But there was another kind of saint, one more akin to St Basil:

> The retired and thoughtful student, who remains years and years in the solitude of a college or a monastery, chastening his soul in secret, raising it to high thought and single-minded purpose . . . such a one is often unsuccessful in his own day . . . he does his work, and so leaves it, and it seems to die; but in the generation after him it lives again, and on the long run it is difficult to say, which of the two classes of men has served the cause of truth more effectually.

In the two portraits it is easy to see suggested the outlines of Manning, a man of 'large plans', and of 'the retired and thoughtful student', John Henry Newman. Newman applied the distinction of the different works to be done, yet in the same Spirit, to himself and his Bishop, William Ullathorne, at the end of one of their last meetings at the Birmingham Oratory in August 1897. As the Bishop was about to leave Cardinal Newman knelt down and asked him for his blessing. Ullathorne recorded:

> I could not refuse without giving him great embarrassment, so I laid my hands on his head and said, "My dear Lord Cardinal, I pray God to bless you and that

the Holy Spirit may be full in your heart." As I walked to the door, refusing to put on his biretta as he went with me, he said, "I have been indoors all my life, whilst you have battled for the Church in the world." I felt annihilated in his presence: there is a saint in that man.

In the words of the future Benedict XVI:

> The characteristic of the great doctor of the Church, it seems to me, is that he teaches not only through his thought and speech, but rather by his life, because within him thought and life are interpenetrated and defined. If this is so, then Newman belongs to the great teachers of the Church, because at the same time he touches our hearts and enlightens our thinking.

SAN GIORGIO IN VELABRO (VIA DEL VELABRO)

The *diaconia* of Cardinals Newman and Gasquet (1914–15) is, of course, an obvious choice for an English cardinal since it is dedicated to the national patron. Part of the head of St George (the 'Great Martyr'), together with his standard and part of his shield, is said to be enshrined below the high altar.

This seventh century church was built over an earlier foundation in former marshland known as the *Velabrum*, and it was ever vulnerable to floods, as witnessed by the high water mark from 1870 in the portico. This church is imbued with a refined sense of beauty, its few artistic treasures – notably the baldacchino over the high altar and the fresco in the apse – are thus shown to best effect. Anarchist bombing in 1993 damaged the church which has since been sensitively restored.

HERBERT ALFRED VAUGHAN
1832 – 1903
CARDINAL PRIEST OF SANTI ANDREA E GREGORIO MAGNO (1893)

It could be said that Herbert Vaughan's motto, *Amare et Servire* ('To Love and To Serve'), vividly captures not only his own life's work but also that of his whole family. Based at Courtfield, Monmouthshire, the Vaughans were distantly related to Blessed Margaret and Reginald Cardinal Pole, and to Cardinal Weld. Herbert was the eldest of a large family of eight sons and five daughters. Their mother, Eliza Vaughan, was a saintly woman of prayerful devotion and charity who prayed a daily Holy Hour that all her children would devote themselves to Christ.

Of Herbert's brothers, Roger became Archbishop of Sydney; John an auxiliary bishop in Salford; Bernard a famous Jesuit preacher; Joseph founded Fort Augustus Abbey in Scotland and Kenelm the Brotherhood of Expiation, which had houses in Chelsea and Hatfield. The two remaining brothers who survived childhood married. Francis, who was made a Papal Chamberlain in 1899, was the father of Herbert (later Superior of the Catholic Missionary Society) and Francis (Bishop of Menevia). Reginald had ten children, three of whom entered the religious life, including Sr Mary Felix Clare, who made her vows in the presence of her uncle, the Cardinal, and ruled as Abbess of the Poor Clares of Notting Hill for thirty-seven years. She lived to see the Second Vatican Council.

Of Herbert's sisters, Gwladys became a Visitation nun at Marquetta, near Boulogne; Teresa a Sister of Charity in London; Clare a Poor Clare at Amiens; and Mary was eventually Prioress of the Augustinian Canonesses of the Lateran at Newton Abbot. Both Gwladys and Mary were subjects of biographical studies by Lady Herbert and Lady Lovat respectively. The remaining sister, Margaret, also tried the religious life, despite being physically limited by a spinal injury. The Vaughan family of Courtfield was a veritable domestic church.

All this lay in the future, however, when Herbert was born on 15 April 1832. He pursued his early studies at Stonyhurst and Brugelette (a Jesuit college in Belgium), where he was known as 'Milord Roast-beef'. Discerning a call to the priesthood he went to study at Downside, where he lived as a cleric in the monastic enclosure and founded the Downside Debating and Literary Society. From 1851 he continued his priestly formation at the *Pontificia Accademia degli Nobili Ecclesiastici* in Rome. He gained a doctorate from the *Collegio Romano* but it was probably his friendship with Manning, a fellow student at the *Accademia*, which proved to be the most influential legacy of his Roman years. Vaughan was ordained at Lucca on 28 October 1854 by the Archbishop, Giulio Arrigoni, and celebrated his first Mass at the Annunziata in Florence, despite 'a good deal of difficulty with the sacristan, who was not satisfied with my papers'. Sadly, his mother never lived to see the day – she had died the previous year giving birth to John.

The first assignment given Herbert by Cardinal Wiseman, on Manning's recommendation, was the Vice Rectorship of St Edmund's College, Old Hall Green. Shortly afterwards Vaughan joined the newly-formed Oblates of St Charles, together with several other members of staff, and their presence in the college led to much opposition from those who mistrusted the 'Romanising' direction of Wiseman. In 1861 the Oblates were forced to leave St Edmund's.

Throughout his ministry Vaughan was a man of zealous evangelising fervour. On leaving Ware he began to turn his thoughts towards his long-held ambition to promote the missions around the British Empire. Encouraged by Wiseman and Manning, Vaughan made a fund-raising tour of the Americas and the Caribbean and in 1866 founded St Joseph's Society of the Sacred Heart for Foreign Missions, with a college at Mill Hill, then eleven miles to the north of London. Vaughan had to work hard to attract students but in 1871 the first group of missionaries were sent out to serve the African–American community of Baltimore in Maryland. These became the nucleus of a separate branch of the Mill Hill family, the Josephites. A notable recent convert, Lady Herbert of Lea, the widow of Sidney Herbert (the War Minister who sent Florence Nightingale to the Crimea) and mother of the thirteenth and fourteenth Earls of Pembroke, became the principal benefactress of Mill Hill and was known as the 'Mother of the Mill'. She enjoyed a close friendship with Vaughan, who once wrote to her:

'You shall be my Paula and I will be your rough and hard old Jerome.'

Vaughan also founded the Catholic Truth Society (1868), which aimed to distribute inexpensive literature defending and explaining Catholicism, and became proprietor of *The Tablet* and eventually also *The Dublin Review*.

In 1872 he was appointed Bishop of Salford, a diocese that included the great industrial city of Manchester. Vaughan's name is so closely associated with Mill Hill and Westminster that it is often forgotten that he spent twenty energetic years as a bishop in Lancashire. He presided over annual diocesan synods and established a college for newly ordained priests, so that the transition from seminary to mission would be as smooth as possible. He founded schools, most notably St Bede's College, Manchester, and helped Rome issue *Romanos Pontifices* (1881), upholding the rights of the English bishops against the Jesuits, who claimed exemptions and had opened a school in Vaughan's diocese without his permission. Vaughan also set up the Voluntary Schools Association in 1884 and, two years later, the Catholic Protection and Rescue Society for children who would otherwise be deprived of their faith through parental neglect, workhouses and aggressive proselytism. Vaughan managed to establish seven Catholic Homes, with the help of the Franciscan Missionaries of St Joseph, founded by Alice Ingham (Mother Mary Francis), a native of Rochdale. This Order also went to Mill Hill to look after the domestic needs of the college.

In March 1892 Bishop Vaughan was named as the third Archbishop of Westminster – an appointment that caused no great surprise – and was enthroned at the Pro-Cathedral of Our Lady of Victories on 8 May 1892. This was despite the fact that Vaughan had written to Leo XIII, urging him to appoint a more worthy candidate:

> The See of Westminster ought to be occupied by a bishop distinguished for some gift of superior learning or by remarkable sanctity, for he ought to be commended to the Church and to the people of England (for whose conversion he may be able to do more than any one else) by some manifest superiority or excellence. Holy Father, it is no mock modesty or fashion of speech which makes the confession that I have no qualification of learning for such a post. I do not excel as a preacher, an author, a theologian, a philosopher, or even as a classical scholar. Whatever I may be in these matters, in none am I above a poor mediocrity. It will be very easy in such a position as the See of Westminster to compromise the interests of religion in England by errors of judgment – and the very quality of a certain tenacity and determination would make these errors still more serious.

Later in 1892 Herbert Vaughan received the pallium from Archbishop

Stonor at the Brompton Oratory rather than in Rome, an occasion which he felt was 'too good a trump-card against the Anglican to throw away'. The preacher at the Mass on this occasion was Dom Aidan Gasquet, who was destined himself to be raised to the sacred purple. On 16 January 1893 Pope Leo created Vaughan Cardinal Priest of the title of Santi Andrea e Gregorio Magno. In a letter to Lady Herbert, Vaughan revealed that the Pope:

> ... desired to give me San Crisogono as my title because it had been his and he thought that to do so would be a mark of special benevolence and an honour for England. But on my representing that England knows St Gregory but not San Crisogono, he graciously withdrew the impending honour and bestowed on me St Gregory.

At a special banquet held at the English College, the new cardinal compared himself to the gilded figurehead on the bow of a warship – the crew did the real work and if they worked hard and in union with each other then all would be well.

True to his character, Vaughan came to Westminster with grand ideas. He was much concerned with the formation of future priests and dreamt of a central seminary to serve the country. With this in mind, he closed down Manning's Hammersmith seminary and sent students to Oscott. The idea was that the central seminary would combine the resources of several dioceses and provide the highest standard of teaching. Vaughan also acted as Cardinal Protector of the English College, Rome, the only English Ordinary to hold the title, and two tapestries bearing his coat of arms, which were displayed on feast days, now hang in the college refectory. According to one student, Richard Burke, 'Vaughan was most anxious to inaugurate reforms whenever he paid a visit to the college and on that account I cannot say that his presence was altogether a source of unmitigated joy.'

He also made the building of a cathedral for the chief city of the Empire one of his great aims, regarding it as both a timely memorial to his predecessors and 'a liturgical, pastoral and intellectual centre for English Catholicism'. Manning had bought a site for his metropolitan cathedral but saw 'the saving of Catholic children from the Protestant workhouses or reformatories' as his priority. In 1894 Vaughan named John Francis Bentley as the architect and began to raise money for the project, boosted by a gift of £1,000 from Pope Leo. A church in the Byzantine style was agreed upon, partly because it could be erected quickly and relatively cheaply, and interior decoration left to successive generations. A more conventional gothic structure would have been hugely expensive, especially if it was going to compare favourably with nearby Westminster Abbey. The foundation stone was laid on 29 June 1895, for which occasion the Cardinal obtained a papal indult in order to wear the pallium over his cope. Vaughan was unable to celebrate the Mass since his health did not allow him to observe the Eucharistic fast until a late hour in the morning, but felt it important to be seen with the symbol of his metropolitan authority at this great moment in his episcopate. Vaughan spoke of his vision of a cathedral at which Benedictine monks would sing the Divine Office daily. It was for this purpose that a monastic community was established at Ealing in 1897, though the Cardinal also entered into negotiations with the French Benedictines of Solesmes. Eventually it was left to the English clergy to ensure the cathedral's liturgical excellence, with the help of the famous choir under the direction of Sir Richard Runciman Terry (appointed in 1901) and his successors. Vaughan inaugurated the cathedral by presiding at Solemn First Vespers of the Ascension 1902 in the cathedral hall (then called Chapter Hall), which acted as a sort of pro-cathedral during the final stages of building work.

Vaughan continued in Westminster some of the characteristics of his Salford years. His concern for Catholic education led to the Voluntary Schools Association and he founded the Crusade of Rescue (1899) after a controversy with Dr Barnado over the Catholic children in his homes. In 1894 he organised a religious census.

Vaughan had to deal with various issues relating to the Anglican establishment. Manning had been opposed to the sending of Catholics to Oxford and Cambridge due to the perceived danger of 'corruption' in a non-Catholic environment, even though a Catholic Club (renamed the 'Newman Society' in 1888) had been established in Oxford in 1878. Vaughan, however, was more flexible and, together with his brother bishops, sent a petition to Rome asking for a change in the Church's Oxbridge policy. This was granted in 1896, on the condition that supplementary talks on Catholic subjects were provided 'with such exhaustiveness and soundness that the minds of the young men may be effectively fortified against errors'. The Universities Board was established and St Edmund's House, Cambridge set up for Church students.

Meanwhile, a group of Anglo-Catholics led by Lord Halifax and supported by the French ecumenist, the Abbé Fernand Portal, were trying to seek corporate 'reunion' with Rome and suggested that the Church should recognise the validity of Anglican orders. Believing that the Church of England was close to Rome, Leo XIII appeared well-disposed and considered offering convert clergy conditional ordination. At this point the Cardinal of Westminster jumped in to warn the Pope that the real situation in England was very different and recommended a commission to study the question, in which Vaughan, Gasquet and Merry del Val played a crucial part. The result was *Apostolicae Curae* (1896), in which the Pope declared: 'Ordinations carried out according to the Anglican rite have been, and are, absolutely null and utterly void.' Expecting an influx of convert clergy, Vaughan set up the Converts' Aid Society (now the St Barnabas Society).

By the turn of the century the Cardinal's health was failing and he complained of having the walking powers of a tortoise. He spent much time recuperating at the houses of friends and at Mill Hill, where he would often contemplate the site of his grave from the comfort of his bath chair. He died there on 19 June 1903 and his funeral on 25 June was the first public service in the almost complete cathedral. His tomb at Mill Hill was inscribed with the words: *Servulus Perpetuus/Gloriosae et Beatae Mariae Virginis/et Sancti Josephi* ('Forever the Poor Little Slave of the Glorious and Blessed Virgin Mary and of St Joseph'). On 14 March 2005, with the closure of Mill Hill imminent, the Cardinal's body was quietly translated to the newly decorated Vaughan Chantry in Westminster Cathedral. The Cardinal Vaughan Memorial School was eventually opened in Kensington in 1914 to honour the memory of the Cardinal.

For the entry on Santa Andrea e Gregorio Magno see p. 156.

RAPHAEL MERRY DEL VAL
1865 – 1930
CARDINAL PRIEST OF SANTA PRASSEDE (1903)

The future Cardinal Secretary of State was born in Portman Square, London on 10 October 1865, the second son of Don Raphael Merry del Val and Josefina de Zulueta. His father was then Secretary of the Spanish Legation (a full Embassy had not yet been established) and later became Spanish Ambassador to Brussels, Vienna and the Holy See. The future cardinal was baptised at the old church of St James's, Spanish Place the day after his birth. The register records his impressive baptismal names: *Raphael Maria Josephus Petrus Franciscus Borgia Dominicus del Vall* [sic] *Gerardus Sanctissimi Trinitatis Merry del Val*. Despite this exotic-sounding name, the Merrys had originated in County Waterford and settled in Spain during the eighteenth century for commercial reasons. They had married into the ancient del Val family, which claimed descent from a child martyr, St Dominguito del Val, who, according to the dubious tradition then held, was crucified by the Jews of Saragossa on Good Friday 1250. Raphael also had a Scottish grandmother, Sophia Wilcox.

The young Raphael went to Bayliss House, a small preparatory school in Slough, and received his First Communion at the Jesuit church of the Sacred Heart in Bournemouth, which was near the house of his maternal grandfather, Don Pedro José de Zulueta, the second Count de Torre Diaz. When Don Raphael became Spanish Minister to Brussels, the future cardinal moved to the Jesuit colleges of Notre-Dame, Namur (1876-77) and St Michel, Brussels (1878-83). Noted for his piety and a strong desire to be a priest, he was also a keen horseman and fencer, and enjoyed playing cricket, tennis and chess.

In 1883 he entered Ushaw to begin his studies for the priesthood, where he was nicknamed 'Merry Devil', and moved to Rome in 1885 as a seminarian for Westminster. Arrangements were made for him to live at the Scots College, which had a good reputation and was deemed to be in a healthier location than the *Venerabile*. On arriving in the Eternal City he and his father were granted a private audience with Leo XIII. The Pope was impressed by the young Raphael and insisted upon his immediate entrance into the elite *Accademia degli Nobili Ecclesiastici*. As the Cardinal's biographer, F A Forbes, wrote:

> The event was of crucial importance, and a turning-point in the young man's life. The procedure was startling and unprecedented, even, it would seem, rash. To single out a young man, untried; to deprive him of the seminary formation he would naturally need, and to thrust honours upon him, seemed hardly wise. Yet apparently the shrewd eye of Leo XIII discovered in the young man peculiar qualities of mind and character.... Thus it was that Providence stepped in, and a high, overruling purpose from the beginning thrust the young man into a career to which he had never given a thought, and which was not only repugnant to his tastes and temperament, but diametrically opposed to his spiritual interests and ideals.

Merry del Val's rise was meteoric. In 1887 he was appointed Secretary to the Pontifical Mission to London for Queen Victoria's Golden Jubilee, on which occasion Raphael was made a Privy Chamberlain to His Holiness, though not yet in major orders. The following year he accompanied the Special Papal Mission to Berlin for the funeral of Wilhelm I and coronation of Emperor Frederick III. Mgr Merry del Val was ordained a priest of the Archdiocese of Westminster on 30 December 1888 at the church of the Daughters of St Anne in Rome and celebrated his First Mass in the rooms of St Ignatius at the Gesù. In 1889 he joined the Pontifical Mission to the Imperial Court of Vienna, where his father was now Spanish Ambassador, and in 1891 he moved to the papal anti-camera as *cameriere segreto partecipante*. He was secretary to the commission that pronounced the invalidity of Anglican orders in the bull *Apostolicae Curae* (1896) and was involved in delicate negotiations with the Canadian Government over the Catholic schools question following hostile legislation. In 1899 he returned to the *Accademia* as President and was consecrated Titular Archbishop of Nicaea at the Spanish church in Rome, Santa Maria di Monserrato, on 6 May 1900. He returned briefly to London in 1902 as Special Envoy for the coronation of Edward VII.

For the conclave which followed Pope Leo's death in 1903, Merry del Val was chosen to act as secretary. Giuseppe Sarto, son of a village postman and Patriarch of Venice, was elected as Pius X and, having been impressed by

Merry del Val during the conclave, chose him as his new Secretary of State. Aged only thirty-eight, he was created Cardinal Priest of Santa Prassede at the Pope's first consistory on 9 November 1903. The new cardinal worked closely with St Pius, who called him 'my Merry', and has become identified with the Pope's policy against Modernism, which was branded a 'synthesis of all heresies' in the decree *Lamentabili* (1907).

Although he has often been painted as a doctrinal watchdog, he had a strong pastoral dimension. As a young priest he founded a club for poor boys and men which grew into the 'Pious Association of the Sacred Heart of Jesus in Trastevere' and he continued to make daily visits, even as a busy cardinal. 'Without seeing my boys,' he would say, 'it seems as if I have not finished my day.'

In 1914 Merry del Val was made Archpriest of St Peter's. Following the death of St Pius X, the newly elected Benedict XV appointed him as Secretary of the Holy Office (the Pope himself was Prefect). He remained in this office for the rest of his life.

As Archpriest of St Peter's, Cardinal Merry del Val was at the heart of many of the great ceremonies and liturgies of that great basilica, yet he did not let this important work weaken his pastoral sensitivity, as one encounter on the last Saturday afternoon of October 1924 with 'a tired and very raw young man', a new seminarian at the English College, demonstrated. Many years later that one-time seminarian wrote of his meeting with Merry del Val:

As I passed the sacristy door I was astonished to meet a procession of prelates who had just taken part in the singing of Vespers in the choir chapel. At the end of the procession was the impressive figure of the Archpriest, Cardinal Merry del Val. I was in a group of English College students. The others were suitably dressed in their black cassocks. I, the new boy, was still wearing lay clothes.

To my joyful embarrassment the Cardinal broke off from the procession and came up to me. "I presume that you are a new student," he said. "Where do you come from?" I told him that I had just left Ushaw. "I am an Ushaw man too," the Cardinal said, "let me give you some good advice. Take things easy in your first year. The climate and the food are different and you need to watch your health. You will be here for seven years, and you will have plenty of time later on to study philosophy and theology. During these first few months enjoy Rome and don't work too hard." . . . I was only later to realize how gracious was the Cardinal's gesture in halting a procession to say a word of encouragement to an unknown young man at the threshold of his Roman course. It was a lesson in the nature of true greatness. A lesser man might have feared a loss of dignity. The Cardinal was guided by affection rather than protocol. It was the same Cardinal who – as most of us discovered only after his death — gladly left the exalted company of diplomats and ecclesiastics in order to be with the poor boys of Rome.

The young seminarian in question was John Carmel Heenan, who was to become the eighth Cardinal Archbishop of Westminster.

Despite working in Rome, Merry del Val always professed to be an Englishman. Indeed, together with Gasquet, he was a potential candidate for Westminster following Vaughan's death in 1903, but was considered too foreign. In Rome, he was closely involved with the Beda College and became Protector of the English College in 1929. He often took holidays with his fellow-countrymen, such as Fr Denis Shiel of the Birmingham Oratory, and he even confessed to dreaming in English.

On 24 February 1930 he visited the boys in Trastevere as usual. The following day he was taken ill with appendicitis and rushed into hospital for an operation. Unexpectedly, he died under the anaesthetic at the age of sixty-four and was buried in the crypt of St Peter's, with his chosen epitaph: *Da mihi animas caetera tolle* (Give me souls, take away all else). The discovery at his death of two hairshirts and a bloodied scourge in the bottom drawer of his desk encouraged the growing call for his beatification. His cause was opened in 1953 and still continues.

Merry del Val composed several hymns and motets. Although he placed little importance on them, they reveal the depths of his inner life. The *Cori dell'Accademia Filarmonica Romana* under the direction of Pablo Colino produced a recording of his music on the 'Audiovisivi San Paolo' label, making Merry del Val the only English cardinal whose music has been made into an album.

For the entry on Santa Prassede see p. 82.

FRANCIS ALPHONSUS BOURNE

1861 – 1935

CARDINAL PRIEST OF SANTA PUDENZIANA (1911)

Cardinal Bourne served Westminster as archbishop for thirty-two years – the longest reign of any archbishop to date. However, he never captured the popular imagination in the same way as his predecessor (Vaughan) and successor (Hinsley). Nevertheless, these were important years in the history of the English Catholic Church, and it is fitting to give credit to Bourne where it is due.

Francis Bourne was born at 10 Larkhall Rise, Clapham on 23 March 1861 and baptised the following day at the Redemptorist church of St Mary's by the Provincial, Fr Robert Coffin. The Fathers had loaned their large relic of St Alphonsus to the Bourne household while the future Cardinal was being born and, in thanksgiving for the saint's intercession, the baby was given 'Alphonsus' as a second name. His father, Henry, was a convert of Frederick Oakley and an up-and-coming clerk in the Receiver-General's branch of the Post Office; his mother, Ellen Byrne, a devout Irish Catholic, had been educated in France by the Faithful Companions of Jesus and had known the Mother Foundress, Mary Madeleine d'Houet.

Francis enjoyed a happy family life at Clapham and, from 1868, at 14 Cobham Terrace, Greenhithe, Kent. However, everything changed in 1869 when Francis joined his brother, Henry, at Ushaw, a place which he later described as 'a hard school for young boys so very far from home'. Shortly after entering Ushaw, his father contracted typhoid after returning from the opening of the Suez Canal (1869), which he had attended due to his work with the P & O Company. Within six weeks he was dead. In 1874 further tragedy struck when Bourne's brother died of consumption. These sorrows, the Cardinal later confessed, had made him 'more serious and pensive than I would otherwise be'. Due to fears for his health, Francis transferred to the milder climes of St Edmund's, Ware in 1875, where he was allowed a daily ration of stout for medical reasons. He entered as a lay student but donned a cassock at Easter 1877, after Fr Stanfield had spontaneously mentioned the idea of the priestly vocation after confession during a retreat. 'The matter then seemed to become quite clear,' he wrote forty years later, 'and I do not think that I ever had any hesitation about it afterwards.' The following year, he received the tonsure at St Edmund's from the hands of Cardinal Howard.

However, the exact nature of his vocation remained open to question. In 1880 he spent several months at Woodchester, testing a possible Dominican vocation that had been inspired by reading the works of Fr Lacordaire. When this did not work out, he spent an unhappy year at the seminary in Hammersmith and then continued his studies at St Sulpice, Paris (1881-83) and the Collège du Saint-Esprit, Louvain (1883-84). Thanks to his boyhood vacations, Bourne already spoke French fluently, though with a strong English accent, and remained a keen Francophile all his life.

On 11 June 1884 he was ordained priest at Clapham by Bishop Coffin of Southwark, who had baptised him in the same church twenty-three years previously. His first Mass was celebrated at Sacred Heart, Camberwell. Bourne's first appointment was to Our Lady, Help of Christians, Blackheath. Though he enjoyed the work, especially with the boys of the parish school, he did not get on with the Rector, Fr Thomas Ford, and poor reports of the young priest were sent to the Bishop. In later life, Bourne would always be sympathetic to curates in a similar situation. He went on to curacies at Sheerness, Mortlake, and the shrine of Our Lady of Consolation and St Joseph, West Grinstead. However, doubts still lingered about his place in the Church. Inspired by his work at the West Grinstead orphanage, he considered joining the Salesians and in 1887 visited St John Bosco in Turin, who told him to return to England where God had other work for him.

Bourne was unexpectedly chosen by Bishop Butt to be the founding Rector of Southwark's new seminary, which was established at Henfield (1889) and later moved to a new building at Wonersh (1891). The seminary also had subsidiary institutions at St Augustine's House, Walworth and St John Berchman's School, Clapham. In recognition of his pioneering work, Bourne became a Domestic Prelate in 1895. The following year he was consecrated coadjutor to Bishop Butt, with the titular see of Epiphania, while retaining the Rectorship of Wonersh. In 1897 he succeeded Butt as Bishop of Southwark, aged only thirty-six. As Cardinal Vaughan's health declined, it was up to the young bishop to take a leading role in fighting for Catholic interests during the discussions around the Education Act of 1902.

In 1903 Bourne was translated to Westminster, even though his name did not originally appear on the *terna* – Abbot Gasquet, Archbishop Merry del Val (soon to become Secretary of State) and Bishop Hedley (the Benedictine Bishop of Newport and Menevia) were initially the favourites. In the meantime Leo XIII died and the new Pope, St Pius X, chose the youngest member of the English episcopate, thanks in part to the recommendation of Cardinal Moran of Sydney. It is said that Gasquet had an audience with the new Pope shortly afterwards and referred to his near escape as Archbishop of Westminster. 'The Holy Spirit has decided otherwise,' he said, to which Pope Pius replied, 'The Holy Spirit? I thought it was Cardinal Moran.'

Bourne soon settled into Westminster and made extensions to Archbishop's House. Although he at first kept two carriages and a pair of fine horses, in about 1907 he made the shift to the motor car, allowing him to travel further around the diocese. His faithful coachman, Morris, who had served Manning and Vaughan, acted as his first chauffeur, although he insisted on retaining traditional coachman's uniform.

Bourne was more a quiet administrator than an inspiring leader, and he has been criticised for concentrating too much on diocesan affairs to the detriment of his role as a national and international leader. In his biography of Hinsley, Heenan wrote that:

> Cardinal Bourne, although an ecclesiastical diplomat of acknowledged ability, rarely made pronouncements. . . . He did not like making pronouncements because he was not a great orator. Experience taught him that when he did make public declarations his interventions were not always happy.

Nevertheless, Bourne oversaw many important events for the Catholic community. 1908 stands out as a particularly significant year. The Apostolic Constitution *Sapienti Consilio* removed England and Wales from the jurisdiction of Propaganda Fide. The country was no longer regarded as missionary territory and could stand alongside its European neighbours without embarrassment.

The same year London was the venue for the International Eucharistic Congress. For the first time since 1554 a papal legate landed at Dover, which was illegal according to the letter of the law. As Vincenzo Vannutelli, Cardinal Bishop of Porto and Santa Rufina, stepped off the Belgian steamer, the *Princesse Clémentine*, he was greeted by large crowds of excited Catholics and curious Protestants, but there was no diplomatic incident. The new Prime Minister, Herbert Asquith, was unhappy about the planned

Eucharistic procession through the streets of London, which sparked off some anti-Catholic feeling, and he suggested that it be cancelled. King Edward had voiced his concern about the procession to Lord Crewe, with whom he was staying in Nottinghamshire attending the races. Lord Crewe wrote to Asquith:

> The King has taken this d----d procession greatly to heart; and asked me to say that he was "greatly cut up about it" – a rather curious phrase. . . . He has received dozens of letters from enraged Protestants, who compare him disadvantageously wth his revered mother, now with God, and hint that his ultimate destination may be directed elsewhere.

Bourne worked towards a compromise. The Blessed Sacrament was not carried outside the cathedral and the clergy only wore 'the full court dress of their respective rank'. Doubts over the legality of the wearing of monastic habits in public meant religious wore ordinary clerical attire and, as a silent protest, carried the habits over their arms. The good will of the participants and a strong police presence meant that no major disturbance occurred. However, it was rumoured that the Government's subsequent defeat in the Newcastle by-election was caused by the loss of the Catholic vote.

The same year, Edward VII, Queen Alexandra and the Prince of Wales attended a Requiem Mass for the assassinated King of Portugal at St James', Spanish Place – the first British monarch publicly to attend Mass since James II. It was a further sign of the Church's new-found maturity.

The Cardinal saw the establishment of many parishes in Westminster and consecrated the cathedral on 28 June 1910, doing much to ensure the continual embellishment of its bare brick vaults. He also supported new ventures such as the Catholic Women's League and the Catholic Scouting Movement.

In 1911 the bull *Si Qua Est* created the Provinces of Liverpool and Birmingham and five years later Cardiff also became an archdiocese. This meant that the Archbishop of Westminster was no longer the only metropolitan archbishop in the country, although it was decreed that he should be chairman of meetings of the English and Welsh bishops, the *Praeses Perpetuus* of the Hierarchy. New dioceses continued to be set up, such as Brentwood (1917) and Lancaster (1924), and Bourne fought hard for the creation of a single London diocese merging together Westminster and Southwark. The ambitious plan also involved the creation of an Archdiocese of Brighton and a rural diocese based in St Albans, Hertford or Colchester. This was resisted by most of the other bishops, who agreed with Amigo of

Southwark that it would create considerable financial difficulties, and it was subsequently shelved.

At the same time that *Si Qua Est* was promulgated, it was announced that Bourne was to be made a Cardinal Priest of Santa Pudenziana. The delay was caused by Bourne's comparatively low standing in the Eternal City: he was not a natural Roman and disliked Vatican bureaucracy. His long standoff with Bishop Amigo and his apparently weak reaction to Modernism had made him suspect in Rome. Moreover, he sent few students to the English College and concentrated instead on supporting his diocesan seminary at St Edmund's, Ware. The situation was delicate, for Vaughan had envisaged Oscott as the central seminary and had invested substantial revenues of the Westminster Ecclesiastical Education Fund into it. Bourne opened the new Divines' Wing at Ware, which eventually became known as Allen Hall. He went on to build new dormitories, classrooms and a beautiful chapel to house the relic of St Edmund and rebuilt Allen Hall in even grander fashion after a fire in 1914. Many expected him to make St Edmund's into a solely ecclesiastical college, without lay students, but the mixed nature of the college continued, partly because Bourne wished to avoid giving the religious orders a monopoly on the education of the laity. Like Manning and Vaughan, Bourne produced a book, *Ecclesiastical Training* (1926), explaining his high ideal of the priesthood.

Much of his time was concerned with the struggle for Catholic schools and negotiations with the Liberal Government over educational legislation. He organised a rally at the Albert Hall on 5 May 1906 and his ongoing opposition helped defeat three bills which were hostile to voluntary schools.

During the First World War he was the guest of Admiral Jellicoe after the Battle of Jutland (1916) and visited soldiers on the Western Front, sometimes at considerable personal risk. His biographer, Edward Oldmeadow, recorded that: 'One night, in gas-mask and steel helmet, he kept an appointment by travelling, in a car without headlights, along a road where bombs from enemy aircraft were exploding abundantly.' Like much of the population, the Cardinal was affected by the war on a personal level, when his godson, Gerald Morrison, was killed in action on 13 October 1915. Bourne also had to demonstrate the patriotism of English Catholics and defended Benedict XV against charges of being 'pro-German'. In 1917 he consecrated the British, French and Italian armies to the Sacred Heart and, in a Pastoral the following year, set down the conditions for a just and lasting peace. He also appealed to the Government for a stop to air-raids on Cologne on the day of the planned Corpus Christi processions in 1918. After the war he had to tiptoe around the Irish Question (he was a moderate Home Ruler) and condemned the General Strike (1926), despite much criticism.

Bourne was the first English cardinal to travel around the world in his official capacity, visiting Canada (1910), the Near East (1918-19) and Poland (1927). In 1929 he presided over the joyful Catholic emancipation Centenary celebrations, and in 1931 he acted as papal legate in France for the Fifth Centenary of St Joan of Arc's death. The following year, he fulfilled the same role at the consecration of Buckfast Abbey.

During a visit to Rome in the winter of 1916-17 Cardinal Bourne enjoyed a surprising and pleasant Roman custom. For the duration of his visit he was a cardinal *in curia*, and thus was presented with the right to become the Cardinal Bishop of the suburbicarian diocese of Velletri, which had become vacant. Not until Bourne formally renounced the right could Velletri be offered to a more junior cardinal. He renounced the right immediately. According to Bourne's biographer, Edward Oldmeadow: 'To become a Cardinal Bishop instead of a Cardinal Priest would not have been a good enough inducement for exchanging the archbishopric of Westminster for the Diocese of Ostia and Velletri.'

David Mathew described Bourne as follows:

> Of middle height, with white hair above a pleasant, frank and rather heavy countenance, he had a dignity of bearing which never left him and he was perhaps seen at his best in some of those great ceremonies in the magnificent setting of Westminster Cathedral which he carried out so perfectly.

Mgr Ronald Knox portrayed Bourne as being rather formal and distant:

> From beginning to end of my relations with Cardinal Bourne I never found it possible to take a conversational initiative. More than once I completely failed to get across what I wanted to say (even on important matters), because he always ran the conversation himself. I never failed, in his presence, to feel like a fag taking a note round to some tremendous blood at school.

The Cardinal was a hard-worker and took few holidays, though he enjoyed visits to his country house at Hare Street (Hertfordshire), which had been left to the Archbishops of Westminster by the convert writer, Mgr Robert Hugh Benson:

> He put aside as far as possible the external marks of his rank, donned a black stock, and sallied forth for long walks over fields and through country lanes,

enjoying the freedom from the restraints of public life. The country round about he knew well, and the old churches would set him wondering how the pre-Reformation clergy passed their lives. He surmised they spent some of their time in discussing the shortcomings of their bishops, as possibly their modern successors did. There was no telephone in the house, and he could get the quiet and freedom from interruption impossible in London. In this peaceful retreat he wrote his Pastorals and public addresses, and the surroundings helped lessen the labour he always found in writing.

Perhaps it was in the congenial surroundings of Hare Street that Cardinal Bourne penned these lines for a child who had told him that she could not pray for him as she was unsure how to pronounce his name:

> Though Heaven might well for prayers of yourn
> Best blessings speed to Cardinal *Boorne,*
> Or even the man you mean discern
> If you miscalled him Cardinal *Burne* –
> Lest Paradisal pedants scorn,
> Pray "God be Guide of Cardinal *Borne!*"

> And if, in childhood's tolerant time,
> You choose to turn a Cockney rhyme,
> Then, lying on your little bed,
> With visions of a fourfold red,
> Say, "England's Wiseman, Manning, Vaughan,
> Be brothers all to Cardinal *Borne.*"

In November 1932 the Cardinal fell ill during his *ad limina* visit to Rome and was only able to return to Westminster in the New Year. His health never fully recovered, though in his final year he was able to celebrate his Golden Jubilee of Ordination and the restoration of the Catholic Shrine of Our Lady of Walsingham. Bourne died in the early hours of 1 January 1935 and was buried in the Galilee chapel of St Edmund's College, Ware, which he had built so that the seminarians and lay students could be separated in the chapel. His heart was enshrined in the seminary he had founded at Wonersh.

Bourne saw many changes during his long period at Westminster. Perhaps the future Cardinal Heenan did not exaggerate when he wrote that: 'When Bourne was enthroned Catholicism was hated. When Bourne was buried Catholicism was not only tolerated but respected.'

For the entry on Santa Pudenziana see p. 150.

FRANCIS AIDAN GASQUET OSB

1846 – 1929

CARDINAL DEACON OF SAN GIORGIO IN VELABRO (1914)
CARDINAL DEACON OF SANTA MARIA IN CAMPITELLI (1915)
CARDINAL PRIEST OF SANTA MARIA IN CAMPITELLI (1924)

Francis Neil Gasquet – known to his friends as 'Frank' – was born into a family of Provençal origin in Somers Town, London, on 5 October 1846. His grandfather had been Vice Admiral of the French fleet that took Toulon in 1793 and had fled to England because of his royalist tendencies. In his youth, Francis had already established relations with members of the Sacred College, present and future – he was altar server to Fr Manning at his parish in Bayswater and had, on one occasion, been trainbearer to Cardinal Wiseman. He was educated at Downside and entered the novitiate in 1866, taking the name of Aidan after the seventh century Bishop of Lindisfarne.

Dom Aidan was ordained in 1874, taught history and mathematics at the school, became prefect of studies, and was elected prior in 1878 at the age of thirty-two. According to his biographer, Shane Leslie:

> He was an uncompromising Englishman, fearless and bluntly outspoken. . . .
> His yea was yea and his nay meant nay. He loved his Order, his abbey and his country with intense feeling and loyalty. He was John Bull in a Benedictine robe, though his appearance was more ascetic and less jovial than the national figurehead. . . . He had a turn for the old-fashioned anecdote, when he had the time, and he lightened the long serious hours of his brethren with unfailing humour and paternal consideration. It was a sense of British fun which caused him one Ash Wednesday to drop the ashes into the open mouth of a Downside schoolboy who had mistaken the ceremony!

Gasquet modernised and enlarged the monastery and built the transepts of the church and the main structure of the tower. The Lady chapel and crypt were beginning to be built when, in 1884, overwork led to heart trouble and he was forced to resign as prior. Gasquet moved to London where he was nursed by his mother, and for a time his life was thought to be in danger. As he recuperated he began researching Tudor history and spent much time at the British Museum and the Public Record Office. He moved to Harpur Street, where he was joined by a friend, the scholar and liturgist, Edmund Bishop. As Gasquet's health recovered the Abbot President expressed his wish to send him to the parish of Acton Burnell, just south of Shrewsbury. Appeals were made to Manning, whose niece had recently married Gasquet's brother, and he sought permission from Leo XIII himself to remain in London and continue his studies. It was, indeed, a good time to pursue such scholarly pursuits, for the Pope had recently issued the Brief *Saepenumero Considerantes* (1883), encouraging historical studies and opening up the Vatican Archives.

Out of Gasquet's research came a series of books on the late medieval and Tudor church, including *Henry VIII and the English Monasteries* (two volumes, 1888 and 1889), *Edward VI and the Book of Common Prayer* (1890) and *The Eve of the Reformation* (1899). These used previously unexplored sources, including wills, inventories and library catalogues. Gasquet's recognition as a historian was demonstrated when Lord Acton invited him to contribute to the first volume of the *Cambridge Modern History*. However, Gasquet has had his critics. It is unclear how much of Gasquet's work was his own and how much he relied upon the efforts of his companion, Edmund Bishop. Nor was Gasquet always a reliable authority: the Benedictine historian, Dom David Knowles, famously said: 'Towards the end of his life Gasquet's capacity for carelessness amounted almost to genius.' Moreover, Knowles continued, 'Gasquet had inherited from his Provençal ancestors little of the Gallic lucidity of thought,' and 'His three-volume edition of Premonstratension documents for the Royal Historical Society must be one of the worst-edited contributions to the Camden series.' That being said, Knowles was quick to add, 'If it is perilous to accept Gasquet uncritically, it is foolish utterly to neglect or despise him.'

In 1896 Gasquet was called to Rome to work on the question of Anglican orders, because of his expertise on the Reformation period. Having been involved in the reform of the English Benedictine Congregation restoring abbatial government, he was elected Abbot President in 1900, an office that he held for fourteen years. In 1907 Pope St Pius X put him at the head of a commission to revise the Vulgate translation of the Bible.

Gasquet was created a Cardinal Deacon on 25 May 1914, which he described to a friend as 'The most extraordinary event to happen in this extraordinary Pontificate.' It was to be the ailing Pope's final consistory, and one of the other new cardinals, Giacomo della Chiesa of Bologna, would be elected as Benedict XV three months later. In the customary *biglietto* speech at his residence, the Palazzo San Callisto, Gasquet expressed surprise at Pope Pius' decision to elevate him to the Sacred College:

> His selection for the highest position of his gift is the more astonishing and remarkable, inasmuch as I have held no post such is the usual stepping stone to so high a dignity, neither have I occupied any office in the great Roman Congregations, from which many of the members of the Sacred College are naturally taken. Neither can I think for a moment that in myself or in the work I have tried to do for the Church, there was anything to warrant such a favour. No one who has really laboured, as I have tried to do for five and twenty years and more, in any field of learning or research, can ever feel that he is anything more than a mere student. From every height of knowledge that is painfully ascended there are revealed such vast fields of learning to be traversed, that pride in what has been accomplished is impossible.

At the outbreak of the First World War Gasquet fulfilled an important diplomatic role in checking pro-German influence at the Vatican by arranging for a British envoy to be sent to Rome. This was Sir Henry Howard, who also acted as Gasquet's *gentiluomo*, and the post later became a permanent legation under Sir Odo Russell in 1926. Gasquet had strong opinions about the war and, on one occasion, when a German cardinal (Hartmann) rather nervously said, 'We will not discuss the war,' the English Cardinal quickly retorted, 'Nor the peace!' Indeed, Gasquet was isolated in wartime Rome and it was said that Merry del Val was the only other cardinal willing to dine with him.

Gasquet held many other Roman offices: in 1915 he became Cardinal Protector of the English College, for which he wrote a college history (1920) and compiled an *Obit Book* (1929); he also acted as Prefect of the Vatican Archives and Librarian of the Holy Roman Church. In 1924 Pius XI made him a Cardinal Priest. He was a close friend of this Pope, himself a former historian and librarian, who had stayed in Gasquet's quarters the night before entering the conclave that elected him.

Gasquet was not always an easy character, as revealed by the Downside monk, Dom Herbert Van Zeller:

> For the space of some months each summer Cardinal Gasquet came back to his monastery, where he took up not so much his residence but his position. It was not, of course, a position of authority but rather one of avuncular patronage, interest and sometimes concern. Having laid down the reins of long ago he still liked the feel

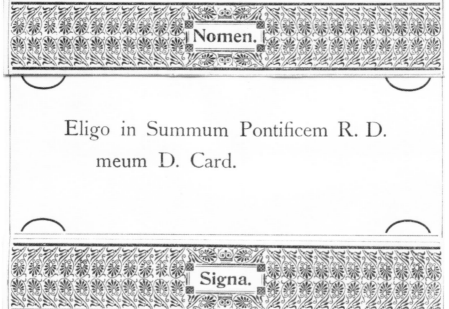

Nomen.

Eligo in Summum Pontificem R. D.
meum D. Card.

Signa.

CLOCKWISE FROM TOP LEFT: *Cardinal Francis Bourne; Bourne on a private view day at the Royal Academy, Burlington House, Piccadilly; an actual voting paper from the papal conclave of 1922 which elected Pope Pius XI, brought back as a souvenir by Cardinal Bourne.*

CLOCKWISE FROM TOP LEFT: *Cardinal Bourne reviewing the Irish Guards on the Western Front during the First World War; the Cardinal – in full clerical attire – on a British Battleship in 1916; embroidery of Bourne's coat of arms; receiving the salute of the Dublin Fusiliers; watching a parachute descend.*

CLOCKWISE FROM TOP LEFT: *Cardinal Francis Gasquet; a portrait of Gasquet which hangs in the refectory at Downside; Gasquet's triumphant return to Downside after his elevation to the Sacred College. The canopy is held by members of the school's Officer Training Corps.*

November 30th 1926

TALES·AMBIO DEFENSORES

FACING PAGE: *Arthur Hinsley, in a photograph to mark his episcopal consecration as Titular Bishop of Sebastopolis.*

TOP: *Cardinal Hinsley at Westminster Cathedral, having returned from Rome with the red hat.*

BOTTOM: *Hinsley attending a lecture in Rome.*

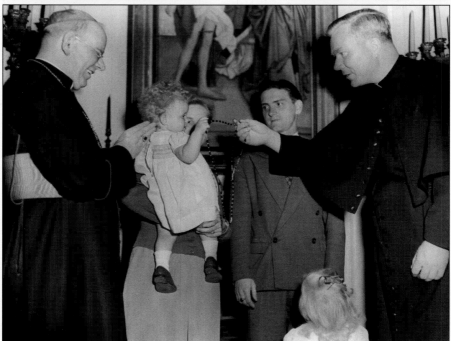

CLOCKWISE FROM TOP LEFT: *Archbishop Griffin on his way to take formal possession of the See of Westminster from the Chapter, 1943; Cardinal Griffin with Pope Pius XII; Griffin with Fr Patrick Peyton who organised a 'Rosary Crusade' at Wembley in 1952.*

TOP: *Cardinal Griffin calls on President Harry Truman at the White House, May 1946.*

LEFT: *Griffin with film stars Patricia Ryan and Stewart Granger, 1946.*

Cardinal William Godfrey

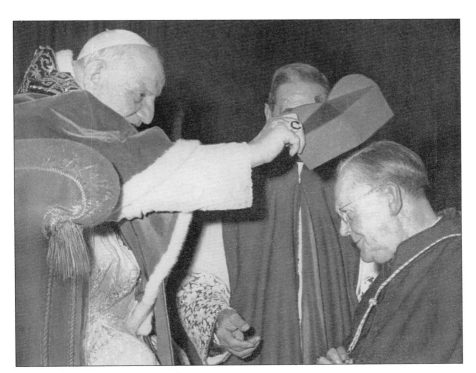

TOP: *Cardinal Godfrey receiving the red hat.*

LEFT: *Godfrey with Blessed Pope John XXIII.*

The English and Welsh Hierarchy meeting in the library of the English College, Rome during the Second Vatican Council. Godfrey, at the head of the table, presides, while the future Cardinal Heenan – then Archbishop of Liverpool – is the second bishop to the left of Godfrey.

Cardinal William Heard

Cardinal Heard, with Archbishop (later Cardinal) Gray of St Andrews and Edinburgh.

SUB UMBRA CARMELI

ABOVE: *Cardinal Heenan with the Archbishop of Canterbury, Dr Michael Ramsey, at a Foyle's Luncheon in November 1971, to mark the publication of Heenan's autobiography,* Not the Whole Truth.

LEFT: *Cardinal John Carmel Heenan.*

Cardinal Basil Hume

The visit of Her Majesty Queen Elizabeth II to Westminster Cathedral on St Andrew's day, 1995.

Cardinal Hume with Pope John Paul II.

At the launch of his book, Basil in Blunderland.

With the Princess of Wales and Pope John Paul II.

CLOCKWISE FROM TOP LEFT: *Archbishop Cormac Murphy-O'Connor is elevated to the cardinalate by Pope John Paul II in the consistory of 21 February 2001; Cardinal Murphy-O'Connor's coat of arms, displayed outside his titular church of Santa Maria sopra Minerva; Cardinal Murphy-O'Connor is welcomed into the Sacred College of Cardinals.*

The opening of the 2005 conclave, which elected the Dean of the Sacred College, Cardinal Ratzinger (seen here standing in the centre in front of the altar), Pope Benedict XVI. Cardinal Murphy-O'Connor can be seen standing in the back row on the right-hand side, second from bottom.

of his foot in the stirrup once a year – a single foot with its prelates buckle – but whether he liked what he saw across the saddle-back is doubtful . . . though the Gasquet smile could work wonders in making people feel at ease, there were days when thunder hung behind those black contrasting brows.

Cardinal Gasquet died in Rome on 5 April 1929 after catching a chill while assisting at the Requiem of Aurelio Cardinal Galli. Shane Leslie gives this account of Gasquet's lying in state, 'carried out with all the Roman ritual':

> For two days and nights the cardinal lay on a bed of purple clothed in his Benedictine robe. On the third day he was vested in his pontificals and the customary eulogy was read over his embalmed body.
>
> Sealed in his casket, surmounted by his Red Hat, he was carried to Santa Maria in Trastevere and placed beneath a blazing cataflaque. . . . The Requiem was sung by the Abbot of Monte Cassino and the Absolutions were given by the Dean of the Sacred College, Cardinal Vincenzo Vannutelli, old "indestructible", as Gasquet used to call him.

His body was brought by rail and sea back to England and after a Solemn Requiem sung by Cardinal Bourne he was, according to his wishes, buried at Downside.

For San Giorgio in Velabro, see p. 172.

For Santa Maria in Campitelli, see p. 133.

Cardinal Gasquet's tomb at Downside.

ARTHUR HINSLEY

1865 – 1943

CARDINAL PRIEST OF SANTA SUSANNA (1937)

The man whom the Daily Mail called 'the best loved cardinal England has ever had' was born at Carlton near Selby, North Yorkshire, on 25 August 1865, the son of Thomas (a joiner) and Bridget (originally from County Galway). The parish priest, Canon George Heptonstall, who had been a contemporary of Nicholas Wiseman at the English College, Rome, baptized the infant Arthur. He went to Ushaw at the age of eleven, where one of his fellow students was Raphael Merry del Val, and proceeded to the *Venerabile* in 1890. Called 'Bocca' by his friends, on account of his habit of frequenting the local bookshops, Hinsley took particular delight in studying the works of Aquinas, which had recently enjoyed a renaissance thanks to Leo XIII's *Aeterni Patris* (1879).

Hinsley was ordained on 23 December 1893 and, on returning to England, spent five years at Ushaw teaching moral philosophy and cataloguing the massive college library. After a brief curacy at St Anne's, Keighley, he became founder-headmaster of St Bede's Boys Grammar School, Bradford (1900). However, Hinsley's early years were not altogether successful – his teaching methods at Ushaw had met with disapproval and a dispute with the Bradford school governors and Bishop Gordon led him to leave the Diocese of Leeds and seek incardination into Southwark in 1904. He acted as chaplain to the Sisters of Charity of Nevers at Withdean, Brighton and, from 1907, administered the historic parish of St Edward's, Sutton Park. He cycled several times a week to lecture at Wonersh.

In 1911 he became parish priest of Our Lady and St Philip Neri, Sydenham, where he did much to help the Belgian refugees who had settled in the area during the First World War. Hinsley liked to relate the story of how he had once stopped to coach some of his altar boys playing cricket in a local park and was told by the attendant that nobody over the age of fourteen was allowed to play there. He also enjoyed a close relationship with his new bishop, Peter Amigo, and was sent to Rome to represent Southwark during Bourne's campaign to create a single London diocese.

Despite the opposition of Bourne and many of the bishops, Hinsley was named Rector of the Venerable English College, Rome in 1917, thanks to the intervention of Cardinal Gasquet, the college's Protector. The college at the time was in decline – as one member of staff put it, 'A down-at-heels college, with a great past, an unworthy present and a problematical future.' Hinsley solved its financial problems, bought a new summer villa in the Alban Hills (Palazzola), saved the college from partial demolition by Mussolini's town-planners and inspired a distinctive type of Anglicised *Romanitas* among his students. These included many future prelates, such as Cardinals Griffin and Heenan, hence the quip that to become an English bishop you had to be male, celibate and an old boy of the *Venerabile* – the first two could possibly be dispensed with, but not the third. Indeed this 'Hinsley tradition' would continue until the 1960s and produced many of the leaders who shepherded the English Church into the third millennium.

Hinsley could be stubborn and moody, as his biographer, the future Cardinal Heenan, described:

> The setting of his jaw was a habit developed through the years in an attempt to conquer shyness and to overcome his distaste for hurting those whom duty might compel him to correct and chastise. The thrusting out of his jaw was not a calculated pose. It was not a trick to inspire awe but an involuntary gesture to help steel his own resolution. To observers the out-thrust jaw was a sign that Arthur Hinsley had set his mind on a course of action likely to be unpopular. It may sound unlikely or even foolish, but the fact is that his intimates learned to base their diagnosis of his moods entirely on the position of his jaw. Until that jaw relaxed no change of policy could possibly be anticipated. In any community ruled by Arthur Hinsley the question: "How is the jaw?" was not a current joke but an anxious search for guidance.

On 30 November 1926 Cardinal Merry del Val consecrated Hinsley as Titular Bishop of Sebastopolis in the college chapel. The following year he was appointed Visitor Apostolic to British Africa, concentrating especially on education. In 1930 he became Apostolic Delegate in Africa, a new post created on Hinsley's recommendation. This more permanent position required his resignation as Rector in Rome, and he was raised to the rank of

Archbishop of Sardes. Pius XI, who had referred to him as 'Romanus', now christened him 'Africanus'. In effect, this meant that Hinsley had jurisdiction over the whole continent, with the exceptions of Egypt, Eritrea, Ethiopia, South Africa, Liberia and the Belgian Congo – a total of about nine million square miles. However, illness forced his return four years later, and he began what he thought would be a peaceful and comfortable retirement at St Peter's, Rome, where he became the first English canon since Bishop Algernon Charles Stanley († 1928).

On 1 April 1935, to everyone's surprise, not least his own, he succeeded Bourne as Archbishop of Westminster. When he protested to Pius XI that he was far too old for such a responsible position, the Pope is supposed to have exclaimed: 'Arise, Lazarus!' It was an astute appointment, given his experience negotiating both with the Vatican (as Rector) and the British Government (as Delegate in Africa). More recently he had come to the Pope's attention through his involvement in the Cause of John Fisher and Thomas More, who were canonised later that year. Indeed, he chose as his motto, Tales Ambio Defensores ('I gird myself with such defenders'), a phrase that he had used in a discourse on the martyrs. However, it was no easy task following Bourne, who had ruled Westminster for thirty-two years, and the new Archbishop knew little about his diocese or his priests (especially since his predecessor sent few students to the Venerabile). His first words in Westminster Cathedral were: 'I come to you in obedience, sent by the Vicar of Christ.' Since he considered himself a mere stopgap he was also surprised when, on 16 December 1937, he was elevated to the Sacred College, with the title of Santa Susanna. Some suggested that he had been passed over in the consistories of 1935 and 1936 after he defended the 'silence' of the Pope during the Italo-Ethiopian Crisis by referring to him as a 'helpless old man'.

According to Evelyn Waugh, the coming of Hinsley to Westminster was

> …a grateful refreshment to English Catholics inside and outside the archdiocese. There was now at the head of the Hierarchy a man amenable to suggestions, of deep human sympathies, who was also a shrewd judge of men, able and willing to recognise diversities of character and talent in his subordinates.

This shrewd judgment led to the appointment of Valentine Elwes, grandson of the Earl of Denbigh, as his private secretary (1935), David Mathew, an Oxford trained historian, as auxiliary bishop (1938), and Mgr Ronald Knox as President of St Edmund's, although Knox turned this down so that he could concentrate on writing. Hinsley also removed The Tablet from the direct control of the Archbishops of Westminster and handed it over to a lay editorial board, led by Douglas Woodruff, who would describe himself as 'the Chesterbelloc of the post-war Church'. The renewed journal aimed: 'To endeavour to interpret not only the Church to the outside world but the outside world to those members of the Church who need a general survey.'

Hinsley inaugurated a General Mission throughout the diocese and set up a Diocesan Council, Schools Commission and Finance Board. He worked hard for social justice and Catholic education, though his style was, for the times, unconventional. He enjoyed a close friendship with Archbishop Lang of Canterbury. His work in Africa had shown him that all Christians were 'marginal' in the modern world and he believed that a show of unity was important in the face of Communism and Fascism. The 'Sword of the Spirit' (SOS) campaign during the Second World War aimed to bring Christians together in a spiritual crusade against totalitarianism. In December 1940 it produced a statement endorsing Pius XII's 'Five Peace Points', which was signed by Hinsley, the Archbishops of Canterbury and York, and the Moderator of the Free Churches. The joint meetings were a bold step for the times and the Holy See reprimanded the Cardinal for publicly saying the Lord's Prayer with Bishop Bell of Chichester. The Cardinal also became a President of the National Council of Christians and Jews (NCCJ).

Hinsley became a leading radio broadcaster and distributed 'Cardinal's Crosses' to thousands of soldiers to remind them of the fight 'for Christian truth and justice'. He called the Nazis 'a pagan clique of upstart tyrants' and such were his public condemnations of Nazism that the Germans retaliated by branding him a 'Bolshevik' and 'lover of the Jews'. So intent was he to demonstrate Catholic patriotism and the Church's opposition to fascism that he condemned the pacifist movement as dangerous for Church and society and banned the *Pax* magazine, which was edited by the artist Eric Gill.

However, his health began to fail with the onset of angina and arterio-sclerosis – Mgr Elwes dated his decline from the Fall of France. On 26 April 1942 he suffered a heart attack minutes before delivering an important broadcast sermon to the forces for Youth Sunday. Despite his pain, he took a tablet and carried on regardless, although it would be one of his last public addresses. On 1 March 1943 he suffered a more severe coronary thrombosis at Archbishop's House. He died shortly afterwards, on St Patrick's Day, at his country residence at Hare Street. During his last night a dose of hyoscine made him delirious and he was seen going through the motions of celebrating Mass – blessing the offerings, elevating the host and even beckoning the communicants to come nearer. His death left only forty-nine members of the wartime College of Cardinals.

The Requiem was attended by General de Gaulle, General Sikorsky and various Cabinet ministers and Anglican bishops. King George VI wrote to his mother, Queen Mary: 'No one was more annoyed than I when I was "advised" not to be represented at Cardinal Hinsley's funeral.' At the time of his death, *The Jewish Chronicle* called him 'An ardent champion of Jewish rights, a great reconciler of communities and creeds, a shining and unfaltering light in a world astray in darkness.' The Cardinal's body was interred in the chapel of St Joseph at Westminster Cathedral.

Despite his fame and popularity, Cardinal Hinsley was a deeply humble man, as Mgr Elwes recalled:

> During his prayers and often even during his Mass (though I am sure that he was unconscious of it) an ejaculation would slip out, sometimes in Latin: *Domine salva nos*, more often in English: "O God, have mercy. . ." with the slight Yorkshire accentuation of the *r* in the last word. At his Mass this usually happened when he was on his way to the epistle side for the washing of the hands and before he began the *Lavabo*. Sometimes I felt like telling him that it was a bad habit that he was getting into. But I never did: that prayer was so much part of him, and I am quite sure he had no idea that its utterance was audible to others: "O God, have mercy on me."

SANTA SUSANNA

The church is best known today as the American Church in Rome, but its origins take us back to the Virgin Martyr, St Susanna, whose house and place of martyrdom was on the site of the present sixteenth century building. Cardinals Lépicier and Hinsley were assigned this church – appropriate for English cardinals since it is the burial place of Pope St Eleutherius (175-89), who, according to tradition, sent missionaries to Britain in the reign of King St Lucius (second century). Since 1946 the titular cardinals have been American.

BERNARD WILLIAM GRIFFIN
1899 – 1956
CARDINAL PRIEST OF SANTI ANDREA E GREGORIO MAGNO (1946)

The 'smiling Eminence', Bernard William Griffin, was born on 21 February 1899 in Oakfield Road, Cannon Hill, Birmingham, the son of a cycle manufacturer's manager and City Councillor. Bernard and his younger twin brother, Walter, decided early on that they wanted to be priests, and their influential parish priest, Fr O'Hagen of Sparkhill, lived to see one a bishop and the other a Benedictine of Douai Abbey. One of his three sisters became a Sister of Mercy.

Bernard was educated at King Edward's Grammar School in Birmingham and Cotton College. In the final years of the Great War he and his brother served in the Royal Naval Air Service and were posted to the Orkneys and Kent. After recovering from an attack of rheumatic fever with cardiac complications in 1918, he proceeded to train for the priesthood at Oscott, where he had a sort of nervous breakdown due to overwork; and, from 1921, at the Venerable English College, Rome, where he was known as 'Griff'. Little did he suspect that twenty-two years later he would succeed Mgr Hinsley, the blunt Yorkshireman who was then Rector, as Archbishop of Westminster.

Fr Griffin was ordained priest on 1 November 1924 and left Rome in 1927 with doctorates in both theology and canon law. He was immediately plunged into curial work in Birmingham, variously acting as Archbishop's Secretary, Chancellor and Vicar General. In 1937 he became parish priest of Coleshill, where he built a new church dedicated to St Thérèse of Lisieux, whose 'Little Way' was at the core of his spiritual life. He was also administrator of the local Father Hudson's homes for children, where he was able to use his excellent fund-raising abilities. He was energetically involved in the Catholic Evidence Guild and sometimes spoke at Speakers' Corner in Hyde Park or the outdoor platform in the Bull Ring. On 30

June 1938 he was consecrated Titular Bishop of Abya and auxiliary to Archbishop Williams. He continued his work with the children of Coleshill and, during the war, served as an air raid warden. Indeed, he was one of the first to enter ruined Coventry in November 1940.

On 18 December 1943 Bishop Griffin was named sixth Archbishop of Westminster, nine months after Hinsley's death. He was just forty-four and his appointment came as a surprise, for many had expected him to go instead to the See of Nottingham, which was also vacant. It seems that Rome favoured a young leader to deal with the inevitable problems during and after the World War. On 18 February 1946 Griffin was created Cardinal Priest of Santi Andrea e Gregorio Magno by Pius XII, who referred to him as 'my beloved Benjamin' on account of his youth. The Bishop of Münster, Blessed Clemens August Graf von Galen, who had won admiration for his opposition to the Third Reich, was one of the others to receive the red hat that day. Griffin liked to jest that the Sacred College was unusual in that it did not have an Old Boys' Association.

Griffin has been cast aside, in the words of Adrian Hastings, as 'the least important Archbishop of Westminster of the century, a nice, hard-working nonentity'. However, it is easy to forget the energy and imagination that characterised his first six years in office. During the war he visited Allied troops in Italy, did much to help refugees and was nearly killed by a flying bomb during a pastoral visit to the East End. He fought the Government over Catholic rights in Butler's Education Act of 1944 (which endangered Catholic schools), Bevan's National Health Service Act of 1946 (which threatened the livelihoods of Irish Catholic nurses) and the National Service Act of 1947 (from which he gained exemption for seminarians). He founded the Association of Catholic Trade Unionists and presided over the slow recovery from wartime, which had left many Catholic churches damaged. He travelled widely: in 1946 he toured the USA, where he had an average of twelve engagements a day and travelled ten thousand miles in a fortnight, and in 1947 he became the first foreign Church dignitary to visit post-war Poland. The Foreign Office called the Cardinal 'Britain's best unpaid ambassador' and Griffin referred to himself as the first jet-propelled cardinal, on account of his frequent air travel. He did not share his predecessor's ecumenical leanings and, following Pius XII's warning against post-war religious indifferentism, opposed joint services and action. This was demonstrated by the Catholic Church's withdrawal from the National Council of Christians and Jews (NCCJ) in 1947.

However, over-work and cigarettes led to high blood pressure and a breakdown in health in January 1949, from which he never fully recovered. Much to his disappointment, he was prevented from attending a rally at the Albert Hall which he had organised to campaign for the release of Cardinal Mindszenty, the Primate of Hungary. He barely made it to Wembley as papal legate for the magnificent Hierarchy Centenary Congress on 1 October 1950. As he processed into the stadium, he limped and leaned heavily on his stick. However, by the end of the day he was walking confidently without any support, smiling at the applauding crowd – a recovery that was attributed to his favourite saint, Thérèse of Lisieux, whose feast it was. He suffered a heart attack in January 1951, after which Edward Myers, who had been an auxiliary in Westminster since 1932, was appointed coadjutor. However, despite the fears of doctors, by September the Cardinal made another recovery – this time the 'cure' was attributed to St Cuthbert Mayne, whose skull had been placed in the Cardinal's room during his convalescence in Torquay. He resumed full duties and encouraged the great Catholic showpieces of the early 1950s: Father Peyton's Wembley Rosary Crusade (1952), the impressive Vocations Exhibition at Olympia (1953), at which thirty priests were ordained, and the Marian Year celebrations of 1954, during which he crowned the statue of Our Lady of Willesden at Wembley. He also visited Rome for Pius XII's promulgation of the Dogma of the Assumption of Our Lady. Nevertheless the Cardinal had to rely increasingly upon his inner circle of Archbishop Myers, Bishop Craven, Mgr Morrogh Bernard, and his indispensable private secretary, Mgr Worlock. Indeed, Westminster priests joked, 'Who is this man Griffin signing Worlock's letters?'

Another heart attack occurred in November 1955, though he made a seemingly rapid recovery. On 28 June 1956 the Cardinal made his last public appearance in the cathedral at a High Mass attended by Catholic VCs and their relatives, and spoke on the theme of 'Valour'. According to Mgr Worlock:

> Those of us who were close to him noticed that after he had been speaking a few moments his hand moved suddenly under his *cappa magna* to his heart. We have read of the crippling effects of heart attacks. That morning Cardinal Griffin, speaking of courage, preached right through a severe coronary thrombosis. Somehow he stood at his throne throughout the Mass, but collapsed immediately upon his return to Archbishop's House. He was genuinely surprised when I suggested that he had earned a VC that morning. "I don't know about that," he said, "but last night I was thinking they should have given one to Blessed John

Southworth" [the martyr enshrined in Westminster Cathedral].

Griffin died shortly afterwards, aged fifty-seven, on 20 August 1956, the feast of St Bernard, while holidaying at a house called 'Winwaloe' in Polzeath Bay, Cornwall. This was a favourite spot, which he had discovered many years previously with his brother. Despite the long years of poor health, his death came as a shock, especially given his powers of resilience. A funeral cortège brought his body back to Westminster, pausing briefly at Bodmin Priory and Ealing Abbey, and he was buried in the crypt of his cathedral under the spot on which the old wooden throne of the Vicars Apostolic had stood for many years. A wreath of flowers was even sent from the imprisoned Cardinal Stepinac (beatified in 1998), addressed 'to the great friend of the oppressed Croatian people'.

Mgr Ronald Knox described Griffin as

> . . . a man of insignificant stature, with a twinkling eye and a merry laugh, a stranger to dignity. . . . No man was ever more determined to burn himself to the socket; but the devoted care of those around him defeated, in some measure, his resolution. It was his heroism that he did so much, his tragedy that he could do so little.

For the entry on Santa Andrea e Gregorio Magno see p. 156.

WILLIAM GODFREY
1889 – 1963
CARDINAL PRIEST OF SANTI NEREO E ACHILLEO (1958)

William Godfrey was born in Leven Street, Kirkdale, Liverpool on 25 September 1889, the son of George (who did not live to see the birth) and Maria. The local parish of St John's, Fountains Road, had a reputation as a seedbed of vocations and, having been educated in the parish schools, Godfrey was accepted as a student for the priesthood in 1903 and sent to Ushaw, where he was eventually elected School Captain. In 1910 he was transferred to the Venerable English College, Rome, where seven years later he followed in the illustrious footsteps of Wiseman and Errington by being selected to defend his doctorate by 'Public Act', in the presence of the professors and students of the Gregorian University. One of his contemporaries wrote that he was: 'An exemplary student and very popular . . . an impersonator of no mean ability . . . very amusing at the piano.'

He was ordained for the Archdiocese of Liverpool on 28 October 1916 and served a challenging curacy at St Michael's, West Derby Road, before going to Ushaw to teach classics, philosophy and theology in 1918. During these years he published *The Young Apostle* (1924) and *God and Ourselves* (1927), played the French horn in the college orchestra and entertained his students by interspersing his lectures with that mimicry that had earned him a reputation in his own student days. His comical impression of Cardinal Bourne was meant to have been especially fine.

In 1930 he succeeded Hinsley as Rector of the *Venerabile*. These were the happiest years of his life. Though a strict disciplinarian, his leadership was always practical – he could often be seen hunting for bargains in the local markets. Godfrey was known to his students as 'Uncle Bill'.

The Rector had a great devotion to the English Martyrs, many of whom had studied in Rome, and found them excellent models for his seminarians, especially in a world where totalitarian regimes were producing a fresh crop of martyrs. He established a Martyrs' Association for the laity, who, through the daily recitation of Wiseman's prayer for the conversion of England, could be united to 'the students praying daily in Rome within the hallowed walls of the college'. He later recalled:

> Sherwin, Walpole, Morse, Hart, Buxton, Lewis and all the rest of the gallant company seemed to me to live again in those young men who were my fellow students, or who, in the days when I was Rector, were given to me to be led to the same priesthood and to the same altar and sacrifice. Together we kept the anniversaries of those brave servants of Christ who were men of our own house. We placed flowers and lights before the picture of the Blessed Trinity which the martyrs themselves had venerated. We asked the Holy Father to grant us a special feast of our college martyrs on December 1, the day of Ralph Sherwin's passion. The special Mass and Office which we submitted were approved, and the feast of the *Venerabile* Martyrs, celebrated as a *Festa nel coro e nel refettorio*, brought us a peculiar domestic joy beyond all telling. . . . While fingering the pages of our own *Liber ruber* we did not think that other books of the same kind were being made and that the day would come when the simple words *Martyr factus est* might be written alongside the names of men with whom we conversed in the halls of the Gregorian University, and whom we saw with books under their arms treading the Roman streets or walking on the Pincio in the evening sunshine. Yet it was so.

As Rector in Rome, Godfrey was given occasional extra responsibilities. He was considered as a possible successor to Hinsley as Apostolic Delegate for British Africa in 1934 but his doctors feared that this would be to the detriment of his health. In 1935 he accompanied the papal legation to Malta, led by Cardinal Lépicier, and was made honorary canon of Vittoriosa. Then, in 1937, he served as Counsellor to Archbishop Pizzardo in the papal delegation sent to the coronation of George VI. During this visit approaches were made to the Foreign Office for the establishment of a permanent papal delegation in London.

Shortly afterwards Godfrey became Apostolic Visitor to the seminaries in England, Wales and Malta, and finally, as war clouds threatened, he was appointed Apostolic Delegate to Great Britain, Gibraltar, Malta and Bermuda. Diplomatic relations between the Holy See and Britain had been broken off in 1559 with Queen Elizabeth's Act of Supremacy. There had been occasional exchanges over the centuries but it was only in 1914 that the British Government sent out a plenipotentiary Minister to the Vatican. Although papal delegations existed elsewhere in the British Empire – Canada, Australia and New Zealand – it was not until 1938 that a Delegation reached London. The appointment was largely arranged by the Holy See and the Foreign Office behind the backs of the Hierarchy, with the notable exception of Amigo of Southwark. Hinsley himself feared that the Apostolic Delegate would be seen as an 'agent of Mussolini' and that it would lead to 'religious bigotry and political bitterness'.

On 21 December 1938 William Godfrey was consecrated Titular Archbishop of Cius by Cardinal Rossi in the chapel of the English College, Rome, and shortly afterwards discreetly set up his Delegation first at Nazareth House, Hammersmith, then on Sheffield Terrace, Kensington, before finding a more suitable base in Parkside, Wimbledon (where the Apostolic Nuncio now lives). His secretary at the Apostolic Delegation, Mgr David Cashman, later became an auxiliary bishop in Westminster (1958).

Godfrey also acted as the *chargé d'affaires* to the Polish Government-in-exile. He set up a wartime office to deal with enquiries about missing persons (such as prisoners-of-war) in the Holy Child Convent on Cavendish Square. After the war he worked with the Pontifical Court Club, which consisted of monsignori and papal chamberlains who were, by virtue of their office, considered members of the *famiglia pontificia*, to publish English translations of papal speeches in the journal, *Papal Documents*. Godfrey managed to balance relations between the Government, the Holy See and the bishops and enjoyed a good working relationship with Hinsley and Griffin. The Delegate took great pride in acting as the Pope's representative. At formal occasions he would often say: 'It is his [the Pope's] hand, not mine, which is held out to you. It is his hand, not mine, which blesses you.'

In November 1953 Godfrey reluctantly left the Apostolic Delegation, where he was replaced by the American Gerald Patrick O'Hara, and returned to his native Liverpool as Archbishop. During his three years in Liverpool he made a complete visitation of the archdiocese, held a Diocesan Synod (1955) and modified Lutyens' ambitious design for the new cathedral.

In December 1956 Godfrey was translated to Westminster, at the age of sixty-seven. The enthronement ceremony on 11 February 1957 was the first to be fully televised. The same year he also became Apostolic Exarch to the Ukrainian Catholics and, on 15 December 1958, was created Cardinal Priest by Blessed John XXIII. One of the other new cardinals that day was Giovanni Battista Montini, the future Paul VI. Godfrey was given the titular church of Santi Nereo e Achilleo, which had once been the *diaconia* of Cardinal Pole (the fourth centenary of whose death was kept that year).

In Westminster Godfrey oversaw the provision of thirty-seven new churches and eleven thousand new school places, and established Commissions for Parochial Development and Schools. He energetically made visitations of his parishes and introduced a four-year programme of catechetical instruction in 1957, with an instruction or sermon to be given at each Sunday Mass. Godfrey's Pastoral Letters were not particularly memorable, although the Press did take note of the so-called 'Poodle' Pastoral for Lent 1961. In response to the National Board of Catholic Women's request to organise a regular family fast day, the Cardinal even suggested that pets could 'benefit by being fed with less expensive foods. A plump and pampered poodle might run all the more gaily after a reduced diet on simpler fare and, perhaps, a denied visit to a hair stylist.' The letter coincided with Crufts and received much attention in the press.

Godfrey had a great love for Westminster Cathedral and regarded it as his parish church. If the timetable allowed, he liked to attend the daily evening Mass, kneeling at the back in a plain black cassock or suit, happy to speak to anyone who approached, to hear confessions or even give directions. According to Worlock, on his walks in the neighbourhood of Archbishop's House he proved to be 'an easy victim to any beggar'.

It was in his beloved Rome that Godfrey spent much of his final years. He sat on the Central Preparatory Commission for the Second Vatican Council and attended the Council's opening session, at which he spoke in the *aula* with his effortlessly polished Latin – the official *Rogito* later placed in his coffin spoke of the 'balanced serenity of his interventions'. He was wary of progressive tendencies and saw himself as following in the footsteps of Manning, who had defended Catholic orthodoxy at Vatican I; indeed, Douglas Woodruff commented that 'Cardinal Godfrey would have been far more at home at the First Vatican Council.' The Cardinal made five major addresses, covering the Sacred Liturgy, the mass media and the schema *De Ecclesia*. On one occasion he argued against the reception of Holy Communion under both kinds on the grounds of hygiene, and mentioned with horror the prospect of women with lipstick drinking from the chalice. On another occasion he said '*debemus levare linguam Latinam*', meaning that the use of Latin in the Church should be increased. He was shocked to read reports in the press that he was promoting the abolition of Latin (in Italian *levare* means to throw away). As Heenan observed in the panegyric preached at his Requiem:

> The press of the world chose to divide the Fathers of the Council into conservatives and progressives. The misapplication of political labels to the pastors of the Church moved him to strong resentment. What, he used to ask, was meant by a conservative prelate? Was it a fault in a bishop to revere tradition? He felt that no Catholic would be truly progressive who compromised doctrine by expressing it in alien terms. As a man of great integrity he refused to disguise the fact that Catholic doctrine is wholly true and, for that reason, wholly unalterable.

On one occasion, the Cardinal delighted English seminarians by adapting the lines from *The Pirates of Penzance* to 'When conciliar duty's to be done, to be done/A bishop's lot is not a happy one, happy one.'

The Cardinal's frequent trips to Rome coincided with a battle against cancer, which was diagnosed in September 1961 but not made public until the time of his death. In Rome Godfrey discreetly visited the Salvator Mundi Hospital for treatment on most days before attending the Council Sessions. On his return to England in December 1962 the Cardinal had a fourth and final operation at St John and St Elizabeth's Hospital. He returned to Archbishop's House but soon had to be admitted into the Westminster Hospital for specialised treatment. He was able to return home at weekends and it was there that he suffered two heart attacks and died at 4.45pm on 22 January 1963, aged seventy-three. He died just as the Archbishop of Canterbury, Dr Ramsey, was due to visit.

Godfrey is one of the least known of England's recent cardinals. His successor, Heenan, later wrote:

> William Godfrey made little mark as a bishop largely because during his robust years he was in the diplomatic service of the Holy See as the first Apostolic Delegate to Great Britain. The good diplomat is anonymous and Dr Godfrey never had the slightest difficulty in keeping silent. He was already sixty-three years of age when as Archbishop of Liverpool he was in a position to exercise overt leadership. It was too late for him to establish himself as a national figure but he was superlatively successful in the more important and much more difficult task of giving his priests and people an example of personal holiness. This was achieved not only by what he said – he was a dull speaker – but by what he was.

For the entry on Santi Nereo e Achilleo see p. 50.

WILLIAM THEODORE HEARD

1884 – 1973

CARDINAL DEACON OF SAN TEODORO IN PALATINO (1959)
CARDINAL PRIEST OF SAN TEODORO IN PALATINO (1970)

William Theodore Heard may not have seen himself as belonging in a book about English cardinals. He was born in Edinburgh on 24 February 1884, the eldest son of a housemaster (later headmaster) of Fettes College, where the future Cardinal was sent to school. Later in life, Heard usually took his vacations in Scotland and, at the time of his elevation to the Sacred College, was declared to be the first Scottish-born Cardinal since the Reformation. However, it was to Balliol College, Oxford that the young William was sent in 1903, and at this quintessentially English institution he took part in Union debates and gained a place in the Boat Race crew of 1907. On this occasion Cambridge won by four and a half lengths. Heard was a contemporary at Balliol of another future Catholic convert, Ronald Knox, who later said that:

> My clearest recollection of him is his coming hurriedly into my room one day and asking my weight. This I gave him, and he was off again in a moment with a murmur of vague dissatisfaction that it was no use at all. Apparently he was looking for a rowing cox and my poundage let him down.

Armed with a second class degree in Jurisprudence and a rowing blue, he was articled to a legal firm in London and admitted as a solicitor in 1910. The same year he was received into the Catholic Church at Farm Street and started running a Catholic boys' club in Bermondsey (the Fisher Club), where he was inspired by the example of the parish priest, Canon Edward Murnane.

In 1913 Heard entered the English College in Rome as a student for the Diocese of Southwark, having spent a brief period at Wonersh. Among his fellow students in Rome was William Godfrey. He also became acquainted with Mgr John Prior, Vice Rector of the Beda College and Auditor of the Rota. After Ordination at the Lateran on 30 March 1918 and the completion of his doctorates in philosophy, theology and canon law, Heard returned to his beloved Bermondsey in 1921 as curate to Canon Murnane.

In 1927 he was called to Rome on the death of Mgr Prior to succeed him as Auditor. As a member of the Southwark diocesan tribunal, he had been involved in annulling the marriage of the Ninth Duke of Marlborough and the American heiress, Consuelo Vanderbilt. As Auditor of the Rota, Heard continued to deal with marriage annulment cases, including that of Evelyn Waugh's first marriage to the Hon. Evelyn Gardner. He also worked for the Congregation of Rites, saying that he preferred to deal with annulments in the mornings and canonisations in the afternoon; the canonisations were less depressing because even the failed candidates had at least tried to be good!

For much of his time in Rome Heard lived at the English College – like Allen and Philip Howard before him – and he acted as confessor, spiritual director and eventually the last Cardinal Protector (1961-73). One student, Gerald Creasey, later wrote:

> He was a very popular figure despite his apparently grumpy exterior . . . I owe much to him since he lent me endless books from his library which distracted me happily from the tedium of scholastic philosophy. He had a very healthy attitude to one's transgressions, usually blaming them on the weather ("that damned *sirocco*").

According to another *Venerabile* student, Anthony Kenny:

> Heard was an impressive figure, and some of us treated him as an oracle. He lived a solitary and austere life, rarely eating in Hall since his health permitted him only the most meagre diet. He slept little and rose early to make himself available for confessions to those who might wish to confess, before communion, any sins that might have been committed during the night. He had decided and outspoken views on a variety of topics from dental surgery to the history of cheese.

Promotion came late in life, although he had been mentioned as a possible successor to Cardinal Bourne in 1935. At the end of 1958 Heard succeeded Cardinal Jullien as Dean of the Rota, and the following December, at the age of seventy-five, was created a Cardinal Deacon with the newly re-established *diaconia* of San Teodoro in Palatino. In 1962 he was consecrated Titular Archbishop of Feradi Maius by Blessed John XXIII, and took part in all four sessions of the Council. He was the only British cardinal at the 1963 conclave, and was raised to the rank of Cardinal Priest in 1970.

In the summer of 1973 he holidayed in Scotland as normal, but returned to Rome in an agitated state and was taken to the hospital of the Blue Nuns at San Stefano Rotondo. He died there peacefully on 16 September at the age of eighty-nine. The Cardinal was buried far from home in the English College vault at the Campo Verano cemetery, but it would have pleased him that his last Mass had been celebrated in Glasgow.

SAN TEODORO IN PALATINO (VIA DI SAN TEODORO)

Cardinal Heard's church on the Palatine Hill was built out of converted imperial grain stores in the fourth century and is popularly known as 'San Toto'. It was formerly the headquarters of a charitable confraternity called the *Sacconi*. The church was one of the original seven deaconries in Rome, although suppressed by Sixtus V (1585-90). It was restored as a *diaconia* by Blessed John XXIII in 1959 and given to Cardinal Heard (whose middle name was Theodore). In the Holy Year of 2000 John Paul II granted San Teodoro to the Greek Orthodox community in Rome.

JOHN CARMEL HEENAN

1905 – 1975

CARDINAL PRIEST OF SAN SILVESTRO IN CAPITE (1965)

John Carmel Heenan was a product of the confident English Catholicism that characterised the first half of the twentieth century, yet it was his unenviable task to guide this Catholic community through a period of bewildering and often painful change.

His background reads as a textbook example of priestly vocation. He was born on 26 January 1905 in Ilford, Essex, to devout Irish parents, James Carmel Heenan, a civil servant, and Anne Pilkington. He was educated (briefly) by Ursuline sisters and then the Jesuits at Stamford Hill. His parents hoped that he would become a chorister at Westminster Cathedral, but Sir Richard Terry, who described Heenan's voice as 'metallic', rejected him at the audition. His great hero was the parish priest of Ss Peter and Paul, Ilford, Canon Patrick Palmer, renowned for the number of converts he received into the Church and the vocations he encouraged. Indeed, Ripley Road, where the Heenan family lived, produced a cardinal, a bishop (Brian Foley of Lancaster) and two parish priests (Alfred Bull of Northampton and Heenan's brother, Frank).

The future cardinal was sent to Ushaw as a student for the recently created Diocese of Brentwood – a period which he described as 'academically boring and wasteful' – and then proceeded to Rome in 1924, where the Rector was Arthur Hinsley. Heenan later described this 'rectorial Mr Chips' as 'admirable, lovable and, above all, unpredictable'. Though, with a few exceptions, Heenan could not recall a single lecture at the Gregorian University that he considered worth hearing, he enjoyed the camaraderie and high spirits of the English College.

Ordained at Ilford on 6 July 1930, he was appointed curate at Ss Mary and Ethelburga, Barking (1931-37). He maintained relations with his old Rector, Cardinal Hinsley, and worked as a sort of unofficial, part-time Public

Relations Officer at Archbishop's House, although Bishop Doubleday of Brentwood resisted any moves to transfer the young priest to Westminster. Heenan even went to the Soviet Union in 1936 on a fact-finding mission, dressed in disguise as a psychology lecturer and with a dispensation from saying the Divine Office.

In 1937 he became parish priest of St Stephen's, Manor Park. He remained there for ten years and guided his flock through a period of heavy wartime bombing. Heenan is unusual among the English cardinals for having spent such a considerable period of his life in pastoral ministry. Even as Cardinal Archbishop of Westminster he essentially remained a parish priest, often receiving regular visits from his former parishioners.

Heenan soon became a national figure and was known as 'the Radio Priest'. As one colleague put it: 'His shining in pulpits, on radio, with Barbara Ward in the *Sword of the Spirit*, round his parish, at prisoner-of-war camps, during air-raids, and up and down the columns of the *Sunday Express* (Irish edition) was steady and at times blinding.' It was said that if he had a spare half-hour he would start a new book and he produced five such works while at Manor Park, including a biography of his mentor, Cardinal Hinsley (1944) and *Letters from Rush Green* (1946), a collection of letters to a niece concerning an agnostic boyfriend. By the end of his life his bibliography amounted to fifteen titles.

In 1947 Fr Heenan became Superior of the re-established Catholic Missionary Society, based at Golders Green, where his 'team' included George Patrick Dwyer (later Archbishop of Birmingham) and Thomas Holland (later Bishop of Salford). They undertook missions around the country, often celebrating Mass on an altar that was carried in a trailer caravan dedicated to Our Lady of the Wayside. Open-air missions began dramatically with a recording of the bells of St Peter's broadcast through amplifiers, which could be heard over a large area.

In his second autobiographical volume, *A Crown of Thorns*, Heenan recalled visiting Archbishop's House one day, where he found Cardinal Hinsley trying on a new mitre. 'In playful mood he put it on my head. It fitted perfectly. The Cardinal's face became serious. "One day ... you will wear a mitre of your own and you will find it a crown of thorns."' So Hinsley's words came to pass. In 1951 Heenan was named fifth Bishop of Leeds and consecrated by Archbishop Godfrey on 12 March. He later wrote that 'during my first years in Leeds I learned much from my mistakes. I assume that while I learned others suffered.' The diocese became known as 'the Cruel See', on account of his penchant for frequently moving his clergy, and there is a story that he even tried to move a priest in a neighbouring diocese. He invited young priests to stay with him for a month so that they could study, familiarise themselves with the diocesan curia, and perfect the art of homiletics. However the priests were often left unattended as the Bishop went about his business and many hours of boredom followed. Heenan soon decided to leave the large Bishop's House and move into the cathedral and act as parish priest. He later admitted that he concentrated too much attention on the city to the detriment of the rest of the diocese. However, he set about visiting his diocese and opened forty churches in six years. Continuing his interest in the media, he celebrated a High Mass in his cathedral on 10 January 1954, with a commentary by Fr Agnellus Andrew. This was the first High Mass to be televised in Great Britain.

In May 1957 he was translated to Liverpool, while his former Catholic Missionary Society colleague, George Patrick Dwyer, succeeded him at Leeds. On the other side of the Pennines, Heenan faced financial difficulties (caused by post-war growth) and took the decision to abandon Lutyens' grand plans for the Metropolitan Cathedral and commission Frederick Gibberd to design a more contemporary – and cheaper – cathedral, with the pews gathered around a central altar. This was near completion by the time Heenan was moved to Westminster in September 1963.

Heenan was a contrast to the introspective Godfrey. Yet Heenan's great strength – his boundless energy and zest for work – was also a great weakness. Writing in 1967, George Scott observed:

> I can well imagine that in his personal catalogue of the Deadly Sins, Sloth comes right at the top. Administration is streamlined; meetings strictly abbreviated; correspondence dispatched with fervour. . . . His efficiency is somewhat chilling. His manner does tend to an abruptness, an impatience that hovers uncomfortably behind the beneficent smile. He is constantly in danger of betraying himself, in public, by his facility with words. As is true of Harold Wilson, he would be even more impressive if it appeared that he had to *search* for an answer occasionally.

Heenan began his ministry in Westminster by making a demanding round of parish visitations, which often included as many as forty lightning visits to sick parishioners alongside the usual church ceremonies and meetings with the parish clergy. He became much concerned with the formation of clergy and laity alike, bringing Heythrop College from Oxfordshire to London in 1969 and establishing the short-lived Corpus Christi College of Religious Education under Hubert Richards.

Heenan's energies were increasingly being taken up by the remaining sessions of Vatican II. Although his role in the conciliar *aula* was limited, Heenan did his best to act as a sure guide and a focus of unity back in his native land during the years following the Council. As his successor, Cardinal Hume, put it:

> He was able to hold, perhaps in precarious balance – but still in balance – a community that found itself pulled in different directions. . . . He was patient and understanding towards those who could not accept the liturgical changes that followed the Council. Yet, at the same time, he gradually put into effect the reforms and the attitudes of the Council with commonsense and shrewdness.

Worlock once commented that Heenan had 'a contempt for jargon and few of the post-conciliar terms escaped his tongue'. He faced much confusion and dissent, most notably in the public defection in 1966 of Fr Charles Davis, a Westminster priest and editor of *The Clergy Review,* and in the widespread opposition to Paul VI's Encyclical *Humanae Vitae* (1968).

Paul VI created Heenan Cardinal Priest of San Silvestro in Capite (the English church in Rome) on 22 February 1965. Two years later he presided over the creation of the Bishops' Conference of England and Wales, as recommended by the Council's *Christus Dominus*. This meant that the Archbishop of Westminster was no longer the *Praeses Perpetuus* of the Hierarchy, as envisaged by *Si Qua Est* (1911), and was replaced by an elected President of the Bishops' Conference (though, in practice, this has tended to be the Archbishop of Westminster). Preferring to work as an individual bishop, Heenan was at first suspicious of this new ecclesiastical structure and feared the endless meetings and commissions would become nothing more than talking shops. However, as first President of the new Conference, he worked hard to ensure unity and consensus, especially in the aftermath of *Humanae Vitae*.

As Vice President of Cardinal Bea's Secretariat for Christian Unity, Heenan was actively involved in the new spirit of ecumenism. He rejoiced over Archbishop Ramsey's historic visit to the Vatican (1966) and enjoyed a close friendship with the Chief Rabbi, Immanuel Jakobovits. He became the first cardinal since the Reformation to preach at both Westminster Abbey and St Paul's Cathedral, on which occasion he quietened down some anti-Catholic hecklers by saying that he had recently visited Belfast and therefore knew what to expect.

However, Heenan's last years were generally marked by pessimism, isolation and ill health – indeed, a parallel could be drawn with the final years of Paul VI's pontificate. As early as September 1971 Heenan circulated to his clergy a request for nominations for his successor. He suffered heart attacks in 1973 and 1974 and died at Westminster Hospital on 7 November 1975, aged seventy. He was buried in his cathedral church, beneath Eric Gill's Twelfth Station – 'Jesus dies upon the Cross'.

Cardinal Heenan's red hat, hanging above his tomb.

SAN SILVESTRO IN CAPITE (PIAZZA SAN SILVESTRO)

Since 1890 the official English church in Rome, this was the *titulus* of Cardinals Heenan and Hume. The original foundation dates back to a church built on this site in the eighth century by two brothers, Pope Stephen II and Pope Paul I. The church was built to enshrine bones brought from the catacombs. The present Baroque church, which is run by the Pallottine Fathers, contains the body of the boy martyr, St Tarcisius, and the head of St John the Baptist.

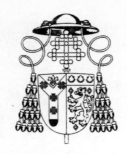

GEORGE BASIL HUME OSB
1923 – 1999
CARDINAL PRIEST OF SAN SILVESTRO IN CAPITE (1976)

Cardinal Hume was one of the most widely admired religious leaders in Britain during the second half of the twentieth century. His inheritance from Heenan was not an easy one. The years following the Second Vatican Council were, in many respects, turbulent and divisive but Hume's prayerful presence at the heart of the English and Welsh Church provided much-needed unity.

George Haliburton Hume was born at 4 Ellison Place, Newcastle-upon-Tyne on 2 March 1923. He remained a devoted Geordie for the rest of his life, especially in his support for Newcastle United – in 1981 he even participated in *This is Your Life* in honour of the footballing legend, Jackie Milburn. Hume's Scottish father, William, met his future wife, Marie Elizabeth Tisseyre ('Mimi'), while serving as an RAMC officer in northern France during the First World War. They married at the end of hostilities and moved to Newcastle, where they raised three daughters and two sons. William (who was later knighted for his services as a heart specialist) was a nominal Protestant, his wife a devout Catholic who, after having given birth to two daughters, prayed for the gift of a son who might become a priest. Like many future priests, the young Hume played at saying Mass. An elderly lady sometimes came to read the children stories and joked that George would one day marry her. One day the future cardinal took her aside and told her apologetically: 'I'm afraid I shan't be able to marry you, because I'm going to be a priest. But if you like, I'll bring you communion on your deathbed instead.'

Hume was brought up to be bilingual – his mother always speaking in French to her children if her husband was not present – and received his education at Gilling Castle and Ampleforth, where he eventually captained the rugby First XV. In 1941, at the age of eighteen, he entered the monastic community, taking the name Basil. Although his vocation seemed clear he anguished over whether he should first join the Army. He later reflected:

> I had a kind of boyish idea that we were going to be invaded, and that priests and people like me would all be strung up on lamp-posts. It seemed like a different kind of heroism.

After his solemn vows in 1945 he was sent to St Benet's Hall, Oxford, where he read modern history and kept up his rugby. He then moved on to the Catholic University of Fribourg in Switzerland, where he lived at the Salesianum and gained a degree in theology. He was ordained a priest at Ampleforth on 23 July 1950.

During his early monastic life he was housemaster of St Bede's, head of modern languages and rugby coach. He also taught the new monks dogmatic theology. In 1957 Hume was elected to represent Ampleforth in the General Chapter of the English Benedictine Congregation and in 1963 he was elected Abbot of Ampleforth aged just forty – the outgoing abbot, Herbert Byrne, was twice his age.

As abbot, Hume was responsible not only for the welfare of his community with its school, but also the needs of his monks engaged in parish work in over twenty-five parishes throughout northern England and Wales, as well as the priory founded in 1956 from Ampleforth in St Louis, Missouri. The Second Vatican Council was in session, and amongst its first pronouncements was a document on the liturgy, the heart of a monk's life. During these years Abbot Hume successfully held together the community of over one hundred and twenty monks and when his eight-year term as abbot expired in 1971 he was re-elected for what was supposed to be a further eight years.

The news of Hume's appointment, on 17 February 1976, as ninth Archbishop of Westminster came as a surprise to many. According to Fr Dominic Milroy, a monk of Ampleforth:

> There were two things of which first-time observers were largely unaware. First, Hume had worn a mitre, as abbot, for thirteen years, and yet had always contrived to look slightly lop-sided in it, giving the impression that he would rather be on the touchline, wearing a woolly hat. In great processions, he lacked, and perhaps still lacks, the suave Anglican glide, and always looks as though he is about to trip up. This has nothing to do with lack of experience; it is a quirk of temperament, and an engaging one. Hume does not particularly like dressing up. . . .
>
> Secondly, the received impression that Hume, before going to Westminster, had been pottering about in a rustic monastery, saying his prayers, studying

ancient manuscripts and tending a herb garden, was wide of the mark. The popular English image of the monk is based less on reality than on a combination of the Black Legend (lines of hooded monks holding candles as they prepare some sinister rite) and Punch cartoons (bell-ringing, illuminated manuscripts and wine-cellars). Hume's 'hidden' preparation for Westminster had been a good deal less romantic and more demanding than many people realized.

Hume had come to the attention of various prominent Catholics, including the Duke of Norfolk and Norman St John Stevas, as well as Archbishop Coggan of York, and there was a feeling in many quarters that a different style was needed after the Heenan era. Like Manning, Hume had to be consecrated bishop before being enthroned as Archbishop of Westminster, which took place on the feast of the Annunciation, 1976. The previous evening he had invited the parishes and religious houses of Westminster to join him in spirit as he made a Holy Hour. He was the first Benedictine Archbishop of Westminster but the twenty-seventh of that Order to lead the Catholic community in this country since St Augustine. On the night of his Enthronement, he led his monks once more in worship – not in his new cathedral but down the road at Westminster Abbey, from which Ampleforth's monks claimed descent.

Just over a month later Paul VI announced that he wished to make Hume a cardinal, inheriting Heenan's *titulus* of San Silvestro in Capite. When he came to Rome for the consistory (24 May 1976), the new cardinal was hosted at the English College by the then Rector, and his eventual successor at Westminster, Mgr Cormac Murphy-O'Connor. Although Hume preferred to wear his simple Benedictine habit, he enjoyed the traditions attached to Archbishop's House and was the last cardinal to employ a *gentiluomo* (gentleman-at-arms), Anthony Bartlett.

In 1978 Hume participated in both conclaves and was even given odds of twenty to one to become the second English Pope. He had indeed become widely respected – the same year he was elected to the presidency of the Council of European Bishops' Conferences and in 1980, as the only Benedictine cardinal, marked the 1,500th anniversary of St Benedict's death by lecturing in America and Europe. Other international responsibilities followed throughout his life as Cardinal Archbishop: he was appointed Relator at the 1994 General Synod on the Consecrated Life held in Rome; President of Churches Together in Britain and Ireland, and also President of Churches Together in England. He was appointed a member of the Congregation for the Sacraments and Divine Worship, the Congregation for Religious and Secular Institutes, the Congregation for Eastern Churches, the Pontifical

Council for the Promotion of Christian Unity and the Pontifical Council for Pastoral Assistance to Health Care Workers.

Within Westminster he was quick to publish *Planning for the Spirit*, which reorganised the diocese into five areas, each with a bishop and a team of pastoral workers, though without compromising his own authority as archbishop. Hume strived to remain true to his Benedictine calling, with a life centred on the worship of God and service to others. These twin poles were exemplified firstly by his role in saving the Cathedral Choir School from closure, encouraging a musical tradition unsurpassed throughout the world. Secondly, he founded the Cardinal Hume Centre for the homeless in 1986, and supported other ventures such as 'The Passage' (Britain's largest day centre for the homeless), and the establishment of the De Paul Trust to work with homeless young people. According to his obituary in *The Tablet*, a homeless person once called out to him, 'Cardinal, I am wearing your old trousers!' which in fact he was – the name-tag of 'Basil Hume' was still sewn inside. Hume also promoted justice and was heavily involved in the case of the Maguire Seven and the Guildford Four.

One of the most notable events of Hume's years as archbishop was the pastoral visit of Pope John Paul II to Britain in 1982, the first such visit to Britain of a reigning Pontiff. The success of the visit was, to a large extent, a tribute to Hume's political tact, since it came in the midst of the Falklands War. The historic climax was the Pope's visit to Canterbury Cathedral. Ecumenical and inter-faith relations remained close to his heart – one of his final engagements was a meeting with the Dalai Lama at Archbishop's House in May 1999. However, he felt that the General Synod's vote for the ordination of women in 1992 was 'an insurmountable obstacle' in relations with the Anglican Communion. Hume dealt sensitively with the consequent influx of Anglican clergy and gained special dispensation from Rome for the ordination of married converts as Catholic priests.

Despite his mixed parentage, Hume appeared more 'English' than his immediate predecessors and this served to bring Catholicism into the heart of national life. That his brother-in-law, Sir John Hunt, was Cabinet Secretary (1973-79) undoubtedly assisted in this, giving the Cardinal an added insight into the most effective way of promoting Catholic interests. A landmark event of Hume's tenure in this regard was the Queen's visit to Westminster Cathedral for Solemn Vespers on the feast of St Andrew in 1995, one of the final events to mark the centenary of the laying of the cathedral's foundation stone. The Queen was known to refer to him as 'my Cardinal', and, after his death, unveiled a statue of him outside St Mary's Cathedral, Newcastle.

Hume was impossible to pigeonhole. He once said that that his head was 'progressive' and his heart 'conservative'. He was not afraid to bring his concerns to the highest level. In the last year of his life he advised the Congregation for the Doctrine of the Faith to take no further action against Sr Lavinia Byrne's book *Woman at the Altar* (1994) and, despite the onset of his final illness, recorded a lecture on episcopal collegiality for the Conference of American Bishops, in which he critically evaluated the relationship between Rome and the diocesan bishops, and suggested regular meetings of the Pope with the heads of the bishops' conferences.

Yet Hume was certainly no maverick. He frequently expressed concern over the decline of respect to the Blessed Sacrament or irreverent celebrations of Mass. In the aftermath of the General Synod's vote for the ordination of women, he famously told the editor of *The Tablet* that he now hoped for 'the conversion of England for which we have prayed all these years'.

Like Heenan, Hume published a number of books, earning him a worldwide audience. These were largely drawn from his talks to monks and, after being appointed Archbishop of Westminster, talks and homilies to many varied congregations, and are solidly grounded in the Catholic spiritual tradition. Perhaps the most popular of these was *Searching for God* (1977), a collection of conferences given by Abbot Hume to his monks. A German edition was prepared at the instigation of the theologian, Hans Urs von Balthasar, who observed in his preface:

> Not without reason, they have found a resonance far beyond the cloister, even among the laity. For the fundamental problem facing every Benedictine abbey, namely how to combine time-consuming work – the *labora* – with silence, contemplation and prayer in choir – the *ora* – is the same problem that every Christian has to face, often with some difficulty. With English realism, but also with French finesse, inherited from his mother, with an incomparable mixture of collegial brotherliness and discreet abbatial authority, he explores and explains in ever new ways the indispensable unity of these two aspects of Christian life.

The Cardinal also made the occasional television programme. *The Return of the Saints* (published in book form as *Footprints of the Northern Saints*) recalled the lives of the great English saints of Northumbria, whilst *Basil in Blunderland* (based on his book of the same title and filmed at the Archbishop of Westminster's country retreat, Hare Street) explored, in the simplest of ways, the quest of every soul that is searching for God. The book's title was inspired by Lewis Carroll's *Alice in Wonderland*. Hume's Benedictine sense of humility was evident throughout:

> Now it is a fact that my spiritual life is more a wandering in Blunderland than a resting in Wonderland. I would guess that most of us would say the same of ourselves. . . . What matters, however, is that minds and hearts should be involved in the search for God, where the seeking and the finding go hand in hand. It is the process of getting to know God and learning to love Him. It is intimacy with Him that we seek. We try to go beyond every experience of knowledge and love, which we have now, to another experience, which is beyond our grasp but not entirely out of our reach.

On 2 March 1998, having reached the end of his seventy-fifth year, Cardinal Hume offered his resignation to John Paul II, but the Pope asked him to remain in office for several more years. Yet within a year he was feeling the effects of what proved to be the onset of his final illness and shortly after Easter 1999 he was diagnosed with terminal cancer. He wrote to his priests:

> I have received two wonderful graces. First, I have been given time to prepare for a new future. Secondly, I find myself – uncharacteristically – calm and at peace. I intend to carry on working as much and as long as I can. I have no intention of being an invalid until I have to submit to the illness. But, nevertheless, I shall be a bit limited in what I can do. Above all, no fuss. The future is in God's hands.

His final weeks were spent at the Hospital of St John and St Elizabeth, although he managed a trip to Buckingham Palace on 2 June to receive the Order of Merit from the Queen, a public recognition of his lifelong service through the Church to the country. The Cardinal died on 17 June 1999 having received the Sacraments of the Church from his last private secretary, Fr James Curry, and was buried, wearing his monk's habit, archbishop's pallium and cardinal's *zucchetto*, in the chapel of Ss Gregory and Augustine in Westminster Cathedral. Over his tomb hangs a cardinal's hat, made by his great niece and shown to him in hospital on the day of his death.

Cardinal Hume's tomb, with red hat hanging above.

For the entry on San Silvestro in Capite see p. 215.

Cormac Murphy-O'Connor
1932 –
Cardinal Priest of Santa Maria Sopra Minerva (2001)

Cormac Murphy-O'Connor was born in Reading on 24 August 1932, the fifth son of Dr George Murphy-O'Connor and his wife Ellen. He was educated at the Presentation College, Reading, before being sent as a border to Prior Park College in Bath. During the Holy Year of 1950 he began to train as a priest for the Diocese of Portsmouth at the Venerable English College, Rome, where he joined his two brothers, Brian and Patrick. He later joked that the Rector, Mgr John Macmillan, needed some persuading since he thought that two Murphy-O'Connors in a seminary were quite enough. Whilst in Rome he gained licentiates in philosophy and theology and was ordained by Valerio Cardinal Valeri on 28 October 1956. He was a keen pianist, singer and, like Basil Hume, rugby player, even making a guest appearance for CUS Roma and taking part in the celebrated match between the *Venerabile* and the Italian national side. The latter won 12-0.

On returning to his home diocese, he served as curate at Corpus Christi, Portsmouth (1956-63) and Sacred Heart, Fareham (1963-66). He especially enjoyed youth work and organising pilgrimages to Lourdes and, in his spare time, played fly-half for Portsmouth Rugby Club. Then in 1966 he became private secretary to the then Bishop of Portsmouth, Derek Worlock, who himself had served as secretary to Cardinals Griffin, Godfrey and (briefly) Heenan. Murphy-O'Connor was also Director of Vocations and helped establish the country's first Diocesan Pastoral Centre at Park Place, Wickham as well as the National Conference of Priests, which first met in 1970.

Fr Murphy-O'Connor was sent to Immaculate Conception, Portswood, in September 1970 as parish priest, but at the end of 1971 the Holy See appointed him Rector of the Venerable English College, Rome, thus following in the footsteps of Cardinals Wiseman, Hinsley and Godfrey. Meanwhile his elder brother, Pat, replaced him at Portswood.

The post-conciliar years were not easy ones for a new seminary rector but Mgr Cormac, as he soon became, managed to create a warm and affable atmosphere while facing some major decisions. He hosted visits to the college made by the likes of Cardinal Karol Wojtyla, Harold Macmillan and Archbishop Coggan of Canterbury.

In 1977 Mgr Murphy-O'Connor was appointed third Bishop of Arundel and Brighton and consecrated on 21 December by the previous bishop, Michael Bowen, who had just been translated to Southwark. Since Gatwick Airport lies in the diocese, Murphy-O'Connor had the privilege of welcoming John Paul II to England in 1982. He undertook various pastoral plans, including the Renew programme (which he later used in Westminster), and planned a Diocesan Synod for 2002, though the plans were shelved with his move to Westminster. He also acted as Co-Chairman of the Anglican and Roman Catholic International Commission (ARCIC) for eighteen years and was eventually awarded a Doctorate of Divinity by the Archbishop of Canterbury, Dr George Carey, in recognition of his ecumenical work.

On 15 February 2000, almost eight months after the death of Cardinal Hume, Bishop Cormac's translation to the Archdiocese of Westminster was announced, even though the bookies had only given him odds of twenty to one. He was installed as archbishop on 22 March and, on the feast of Ss Peter and Paul the same year, received the pallium from John Paul II in St Peter's Square, Rome.

On 21 February 2001 he was created a Cardinal Priest, two centuries to the day after the birth of Cardinal Newman. He was presented with the prestigious *titulus* of Santa Maria sopra Minerva in the very heart of Rome. This church contains the remains of St Catherine of Siena and Blessed Fra Angelico as well as numerous famous works of art. It was also the *titulus* and final resting place of Cardinal Philip Howard — making the choice of church highly appropriate, given the new cardinal's previous connections to Arundel, the seat of the Howard family.

Two major initiatives marked Cardinal Murphy-O'Connor's early years in Westminster. Firstly he commissioned Lord Nolan to chair an independent review on child protection in the Catholic Church in

England and Wales, the final report of which pointed to the establishment of an independent office (COPCA) to oversee the protection of children and vulnerable adults. Secondly, he oversaw various developments in the life of the Archdiocese of Westminster. In 2001 he replaced the geographic episcopal areas with four key areas of responsibility (Education, Clergy and Consecrated Life, Pastoral Affairs, and Ecumenism and Interfaith relations), each one under the supervision of a different auxiliary bishop. In 2003 he launched a diocesan process of spiritual and pastoral renewal called *At Your Word, Lord*, which responded to John Paul II's Apostolic Letter *Tertio Millennio Adveniente* (1994) and brought together thousands in small prayer groups, promoting his vision of the Church as 'a communion of communities'. This was followed by the publication in February 2006 of a 'White Paper', *Communion and Mission*, which identified the priorities for the local Church in the twenty-first century: the call to holiness, the formation of adults and young people, small communities, priesthood and vocations, and increased participation, collaboration and accountability.

In January 2002 the Cardinal became the first Catholic bishop to preach before the monarch since the reign of James II, when he attended a morning service at Sandringham. In October 2003 he made an unprecedented visit to Rome together with the Archbishop of Canterbury, Dr Rowan Williams, and allowed the celebration of evensong in his titular church. The following week he attended the Golden Jubilee celebrations of the Diocese of Stockholm as the representative of John Paul II. On Boxing Day 2005 he commenced a twelve-day visit to Sri Lanka on the first anniversary of the devastating tsunami.

Ecumenical searching has always marked the ministry of Cardinal Murphy-O'Connor. This was seen in the November 2006 gathering of the Catholic and Anglican hierarchies in Leeds. That same month he once again visited Rome with Dr Williams and at Christmas 2006 made a pilgrimage to Bethlehem with the Archbishop of Canterbury, the Primate of the Armenian Church of Great Britain and the Moderator of the Free Churches.

On 28 October 2006 Cardinal Cormac Murphy-O'Connor celebrated his Golden Jubilee of priestly ordination. To mark the occasion the Pope sent him a personal message:

> *To Our Venerable Brother Cormac His Eminence Cardinal Murphy-O'Connor, Archbishop of Westminster*
> Soon the whole Catholic community in Britain will experience a special

joy when it will be able and indeed will want to honour you, our venerable brother, as a renowned spiritual leader. This is because you have been for a long time a distinguished teacher in the ways of the Gospel of Jesus Christ and now celebrate a truly memorable event in your life and ministry, namely, the Fiftieth Anniversary of your Ordination as a Priest on 28th October 2006.

From afar, we have always and with admiration followed the course of your life and so would wish also to share in the congratulations and the festivities of this occasion. We are therefore writing this letter in a spirit of sincere affection and brotherly love so that we can also be near to you at this time and with the whole flock of the Diocese of Westminster which is so dear to you. Together we give thanks to God, the giver of all blessings, for the great achievements of your long apostolate among your people and where you will surely be honoured and our joy shared by everyone.

We remember in particular three blessings of your priestly life. First of all, we remember that you served happily as a priest of the Diocese of Portsmouth for over twenty years until Mother Church thought you worthy to be appointed as Bishop of Arundel and Brighton. Then our predecessor of recent memory, John Paul II, appointed you Metropolitan Archbishop of Westminster where you continually build up and renew the Church of God with worthy and fruitful initiatives and with great authority.

Likewise, dear brother, here at Rome, we remember your particular service as Rector of the English College and the continual help you give to us in the tasks given to you as Cardinal and Member of several Congregations and Councils of our Apostolic See.

Thus it is with a spirit of gratitude to God and in recognition of the gifts of your priesthood that we wish to be truly united with your clergy and faithful people as you celebrate the anniversary of your ordination as a priest. For this reason, we warmly congratulate you and extend our best wishes for the future. We pray that our Merciful Redeemer Himself may even now reward and console you as you remember your past life which is indeed a pledge of the eternal rewards in the Kingdom of Heaven.

With affection, we extend to you, dear brother, our Apostolic Blessing.

From Castel Gandolfo, 30th September 2006, the second of Our Pontificate.

Benedict PP XVI

For the entry on Santa Maria Sopra Minerva see p. 127.

Appendix I

The Huguenot Cardinal of Canterbury

Odet de Coligny
1517 – 1571
Cardinal Deacon of Santi Sergio e Bacco (1533)
Cardinal Deacon of Sant' Adriano al Foro (1549)

Canterbury Cathedral boasts a whole array of cardinalatial bones in its vaults: Langton, Kemp, Bourchier, Morton and Pole. However, Pole was not the last cardinal to be buried in the cathedral. At the southeast end of the Trinity Chapel is a plaque marking the tomb of Odet de Coligny, an apostate prelate who was known as the 'Cardinal de Châtillon'. He died mysteriously in a guesthouse at Canterbury in 1571, as he was returning to France. Most historians agree that he was poisoned by his *valet de chambre*, who may have been in the pay of Catherine de' Medici, well known for her opposition to the Huguenots. He was buried in a temporary tomb in the cathedral awaiting translation to France.

Some writers claim that he was eventually buried in his homeland and that the incumbent of his tomb at Canterbury is someone much more worthy: St Thomas himself, whose magnificent shrine once stood nearby. It is certainly unusual that a visiting Frenchman should have been buried in such an important position, surrounded by the likes of Henry IV and the Black Prince. However, the theory is questionable, especially given the gap of over thirty years between the destruction of Becket's shrine (with the possible hiding of his body) and the death of Coligny.

Odet de Coligny was born on 10 July 1517 at Châtillon-sur-Loing, the second son of Gaspard de Coligny, *maréchal de France*, and a member of one of the most influential French families of the time. He received the red hat from Clement VII on 10 November 1533 at the request of the King of France, Francis I. He was aged just sixteen. The following year he became Archbishop of Toulouse, even though he was not yet in major orders, and participated in the conclave that elected Paul III. As well as holding a number of abbacies *in commendam*, which guaranteed him a stable income, he became in 1535 Administrator of the diocese of Beauvais. In 1560 Pius IV appointed him Grand Inquisitor of France, but he was prevented from taking up the position because of the opposition of the powerful *Parlement* of Paris.

In 1561, encouraged by his family, he rejected his Catholic Faith and became a Calvinist. His *volte face* caused great scandal, especially coming one year after his papal appointment as Grand Inquisitor. In 1563 he was deprived of his cardinalate and other benefices, and excommunicated. However, he continued to wear his scarlet robes, most famously on the occasion of his marriage, in 1564, to Isabelle de Hauteville, who was presented to fashionable society as *Madame la Cardinale*. In 1567 he fought with the Huguenots at the Battle of St Denis and travelled to England in 1568, disguised as a sailor, partly to flee persecution and partly to secure negotiations with Queen Elizabeth. He was never to return to his homeland and he still lies awaiting judgment day at the Cathedral of Canterbury.

APPENDIX II
THE ENGLISH CARDINALS OF LEO XII

Pius VIII's pontificate lasted twenty months, but he managed not only to witness the passing of the Catholic Relief Act in Great Britain (13 April 1829), but also to raise the first native Englishman to the Sacred College since 1675 – Thomas Weld. However, it seems that two Englishmen were very nearly given this dignity by Pius' predecessor, Leo XII, and some claim that one of these, John Lingard, was actually created a cardinal *in petto*.

Peter Augustine Baines OSB
1787 – 1843

Between 1826 and 1829 Peter Augustine Baines, the coadjutor to Bishop Collingridge, Vicar Apostolic of the Western District, took a long European holiday in order to recover from a breakdown in health. Much of this recuperation took place in the Eternal City. He arrived there in the winter of 1826, accompanied by his ward, Anna de Mendoza, and her other guardian, Madame Chaussegros. The move to Rome benefited his health – as Wiseman put it: 'At some due period, the interior enemy capitulated, in that Englishman's stronghold of misery and pain – the liver; and a visible change for the better was observable by spring.'

Feeling stronger, his reputation began to spread. Based at the Palazzo Nicosia, he mixed with the Roman nobility, preached English sermons to packed audiences at the Gesù e Maria on the Corso and soon attracted the attention of the new Pope, Leo XII. He was granted two audiences soon after his arrival and was even asked to sing High Mass at the Sistine Chapel in the Pope's presence. It was customary for a new Pontiff, who by virtue of his election had left the Sacred College, to 'restore the hat' on a relation or, if he belonged to an Order, a member of that body. Leo had himself been created a Cardinal by Pius VII, a Benedictine. According to Wiseman, Leo wished to show his gratitude to that Order by raising one of their number to the sacred purple. Many of the candidates were either too old or too young and Baines, who had been educated at the English Abbey of Lamspringe (in Lower Saxony) and was a former Prior of Ampleforth, seemed to be a promising candidate. Baines was asked to move into the monastery of San Callisto to prepare for his imminent elevation. However, the death of the Pope on 10 February 1829 prevented this plan from being carried out. Pius

VIII is also said to have repeated the offer, which was declined and granted instead to the Benedictine Bishop of Parma, Remigio Crescini.

1829 would prove to be a momentous year for Baines – not only had he been promised the red hat, but he returned to England as the Vicar Apostolic of the Western District after the death of Collingridge. He was thus able to witness Catholic emancipation. However, he was soon drawn into controversy. As coadjutor he had hoped to gain control over the newly opened school at Downside and he now returned to his scheme as Vicar Apostolic. The monks protested and he claimed that Downside and Ampleforth had never in fact been canonically erected and that consequently their properties now belonged to the local Ordinary. In the end, Rome came down on the monks' side, granting a *sanatio* that rectified any previous canonical defects. A disgruntled Baines founded a school at Prior Park, outside Bath, with the help of four secularised monks from Ampleforth – he hoped that this foundation would develop into the first post-Reformation Catholic University. Baines boldly invited the Rosminian, Fr Luigi Gentili, to teach at the college and eventually became its President, before a disagreement led to his departure and his subsequent missionary endeavours in the Midlands and Ireland. Hampered by financial difficulties and a devastating fire in 1836, Prior Park was eventually closed in 1856 (although it was eventually resurrected as a successful independent school). However, Baines was saved from this final disappointment by his sudden death on 6 July 1843.

John Lingard
1771 – 1851

Leo XII not only intended to raise Baines to the sacred purple, but it has been claimed that the Pope actually made John Lingard a cardinal *in petto* at the consistory of 2 October 1826. Leo referred to this 'secret' cardinal as 'A man of great talents, an accomplished scholar, whose writings, drawn *ex authenticis fontibus*, had not only rendered great service to religion, but had delighted and astonished Europe.' Many, including the Rector of the English College and agent of the English Bishops, Robert Gradwell, assumed that the Pope was referring to Lingard, who had become internationally renowned for his historical research. Fordyce, in his *History of the County Palatine of Durham* (1857), even suggests that Lingard was to become the 'Cardinal Protector of the English Missions'. Lingard's elevation to the sacred purple *in petto* meant that he could finish his great English *History* before accepting the title and taking up residence in the Eternal City.

In his *Recollections*, Wiseman suggested that the Pope had, in fact, created the Frenchman, Lammenais, not Lingard, a cardinal. Following an adverse reaction in the correspondence pages of *The Rambler* in June 1858, Wiseman privately circulated *A Letter to the Canons of the Cathedral Chapter of Westminster*, in which he defended his theory. In 1826 Lammenais had been at the height of his powers. Leo XII clearly thought highly of him – his portrait hung in the papal chamber and he was exempted from reciting the breviary so that he could concentrate on scholarship – and the general opinion in Rome was that Lammenais was the secret cardinal. However, it is clear that Lingard believed the rumours of his own elevation and in a letter written the year before his death he bluntly told a friend: 'He [Leo XII] made me a cardinal.'

Lingard was born at Winchester in 1771, the son of a Lincolnshire yeoman, and entered the famous college at Douai in 1782. Here he was consistently top of his class and he stayed on to teach. As the Revolution took increasingly radical turns, Lingard left France in 1793, accompanied with three of his students, and became house tutor to one of them, the future Lord Stourton. Lingard was ordained in 1795. The next decade and a half of his life was spent with the Douai refugees who eventually settled at Crook Hall and then at Ushaw (1808). He acted as Vice President, Prefect of Studies, and Professor of Moral and Natural Philosophy – and between May 1810 and June 1811 was acting President. Years later one of his students, Nicholas Wiseman, recalled his many 'specific acts of thoughtful and delicate kindness, which showed a tender heart mindful of its duties, amidst the many harassing occupations just devolved on him . . . and his own literary engagements'.

He retired in 1811 to the peaceful mission of Hornby, near Lancaster, so that he could concentrate on these 'literary engagements'. Though poor health meant that he seldom left his country retreat, Lingard became a famous scholar, with an international correspondence network. His first major success had been with his *History and Antiquities of the Anglo-Saxon Church* (1806), written while teaching at Crook Hall, while in the 1830s he worked on a version of the New Testament, but the project that dominated much of his life was the *History of England to the Accession of William and Mary* (1819-30). Lingard was a mild-tempered historian who avoided controversy and hoped to win the hearts of his readers (Catholic and non-

Catholic alike) by the simple presentation of incontrovertible truth, backed up by careful research, *ex authenticis fontibus*. He was in Rome to work in the Vatican Library in 1817–18, though he also found time to act as Bishop Poynter's agent and to become heavily involved in the restoration of the Venerable English College, closed during the French occupation. His many contacts also helped him in his research – the Archbishop of Paris, for example, sent him information from the correspondence of Simon Renard, the Spanish Ambassador in Marian England. Lingard's great maxim was 'to take nothing on trust' and he took pride in tracing every statement to its original source – as Lord Acton put it, 'Lingard never gets anything wrong.'

In other words, Lingard was what we might call today a 'revisionist' historian, though his frequent deviations from conventional (Protestant) historiography meant that he was ostracised from many academic circles. Thus, he thought the burning of Joan of Arc by the English was 'a cruel and unjustifiable tragedy', described England under Henry VIII as 'a nation of slaves' and called Elizabeth 'irresolute', 'vain', and 'bloodthirsty'. However, he was honest enough to see the Marian persecution of Protestants as 'the foulest blot'. His *History* won him great fame: there were five English editions during his lifetime as well as French, Italian and German translations. Pius VII awarded him a triple doctorate in 1821 and it is unsurprising that Leo XII may have wished to raise this 'English Baronius' to the sacred purple. However, it was not to be. Father John Lingard died in 1851 and was buried in the cemetery cloister at Ushaw.

APPENDIX III

THE CARDINAL OF THE FULHAM ROAD

Alexis Henri Marie Lépicier OSM
1863 – 1936
Cardinal Priest of Santa Susanna (1927)

Cardinal Lépicier was born on 28 February 1863 at Vaucouleurs, not far from Verdun, the sixth child of François-Henri and Marie-Claire Lépicier (nee Hette). However his formation and 'birth' as a religious occurred in London, hence his inclusion in this book. On 10 March 1878, aged 15, he entered the Order of the Servants of Mary (Servites) at their recently established priory on the Fulham Road and studied at St Thomas' Seminary in Hammersmith. He was ordained priest in the seminary chapel by Bishop William Weathers (Auxiliary Bishop of Westminster) on 19 September 1885.

Lépicier then went to study in Rome, eventually returning to London and becoming, in 1890, Novice Master at the Servite house of Our Lady of Dolours in Bognor Regis. The intention was that he would remain in England but he was unexpectedly appointed Professor of Dogmatic Theology at Propaganda Fide, on the insistence of the outgoing professor, Archbishop Satolli, who had taught Lépicier in Rome and was now travelling to the U.S.A. as Apostolic Delegate. Lépicier produced some important theological and spiritual works, especially in the field of Mariology, and was a great promoter of the neo-scholastic revival. Many of these books were translated into English, including *Indulgences: Their Origin, Nature and Development* (1895), *The Unseen World* (1906 – against Spiritism), *Jesus Christ the King of Our Hearts* (1921), *The Fairest Flower of Paradise* (1922), *The Mystery of Love* (1925), *The Eucharistic Priest* (1927), *Behold Thy Mother* (1935) and expositions on the Our Father (1936).

In 1895 Lépicier became the first Rector of the Collegio Internazionale Sant' Alessio Falconieri in Rome (later called the Marianum) and, in 1901, the Order's Procurator General. His knowledge of England proved invaluable when he came as Apostolic Visitor to oversee plans for diocesan restructure. The ambitious proposals to merge Westminster and Southwark and create an Archdiocese of Brighton and a rural diocese based in St Albans, Hertford or Colchester ultimately came to nothing. In 1912 he went to Scotland as Apostolic Visitor and soon after became Apostolic

Delegate without the obligation of residence.

Between 1913 and 1920 Lépicier served as Prior General of the Servites and it was his happy task in 1914 to establish the English Province. From 1916 he was responsible for publishing the Acta of the Order. Between 1920 and 1924 he taught at the Collegio Sant' Alessio and, also, the Beda College, before being consecrated titular Archbishop of Tarso on 29 May 1924. The Archbishop acted as Apostolic Visitor to the East Indies (1924–26) and Abyssinia and Eritrea (1927). On 22 December 1927 he received the red hat from Pius XI and was given the titulus of S Susanna. The following year he was appointed Prefect of the Sacred Congregation for Religious. He fulfilled this role for eight years, before resigning in 1935.

In 1930 he succeeded Merry del Val as Cardinal Protector of the English College, Rome – in recognition of his close links to England – and one of his first tasks was to appoint the future Cardinal Godfrey as Rector. He was a regular visitor to the college, giving conferences and addressing the Literary Society on his journeys to India and Abyssinia as Apostolic Visitor. The college magazine, *The Venerabile*, records: 'Once in his determination to create the right atmosphere, he enhanced his attire with a pith helmet and made an impressive entry, waving an African plume.'

Lépicier died on 20 May 1936. After lying-in-state at his house on the Via Mercadante, his Requiem was celebrated at Sant' Andrea della Valle. He is buried in the Servite vault at the Campo Verano cemetery in Rome, not far from the final resting place of Cardinal Heard.

APPENDIX IV
THE SUBURBICARIAN DIOCESES

These are the ancient dioceses on the outskirts (or 'suburbs') of Rome that are allotted to the Cardinal Bishops. Today these are Velletri-Segni, Porto-Santa Rufina, Frascati, Palestrina, Albano, Sabina-Poggio Mirteto and Ostia, but over the centuries they have varied slightly. The Cardinal Bishops are titular bishops and each diocese also has a separate bishop with ordinary jurisdiction, though before 1914 the Cardinal Bishops were also the Ordinaries (as can be clearly seen from Cardinal York's reign at Frascati). Thus, at the time of the election of Pope Benedict XVI (2005) the Cardinal Bishop of Frascati was Cardinal Alfonso López Trujillo, President of the Pontifical Council of the Family, but the bishop with ordinary jurisdiction was Bishop Giuseppe Matarrese. Ostia is administered by the Cardinal Vicar of Rome. The English Cardinal Bishops were given the following dioceses:

Albano

Nicholas Breakspear (1146-54) and Lorenzo Campeggio (1534-35) were Cardinal Bishops of Albano.

Frascati (Tusculum)

Henry Benedict Stuart (1761-1803) and Edward Henry Howard (1884-92) were Cardinal Bishops of Frascati. The Cardinal Duke in particular left his mark on this *Castelli* town. According to Alice Shield, 'The very stones cry out its affection and gratitude in the numerous white inscriptions all about Frascati, testifying to this day on wells, walls, and other buildings to the munificence of Henry, Duke of York and Cardinal.'

Ostia and Velletri

Between 1150 and 1914 the dioceses of Ostia and Velletri were united and the Cardinal Bishop was Dean of the Sacred College of Cardinals. The only English cardinal to have held this position was Henry Benedict Stuart, Duke of York (1803-07), although he was granted permission to remain in his episcopal palace at Frascati. Velletri was separated from Ostia in 1914 and joined with Segni in 1986. Joseph Ratzinger was Cardinal Bishop of Velletri-Segni between 1993 and 2002, when as Dean he became Cardinal Bishop of Ostia (until his election as Benedict XVI).

Palestrina

Simon Langham (1373-76) and Lorenzo Campeggio (1535-37) were Cardinal Bishops of Palestrina.

Porto and Santa Rufina

John of Toledo, Robert Kildwardby (1278-79) and John Kemp (1453-55) were Cardinal Bishops of Porto and Santa Rufina. These dioceses were united by Calixtus II in 1119 and between 1825 and 1854 joined to Civitavecchia. For a time the title was given to the Sub-Dean of the Sacred College.

Sabina

Lorenzo Campeggio (1537-39) was Cardinal Bishop of Sabina (not to be confused with the *titulus* of Santa Sabina, which has been held by three English cardinals). In 1925 Sabina was united to the diocese of Poggio Mirteto.

APPENDIX V
TITULAR AND DIACONAL CHURCHES

Tituli: The first churches of Rome were called *tituli*, originating from the slabs by the door that identified the owner of the house church (*domus ecclesia*). Thus, the Basilica of San Clemente was originally the *Titulus Clementis* (probably the consul and martyr, Titus Flavius Clemens, a contemporary of Pope St Clement). According to the *Liber Pontificalis*, Pope Evaristus (97–105) assigned twenty five Roman priests to tituli, the first parish churches of Rome. These gradually grew in number and the parish priests (who were the proto-cardinals) had an important role in assisting the Pope in his ministry. As the creation of cardinals became increasingly formalised and international, the custom of assigning each to a *titulus* continued. Today, after receiving the red hat, each cardinal 'takes possession' of his titular church, though this is little more than a symbolic act.

Deaconries: Originally in charge of the seven regions of Rome on behalf of the Pope, the Cardinal Deacons are now senior curial officials, as was Cardinal Heard, Dean of the Roman Rota. The senior Cardinal Deacon (or Protodeacon) has the privilege of announcing the name of the new Pope to the world at the end of a conclave. Like the Cardinal Priests, the Cardinal Deacons are assigned one of the churches in Rome as their *diaconia*. If a Cardinal Deacon is elevated to be a Cardinal Priest (as often happens after ten years), the *diaconia* becomes a *titulus*. Thus, when Heard became a Cardinal Priest in 1970, his *diaconia* of San Teodoro in Palatino became a *titulus*.

APPENDIX VI
THE HERALDRY OF THE ENGLISH CARDINALS

Throughout this book two sources have been drawn on to provide most of the images of the heraldic achievements of the English Cardinals. The majority of line drawings up until the entry on Cardinal Bourne are the work of Major Thomas Shepherd FSA who published them in the mid 1920s. The colour illustrations of these coats of arms, up until the entry on Cardinal Manning, are mostly the work of a Cistercian monk, Dom Anselm Baker, painted circa 1875.

Comparing the two sets of images reveals certain discrepancies of style and content. For a concise analysis of the English cardinals' heraldic achievements, Mark Turnham Elvins' *Cardinals and Heraldry* (London, 1988) is an essential point of reference. The Shepherd line drawings are considered to be, for the most part, accurate representations of each cardinal's arms. Dom Anselm Baker's work, whilst always most beautiful in itself, employs a greater degree of artistic licence, yet sometimes with the occasional error. When comparing the two sets of arms Shepherd gives a surer lead with regards linear design whilst Baker provides the colour with which the arms captivate the eye.

Later achievements of arms are drawn from a variety of sources and are portrayed in a variety of media, often bearing the cardinalatial motto as part of the design.

BIBLIOGRAPHY

General Works

Baxter, D., *England's Cardinals with an Appendix showing the Reception of the Sacred Pallium by the Archbishops of Canterbury and Westminster* (1903).

Bellenger, D.A. & Fletcher, S., *Princes of the Church: A History of the English Cardinals* (2001).

Bellenger, D.A. & Fletcher, S., *The Mitre and the Crown: A History of the Archbishops of Canterbury* (2005).

Bence-Jones, M., *The Catholic Families* (1992).

Champ, J., *The English Pilgrimage to Rome – A Dwelling for the Soul* (2000).

Champ, J., *William Bernard Ullathorne: A Different Kind of Monk* (2006).

Elvins, M.T., *Cardinals and Heraldry* (1988).

Heseltine, G.C., *The English Cardinals with some Account of those of other English-speaking countries* (1931).

Isaacson, C., *The Story of the English Cardinals* (1907).

Kenny, A., *A Path from Rome* (1985).

Luff, S.G., *The Christian's Guide to Rome* (1990).

Mason, G., *The Companion Guide to Rome* (1967).

Maxwell-Stuart, P.G., *The Archbishops of Canterbury* (2006).

Quinlan, J., *Our English Cardinals including the English Pope* (1972).

Wilkie, W.E., *The Cardinal Protectors of England: Rome and the Tudors before the Reformation* (1974).

Williams, F., *Lives of the English Cardinals including Historical Notices of the Papal Court from Nicholas Breakspear (Pope Adrian IV) to Thomas Wolsey, Cardinal Legate*, 2 vols (1868).

Selected Works on Individual Cardinals

Oxford Dictionary of National Biography.

Buehrle, M.C., *Rafael Cardinal Merry del Val* (1957).

Butler, C. (ed.), *Basil Hume: by his friends* (1999).

Castle, T., *Basil Hume – a portrait* (1986).

Champ, J., 'Cardinal Philip Howard – Rome and English Recusancy', in Schofield, N. (ed.), *Roman Miscellany: The English in Rome 1550-2000* (2002).

Corp, E., *The King Over the Water* (2001).

De La Bedoyere, M., *Bernard Cardinal Griffin* (1955).

Duffy, E., 'William, Cardinal Allen, 1532-1594', in Schofield, N. (ed.), *Roman Miscellany: The English in Rome 1550-2000* (2002).

Forbes, F.A., *Rafael, Cardinal Merry del Val* (1932).

Fothergill, B., *The Cardinal King* (1958).

Fothergill, B., *Nicholas Wiseman* (1963).

Gilley, S., *Newman and his Age* (1990).

Gray, R., *Cardinal Manning: A Biography* (1985).

Gwyn, P., *The King's Cardinal: The Rise and Fall of Thomas Wolsey* (1990).

Harriss, G.L., *Cardinal Beaufort: A Study of Lancastrian Ascendancy and Decline* (1988).

Heenan, J.C., *Cardinal Hinsley* (1944).

Heenan, J.C., *Not the Whole Truth* (1973).

Heenan, J.C., *A Crown of Thorns* (1974).

Howard, A., *Basil Hume: The Monk Cardinal* (2005).

Ker, I., *John Henry Newman: A Biography* (1988).

Knowles, D., *Cardinal Gasquet as a Historian* (1957).

Leslie, S., *Cardinal Gasquet: A Memoir* (1953).

MacCormack, A., *Cardinal Vaughan* (1966).

Mayer, T.F., *Reginald Pole: Prince and Prophet* (2000).

McClelland, V.A., *Cardinal Manning: His Public Life and Influence, 1865-1892* (1962).

Moloney, T., *Westminster, Whitehall and the Vatican: The Role of Cardinal Hinsley 1935-43* (1985).

Newsome, D., *The Convert Cardinals: John Henry Newman and Henry Edward Manning* (1993).

Oldmeadow, E., *Cardinal Francis Bourne*, 2 vols (1940 and 1944).

O'Neil, R., *Cardinal Herbert Vaughan* (1989).

Pereiro, J., *Cardinal Manning: An Intellectual Biography* (1998).

Powicke, F.M., *Stephen Langton* (1928).

Quirk, R.N., 'Robert Hallum and the Council of Constance', in *Friends of Salisbury Cathedral* (1952).

Reynolds, E.E., *Saint John Fisher* (1972).

Rex, R., *The Theology of John Fisher* (1991).

Schofield, N., 'Not Accepted by Men but Chosen by the Will of God – The Cardinal Duke of York', in Schofield, N. (ed.), *Roman Miscellany: The English in Rome 1550-2000* (2002).

Schiefen, R.J., *Nicholas Wiseman and the Transformation of English Catholicism* (1984).

Sewell, B., *The Cardinal of Norfolk: Philip Thomas Howard OP* (Royal Stuart Papers XV).